PRAISE FOR *ON THE EIGHTH DAY*

"The authors . . . have managed to weave theological and philosophical ideas alongside stories from across the world of sports. This book is an important and much-needed addition to the ever-expanding academic work addressing sports and religion which will encourage others to explore how their Catholic faith has helped them make sense of this wonderful human pursuit."

—MARK NESTI, Sport Psychologist at SportinSpirit Limited

"Hoven, Carney, and Engel speak profoundly of transcendence, leisure, and virtue as fundamental points of connection between faith and sport. . . . All things authentically human can lead us to God. I highly recommend this book for all who coach athletics, play sports, or are just interested in the game!"

—DONALD HYING, Bishop, Diocese of Madison

"With its playful title, functional formatting, and critical questions, *On the Eighth Day* offers in-depth thought, reflection, and insight into the connection between theology and sports. Hoven, Carney, and Engel lend three voices that truly become one. The result? A text that enables the reader to find grace in sports and beyond."

—ANNE STRICHERZ, author of *Sport and Spirituality* (blog)

"*On the Eighth Day* is an intelligent and engaging book on the theology of sports. It sparked my faith to be a more authentic sports chaplain. We can and should commune with the Father, Son, and Holy Spirit as much on the volleyball court as in the church sanctuary."

—BRENT "CHAPPY" KASSIAN, pro-ministry sports chaplain

"In *On the Eighth Day*, we find a proper framework in which to experience and enjoy the role of sports in our lives. The authors remind us that sports ought to be a stage for the development of our relationship with God. . . . I recommend this book as a corrective for our culture. I also commend the authors for showing us how sports can be an arena for God's interaction in our lives."

—JAMES R. GOLKA, bishop, Diocese of Colorado Springs

"Hoven, Carney, and Engel dig deep in *On the Eighth Day*. This book dives into the theology of sports, the history of the Catholic church, and the impact of sports on culture to create a mash-up unlike any other. Readers beware, this book is not the easy way out . . . *On the Eighth Day* is for the guys who sit in the front row of class."

—BILL KRAMER, football coach, Florida High School Athletic Association Hall of Fame

"This is a groundbreaking book, standard reading for anyone interested in sports and Christianity—whether Catholic or not. This is basic Catholic theology and basic sports studies at its best!"

—CHAD CARLSON, Hope College

"A clearly-written, eminently accessible, and theologically perceptive reflection on sports. . . . The authors' balanced approach considers carefully the dangers and ethical challenges that are often encountered in the world of sports. Yet, drawing on the riches of the Catholic theological tradition and a wide range of historical and contemporary illustrations, they also help us recognize that participation in sports may offer nothing less than a sacramental encounter with the divine."

—RICHARD R. GAILLARDETZ, Boston College

"Laced with lively sports stories, this thought-provoking and accessible book is more than a Catholic theology of sports. It is also a sports theology. While theological guideposts for bringing out the best in sports abound in this book, so do sports guideposts for bringing out the best in faith and life. The authors go head-on with tough questions about flourishing, suffering, doping, social justice, and what it means to be faithful humans in sports."

—TRACY J. TROTHEN, Queen's University

"Hoven, Carney, and Engel have written a wonderful new book that introduces undergraduate students and others to Catholic theology and spirituality at the same time that it helps them to gain new insight into the problems and possibilities of sports itself. I highly recommend it!"

—PATRICK KELLY, SJ, University of Detroit Mercy

On the Eighth Day

On the Eighth Day

A Catholic Theology of Sport

MATT HOVEN
J. J. CARNEY
MAX T. ENGEL

CASCADE *Books* • Eugene, Oregon

ON THE EIGHTH DAY
A Catholic Theology of Sport

Copyright © 2022 Matt Hoven, J. J. Carney, and Max T. Engel. All rights reserved. Except for brief quotations in critical publications or reviews, no part of this book may be reproduced in any manner without prior written permission from the publisher. Write: Permissions, Wipf and Stock Publishers, 199 W. 8th Ave., Suite 3, Eugene, OR 97401.

Cascade Books
An Imprint of Wipf and Stock Publishers
199 W. 8th Ave., Suite 3
Eugene, OR 97401

www.wipfandstock.com

PAPERBACK ISBN: 978-1-6667-0114-2
HARDCOVER ISBN: 978-1-6667-0115-9
EBOOK ISBN: 978-1-6667-0116-6

Cataloguing-in-Publication data:

Names: Hoven, Matt, author. | Carney, J. J., author. | Engel, Max T., author.

Title: On the eighth day : a catholic theology of sport / Matt Hoven, J. J. Carney, and Max T. Engel.

Description: Eugene, OR : Cascade Books, 2022 | Includes bibliographical references.

Identifiers: ISBN 978-1-6667-0114-2 (paperback) | ISBN 978-1-6667-0115-9 (hardcover) | ISBN 978-1-6667-0116-6 (ebook)

Subjects: LCSH: Sports—Religious aspects—Catholic Church. | Sports—Religious aspects—Christianity. | Sports—Religious aspects—History. | Sports—Moral and ethical aspects.

Classification: GV706.42 .H68 2022 (paperback) | GV706.42 .H68 (ebook)

06/07/22

For Mom & Dad, and my St. Joe's students (MJH)
For my Creighton students, who inspired this book (JJC)
For my father: a great coach, man, and dad (MTE)

Deus Lux Mea Est.

Contents

Acknowledgments		xiii
Introduction	Why a Catholic Theology of Sport?	1
Chapter 1	From Saint Paul to Pope Francis *Sport in Catholic History*	13
Chapter 2	The Spirit of Play *The Heart of Sports and Religious Faith*	29
Chapter 3	Seeing What Is There *Sports, Transcendence, and Sacramental Perspective*	46
Chapter 4	The Human Team *God, Anthropology, and Sports*	66
Chapter 5	Sports Can Hurt *The Problem of Suffering and Loss in Sports*	86
Chapter 6	Kneeling in the End Zone *Ritual, Superstition, and Prayer in Sports*	104
Chapter 7	The Virtuous Life *Morality and Human Flourishing in Sports*	125
Chapter 8	Building a Culture of Encounter *Sport and Catholic Social Teaching*	145
Conclusion	Sport and Eschatology on the Eighth Day	166
Bibliography		177

Acknowledgments

WE WISH TO THANK all the people who supported this book project—it was definitely a team effort. Richard Gaillardetz, Chad Carlson, and Anne Stricherz each reviewed the first draft of the manuscript. Their careful reading and insightful feedback made for a much clearer, more rounded text. Other colleagues reviewed individual chapters of the book: Jesse Donoghue; Paddy Gilger, SJ; Michael Lawler; Christina McRorie; and Todd Salzman. We very much appreciated their expertise and generous offer of time. Thanks to Michelle Rochard for reviewing the bibliographic references, merging documents, and putting together the full manuscript. Finally, over 100 students at Creighton University and University of Alberta read chapters while enrolled in our courses; thanks to them for their enthused responses, critical eyes, and gentle prodding of our early drafts.

We are also grateful to Charlie Collier and the editorial crew at Wipf & Stock, who took up our project with vigor and guided it successfully to its end. We wish to thank Creighton University and St. Joseph's College for their support of the project, especially with funding assistance from the Peter and Doris Kule Chair in Catholic Religious Education. We also appreciate the feedback we received on several early ideas for this book at the Third Global Congress on Sport and Christianity at Calvin University in October 2019. The last word of appreciation goes to our families, particularly our wives Crystal, Becky, and Beth, for their support, encouragement, and love.

This book is ultimately the fruit of friendship. We first met each other as graduate students at The Catholic University of America in Washington, DC. Yet our shared love of sports, collaborative teaching in the field of sport and spirituality, and ultimately this book project, brought us even closer together. Whether talking about this book during vacations, innumerable

Zoom calls, or on longer-than-usual bike rides home from work, we grew in appreciation and respect for one another. Like sport, this book crosses the finish line due to a collaborative spirit, hard work, and the ability to have fun along the way. We are grateful to have competed together.

MATT HOVEN, JAY CARNEY, AND MAX ENGEL
JANUARY 2022

Introduction

Why a Catholic Theology of Sport?

A BANNER AT AN Edmonton Oilers ice hockey game in the early 1980s announced, "On the eighth day, God created Gretzky." For one very young Oilers fan, the sign declared something impossible, yet conceivably true. Could the Creator of the universe make all things in six days, rest on the seventh, and then create the greatest hockey player ever? Surely not, but Wayne Gretzky seemed heaven-sent. He established a new record for most goals scored in a season. He played the game in unusually new ways, making passes that no one had made before and revolutionizing how players used the space behind the goal. Elsewhere on the ice, he inexplicably appeared in the right place at the right time, a trait learned from his father who sounded more like a mystic than a coach: "Don't go to where the puck is, but where it is going to be."[1] In truth, a young fan could believe that God had created Gretzky on the eighth day, as was claimed on the banner unfurled at Northlands Coliseum in the 1980s.

Connections between sport and religion do not end with Gretzky: consider Doug Flutie's last-second "Hail Mary" pass; Tim Tebow's prayerful, kneeling gesture in the end zone; or baseball players making the sign of the cross before batting. Some athletes write biblical passages on their basketball shoes. Others privately carry a rosary in their athletic bag or light a candle to St. Sebastian, the patron saint of athletes, as has the most successful women's gymnast ever, Simone Biles.[2] Many coaches endorse pregame prayers, while fans complete private rituals imploring divine assistance.

---

1. Gretzky, with McLennan Day, 99, 163–64.

2. These examples are found in Davis, "Spiritual Strength of Simone Biles"; Farrow, "These Two Game-Changing Olympians"; Windle, "'God Is the One'"; Armour, "Simone Biles."

Religious organizations, like the Catholic Church, have become well-known for their institutional commitment to sport in their schools and colleges. It appears that the combination of religion and sport is as commonplace as that young Oilers fan had hoped.

What is one to make of these instances of religious expression in sport? This book provides a critical overview of how religious thinking can engage the phenomenon of sport and, with the help of theological knowledge and values, promote what is best in sport for the benefit of its participants. We offer a contemporary theological framework that gives a richer understanding of sport for people of faith, provides deeper reflection on the meaning of sport for the nonreligious reader, and tacitly argues why religious believers like Biles and others should remain involved in sport now more than ever.

THEOLOGY AND SPORT

Let us clarify what we mean by theology. Traditionally, theology is described by the medieval monk Anselm's dictum, *fides quaerens intellectum*, or "faith seeking understanding," where reflection and discussion about faith take place within a community of believers and in dialogue with society at large.[3] Theology wonders about who God is, what the purpose of human living is, and how humans can love and serve God. While theology is done for humanity's sake and for building God's kingdom on earth, it is not a closed-off system of thought and thus engages other academic fields and the lives of Christians today.[4] The work of theology isn't limited to the intellectual side of things either, but also includes "faith seeking justice," "faith seeking mercy," and "faith seeking contemplation."[5] Similarly, Agbonkhianmeghe E. Orobator, a Nigerian Jesuit, defines theology more broadly as "faith seeking understanding, hope, and love."[6] He connects the work of theology to all three theological virtues, where they inform and animate human beings by divine grace. Thus, we can say that theology is a human practice of the mind, hands, and heart, where all people are called to live a grace-filled life or, simply, to become holy.

A theology of sport is unique because it is focused on faith seeking understanding, justice, mercy, and contemplation *in* and *through* sport. In this book, we wonder about how play and sport might speak to us about God and living the Christian life. Does God care about play? Should people

---

3. Marthaler, *Creed*, 50.
4. Cunningham, "Perspectives in Catholic Theology," 60–61.
5. Cunningham, "Perspectives in Catholic Theology," 49.
6. Orobator, *Theology Brewed*, 3.

of faith participate in competitive sport? If so, how can their involvement develop a deeper connection to Jesus? In this sense, a theology of sport is practical, but should not be understood as a naïve transition from theory to practice. A theology of sport engages in a dialogue between sport and faith that is both reflective and critical. Further, given the ambivalent ethical impact of sport, theology should both bless and challenge the many features of sport, seeking liberation from oppressive social assumptions and working toward solidarity with other human beings.[7]

Theologian Robert K. Johnston specifies that a theology of sport must answer two fundamental questions.[8] First, with the combined occurrences of a global pandemic, ongoing wars, gun violence, and growing polarization in Western society, should we even be playing sport, let alone writing books about it? Amidst the martyrdoms of unprecedented numbers of Christians in the twentieth and twenty-first-century world, is sport too frivolous for Christians to really care about? Johnston sums up this critical introspection about the value of sport with his first question: "What the hell are they doing?" That is, should we be affording so much time to sport, especially when it seems trivial or causes factions in our communities? In theological terms, we can speak about sport as sinful in many ways, or as a part of our fallen world. Whereas Christians have often named the sins of sport, like its over-commercialization and physical violence, sport sociology analyzes more specifically the deeper problems of sport. Forms of discrimination (e.g., race and gender), systemic issues (tied to globalization, sport systems, labor migration), and the use of performance-enhancing drugs require careful analysis and cry out for justice. These issues cause Johnston to question, "What the hell are they doing?"

Second, Johnston offers a contrasting viewpoint with a different question: "What in heaven's name is going on?" Instead of only narrowly persisting with skepticism, suspicion, and ethical questions, Johnston invites inclusion of a second hermeneutic, one of engagement and appreciation, where it is possible to find God in all things (as promoted by the Jesuit spiritual tradition). Johnston concludes: "Rather than focus on the question of sin, this alternative question centers on play's ability 'to make us more fully human, more fully in the image of the playful, powerful, Creator.' When we are truly at play, we participate in God's creative life; it is a foretaste of heaven."[9] Whereas moral concern and sport sociology try to pull back the

---

7. Hoven, "'Sport as a Celebrative and Worshipful Act,'" 3.
8. Johnston, "How Might Theology of Play?," 11.
9. Johnston, "How Might Theology of Play?," 12.

veil on the magic of sport, a theology of sport must make room for aesthetics and possibilities for finding grace.

Manifold examples underline Johnston's positive point about sport. Consider the unpredictability of sport, which can capture one's imagination in an otherwise automated and programmed world. Older players can still inspire greatness in a special moment, like forty-two-year-old Bartolo Colon hitting his first major league home run in 2016, or Phil Mickelson winning a major golf tournament at the half-century mark in 2021. Teams or players can stumble when victory is within reach, as the Atlanta Falcons blew a 28–3 lead in the second half of Super Bowl LI. We stay glued to our television or laptop in case lightning flashes and the impossible happens. Unlike a movie or reality TV series, however, a highly unusual sports happening is not *deus ex machina*, as if fabricated to appease the audience, but is a natural occurrence that surprises viewers. When Deandre Ayton of the Phoenix Suns won a 2021 playoff game on an alley-oop slam dunk on an inbounds play with less than a second left, even the NBA referees completed a video review to make sure that the implausible moment was legitimate. In 1988, on two injured legs, the LA Dodgers' Kirk Gibson hit a game-winning home run with two outs in the bottom of the ninth inning in the World Series. Radio announcer Jack Buck dramatically called out, "Unbelievable ... I don't believe what I just saw ... is this really happening?"[10]

A theology of sport must be informed by the skeptical mindset stemming from the question, "What the hell are they doing?" And yet despite the problems in sport, such a theology must also rise above and ponder, "What in heaven's name is going on?" Our book exists in dialogue with both questions.

RELIGIOUS STUDIES AND SPORT

The field of religious studies has offered rich theoretical insight into an understanding of sport. Because of the growing prominence of sport throughout the twentieth century, some religious studies scholars began to carefully examine similarities between religion and sport. One helpful theoretical framework comes from scholar Ninian Smart, who analyzed religion as a complex phenomenon that fuses together both external and internal meanings.[11] For instance, the event of the birth of Jesus of Nazareth is an external, historical fact (which the Christian calendar commemorates as its first year), while its internal meaning for Christians is that the incarnation

---

10. Posnanski, "32 Best Calls in Sports," para. 5.
11. Smart, *Religious Experience of Mankind*, 3.

of the Son of God brings ultimate hope into a broken world. Smart's two-pronged approach is more interested in finding an accurate description of the many dimensions of religion than in determining the truth claims of each religion.[12] We will briefly examine two dimensions described by Smart which reveal how sport can act like a religious phenomenon.[13]

First, the mythological dimension highlights the central stories of religious traditions. A myth does not mean "false" or "ahistorical" in Smart's understanding. Instead, myths are foundational, meaning-making stories that anchor a religious community (e.g., Jesus' parable on the prodigal son teaches about God's forgiveness and mercy). Propagated by modern media, contemporary sport also contains central myths that reveal core values and origin stories. For example, Babe Ruth may or may not have called his home run at Wrigley Field in the 1932 World Series, but this famous myth reflects Ruth's identity as the unparalleled home run king of his era.[14] More recently, the 2020 Netflix docuseries on the life of Michael Jordan promoted a myth about Jordan's relentless drive for supremacy, where basketball enthusiasts were shown what it takes to become a champion.

Second, Smart's experiential dimension describes how people encounter God not only externally but also internally, where divine-human communion is the ultimate life purpose for Christians. This experience of the invisible, spiritual world is captured in examples like the dramatic conversion story of Saul of Tarsus (who became Saint Paul) or the spiritual growth of Saint Teresa of Avila in the solitude of a monastery. Similarly, Olympic athletes can seem to reach a transcendent realm: a rower realizes sporting triumph after years of training and past defeats, or audiences become captivated by the speed and elegance of sprinting bodies viewed on high-definition television. Moving past external results of a race, remarkable moments and sensations feel possible through sport. Smart's framework and others' subsequent analyses reveal how sport can function or act like a religion through the power of myth and the human desire for peak experiences. But can we conclude from this that sport *is* a religion?

On one hand, it seems that sport's increasing cultural influence parallels the traditional role of religion in society. The discourses and practices of sport and religion have blurred, and people move easily between the sacred and profane in both realms.[15] This is seen in many places. Since 1922, there

---

12. Smart, *Religious Experience of Mankind*, 4.

13. Bain-Selbo and Sapp, *Understanding Sport*, 9–38. See also Ellis, *Games People Play*, 109–22.

14. Bain-Selbo and Sapp, *Understanding Sport*, 17–19.

15. Scholes and Sassower, *Religion and Sports*, 149.

have been newspaper reports of Catholic college football teams and Catholic players saying a Hail Mary prayer before an important play, leading to the renaming of a last-minute play as a "Hail Mary."[16] Most memorably in a 1975 NFL playoff game, Roger Staubach, the Dallas Cowboys quarterback (who was raised a Catholic), threw a pass halfway down the field for the winning touchdown in the dying seconds of the game. Staubach famously told reporters after the game, "It was a Hail Mary pass."[17] With the help of incredible moments viewed on television, like Doug Flutie's 1984 game-winning touchdown pass for Boston College, the phrase became part of the common football lexicon, where any football fan knows a Hail Mary pass but is unlikely to be able to recite the prayer. Another example of this blurring between sport and religion is the idea of redemption.[18] Whereas Christianity offers a complex theological explanation of its meaning—which essentially is about the deliverance of someone from sin, or their return to God—today's sports broadcasters generally understand redemption as a comeback from the worst of situations or a terrible previous defeat, such as "she is back from the dead." Examples abound, including LeBron James's triumphant return to lead his hometown Cleveland Cavaliers to the 2015 NBA championship. Not surprisingly, sports reporters have often found a comfortable home for religious metaphors in sport.

Sociologically, one could argue that since modern sport's origins in the mid-nineteenth century, sport has gradually displaced traditional religion on a functional level. Today, many spend their Sundays with sport rather than in church. Sport gives people the type of social connections, traditions, identity, and even meaning that is usually found in religion. To put it simply, the pews are empty, but the bleachers are full. Thus, concerns arise from both religious and sporting people. Christians might have good reason to be concerned about sport usurping religious practices, where sport can become a form of idolatrous self-worship that foolishly confuses athletes with God.[19] At the same time, sporting enthusiasts may worry that sport cannot properly tend to deep human existential concerns because, as a social institution, sport is not structured to replace transcendent religious traditions.

Consider that the term "religion" derives from the Latin root *religare*, which means "to bind"; thus, for authentic religion there needs to be a connection, a binding to something other than oneself.[20] The claim that sports

16. Sheridan, "How Roger Staubach," paras. 2–6.
17. Sheridan, "How Roger Staubach," para. 9.
18. Scholes and Sassower, *Religion and Sports*, 130–46.
19. Harvey, *Brief Theology of Sport*, 103.
20. O'Malley, *God*, 6.

bind people together in some way is certainly true. However, religion necessitates a binding to something beyond oneself, a group of people, or even the sum of one's experiences. Religion necessitates a connection between an individual, other people, and the Ultimate Reality, which Christians recognize as God.[21] Without an explicit, felt connection to an Ultimate Reality within a worldview open to God's grace, something can be powerful and profound, but it is not real religion.

This blurring of reality challenges us to think about new ways of understanding the relationship between sport and religion.[22] Viewing reality as a relativistic chaos is extreme, where religious and sport meanings mix randomly like a high-performance protein shake. Instead, people should name the basic truth of the sport-religion relationship: religion is often associated with the growing importance of sport, and historically religious themes and persons have often animated the deeper meanings of sport.[23] Philosophers Scholes and Sassower argue that religion will always remain a crucial social enterprise to help people transcend their daily existence through reflection on their convictions, behaviors, and place in the universe.[24] Fundamental values and ideals are rooted in religious traditions, where religion can help direct sport and, when religion loses its way, sport can help religion recall its core mission and role in human affairs.

Our theological book adheres to this dialogical, cooperative model that sees something of great value in sport. The excitement and magic of sport means that it will play an important role for many in expressing their religious impulses.[25] This need not mean the end of religious institutions, even as the trajectory of decline is a major trend in the twenty-first-century West. Rather, the growth of sport globally points to something larger, something very religious. The growth of sport reveals the relationality of humans, the need to belong to something greater, and how a human identity must be shaped by something bigger than one's own merit. Sport speaks to the appeal of those things that are spiritual, where our spirits are drawn toward that which is beautiful, glorious, and even awe-inspiring. It confirms that drive for something of substance. It says that even amidst the apparent frivolity of play and sport, there is also a desire for larger, substantial purposes. Ultimately, sport can be a road that takes us to revered places

---

21. Hill et al., *Faith, Religion, & Theology*, 159–61.
22. Scholes and Sassower, *Religion and Sports*, 149.
23. Scholes and Sassower, *Religion and Sports*, 150.
24. Scholes and Sassower, *Religion and Sports*, 150.
25. Bain-Selbo and Sapp, *Understanding Sport*, 135.

beyond human words and that lead to the sacred realm of human living.[26] This need not lead to idolatry but can point human persons toward what matters most. Given sports' symbolic strength, its educational potential, and universal appeal, it is little wonder that Pope Pius XII asked decades ago: "How can the Church therefore not be interested in sport?"[27]

TOWARD A CATHOLIC THEOLOGY OF SPORT

We believe the time is ripe for offering a robust theological vision of sport because of major research trends over the past three decades. Broadly speaking, recent years have seen an increased emphasis on interdisciplinary, contextual research to better understand human experience of the world. For its part, Catholic theology began an anthropological turn in the mid-twentieth century, where theological understandings needed to consider more deeply what belief meant for human persons and, more particularly, reflect on marginalized human communities in the midst of suffering (e.g., the Global South, women, people of color). Also in the middle of the twentieth century, research into different areas of sport (e.g., history, philosophy, kinesiology, sport psychology) began a great expansion, revealing the social significance of sport and its impact on human cultures.

The Catholic Church has shown great interest and involvement in sport since the birth of modern sport in the late 1800s; this nexus of faith and sport was also promoted by Protestant Christians. Modern Catholic pedagogies began to more fully embrace sport and recreation, Catholic sporting institutions contributed to athletic organizations and activities,[28] and papal speeches on sport flourished.[29] At the Second Vatican Council (1962–65), some bishops voiced reservations about sport as a moral danger to human bodies and communities—especially because sport could distract and mislead church attendees on Sunday mornings.[30] Importantly, however, the council's brief pronouncement on sport was highly positive, following the lead of Pope John XXIII, who sought to situate the church in a more conciliatory dialogue with the modern world—even claiming that sport could assist in the work of world peace and in defense of human dignity.[31] Postconciliar papal teaching on sport expanded on this constructive

---

26. Sexton, *Baseball as a Road to God*. See also Price, *Rounding the Bases*.
27. Holy See Dicastery for Laity, Family and Life, "Giving the Best of Yourself," 1.1.
28. Vanysacker, "Attitude of the Holy See," 797–98.
29. Bosschaert, "Discerning Sports," 130.
30. Bosschaert, "Discerning Sports," 116–18.
31. Bosschaert, "Discerning Sports," 109–10. See Vatican II, *Gaudium et spes*, §61.

foundation, especially under Pope John Paul II, the "athlete pope," and culminated recently with the 2016 Sport at the Service of Humanity Conference. Held at the Vatican under the leadership of Pope Francis and in collaboration with the United Nations and the International Olympic Committee, this interfaith conference brought leaders from sport, business, academia, and media to determine how sport and faith can improve the dignity of human persons and peace among nations.[32] While some might complain of an aggressive politicization of American sport today, no one can argue that the church has understood sport as only a competitive game to determine a victor, or a way to stoke national pride.[33] Its stance of dialogue and its desire to seek the flourishing of human persons mark the Catholic Church's modern relationship to sport.

Scholarly foundations for a Christian theology of modern sport can be traced to post-World War II books that celebrated the nature of play and leisure. As the modern world strove to rebuild Europe in a mindset driven by productivity, authors like Josef Pieper, Hugo Rahner, and later Michael Novak described the power of the human spirit in moments of play, which could enliven communion with the divine.[34] Greater interest in the connection between sport and theology surfaced around the turn of the twenty-first century, where North American and British Protestant writers like Robert K. Johnston, Shirl Hoffman, Jim Parry, Andrew Parker, and Nick J. Watson led the charge from backgrounds in sport, kinesiology, cultural studies, or theology.[35] Theologian Robert Ellis produced the first full-length, comprehensive theology of sport manuscript in English, while Lincoln Harvey's concise book critiqued overly positive assessments of Christian engagement in sport.[36] Scholars such as the Canadian Tracy Trothen and the American Marcia W. Mount Shoop have broadened the field, using lenses of gender, race, and other facets of social identity.[37]

These predominantly Protestant authors encouraged further development in the Catholic world, where Jesuit scholar Patrick Kelly's expansive corpus presented foundational theological and historical work throughout

---

32. Edmonds, "Vatican View," 20–21.

33. Leithart, "Mystical Game."

34. H. Rahner, *Man at Play*; Pieper, *Leisure*; Novak, *Joy of Sports*.

35. Johnston, *Christian at Play*; Hoffman, *Good Game*; Parry et al., *Sport and Spirituality*; Watson and Parker, *Sport and the Christian Religion*.

36. Ellis, *Games People Play*; Harvey, *Brief Theology of Sport*.

37. Trothen, *Winning the Race?*; Mount Shoop, *Touchdowns for Jesus*. See also, Alpert and Remillard, *Gods, Games, and Globalization*; Scholes, *Christianity, Race, and Sport*.

the 2010s.[38] Drawing from patristic, medieval, and early modern thought on sport and leisure, Kelly made a persuasive argument for a more positive attitude toward sport that could be traced throughout the historical Catholic tradition. In some ways, Kelly's work paved the way for the Holy See's first ever document on sport, "Giving the Best of Yourself: A Document about the Christian Perspective on Sport and the Human Person."[39] Other Catholic writers have completed works developing a faith-informed approach to different subfields of sport thinking: history and theology, youth sport, sport psychology, morality and ethics, social justice, and spirituality.[40] Theological studies drawing from these fields can create a multifaceted perspective for reshaping our understanding of sport on both a personal and institutional level. Based on the Jesuit principle that faith can find God in all things, writers have uncovered a rich tradition where sport's capacity can create community, develop character and advance moral thought, promote hope and encourage justice, and become profoundly revelatory in the lives of sporting enthusiasts.

OVERVIEW OF THE BOOK'S CHAPTERS

As previously mentioned, the title of our book, *On the Eighth Day*, finds inspiration from a banner at a 1980s Edmonton Oilers hockey game: "On the eighth day, God created Gretzky." "The Great One" revolutionized the offensive side of the sport and became the greatest scorer in the history of the National Hockey League. Thus, according to the banner, Gretzky's scoring magic on ice rinks represented an astounding feat that could compare to the biblical six days of creation, which was followed by the sabbath day of rest on the seventh day (Gen 1). Theologically, "on the eighth day" recalls the playful, creative work at the beginning of creation, and it also marks Christ's reinvention of the first day of creation through his resurrection on Easter Sunday morning. As the *Catechism of the Catholic Church* proclaims: "The

---

38. Kelly, *Catholic Perspectives on Sports*; Kelly, *Youth Sport and Spirituality*; Kelly, "Catholics and Sport in a Global Context."

39. Holy See Dicastery for Laity, Family, and Life, "Giving the Best of Yourself."

40. Writings include: about history and theology—Lixey, *Sport and Christianity*; about youth sport—Power, "Playing Like a Champion Today," 88–110; Power and Rodgers, "From Play to Virtue," 23–44; about sport psychology—Nesti, "Persons First, Athletes Second," 94–105; Maranise, "Superstition & Religious Ritual," 83–89; about morals and ethics—McNamee, "Youth Sport and the Virtues," 74–87; McNamee, "Whose Prometheus?," 214–23; about social justice—Barbieri, "'Sport Is a School of Peace,'" 557–81; and about spirituality—Kelly, "Flow, Sport, and Spiritual Traditions," 47–58; Rodgers and Power, "Athletics as Sacrificial Offering," 97–108; Haeg, *Saint Benedict's Rule*.

eighth day begins the new creation.... The first creation finds its meaning and its summit in the new creation in Christ, the splendor of which surpasses that of the first creation."[41] In this sense, this book captures this "new day" in Catholic attitudes toward sport in the modern era and the continuing call to redeem and elevate sport in service to the human person and the glory of God.

Accordingly, the book is divided into eight chapters. Chapter 1 reviews the Christian and Catholic tradition's evolving relationship to, and understanding of, sport in several historical periods: the early church, medieval, early modern, and modern. This overview concludes with five major themes that act as the launching point for our theological investigations in subsequent chapters. Chapter 2 examines the importance of the spirit of play in sport, society, and theology. In a scientifically oriented world, we can easily overlook how the childlike action of play contains essential human elements of freedom, connectedness, and transcendence. A theology of play undergirds a theology of sport.

Chapters 3–6 provide an in-depth look at sport from a sacramental worldview, where different chapters explore the meaning of the human person from a religious perspective. Chapter 3 examines how a sacramental perspective—the belief that all of creation has the capacity to mediate God's grace—challenges a stale, materialist view of sport and thus reveals sport's capacity to act as a conduit of transcendence. Drawing on principles like "all experience is mediated" and "whatever humanizes divinizes," this chapter shows how sport is ripe for theological reflection and spiritual engagement. Chapter 4 focuses on what it means theologically to be human in sport. It offers several traits—such as "humans are restless and filled with yearning" and "humans are embodied and corporeal realities"—that provide a lens to evaluate sports and its role in communities. Chapter 5 considers how sport wrestles with pain, suffering, and loss. Because athletes must face their worst fears, this chapter offers the paschal mystery of Jesus Christ as a pattern for uniting themselves to God and journeying to new life through—not around—loss and failures. Chapter 6 completes this section by examining how sporting participants are spiritual persons. In light of the widespread phenomena of players pointing to the heavens or making the sign of the cross, we argue that ritual practices should be seen as potentially beneficial ways of engaging sport. However, we carefully differentiate ritual from routines and superstitions and conclude with some guidelines for "what" and "how" to pray in sport.

---

41. *Catechism of the Catholic Church*, 349.

The final two chapters address how human persons can act morally in sport. Chapter 7 analyzes sport as a place of human stories where people interact and develop habits that can either enable their flourishing or precipitate their downfall. Moral issues within sport including violence, rivalry, and the use of performance enhancers are moments when humans make decisions that over time become habits that shape their personhood. Chapter 8 addresses larger structural issues of social justice, like the professionalization of youth sport, where Catholicism's deeply social vision critiques and offers insight into larger structural influences within sport. Drawing on the tradition of Catholic social teaching, the chapter also describes Catholic pastoral practices—including a refugee sports program in Uganda—that reflect Pope Francis's call for dialogue and encounter in the sporting world. Combined, these two chapters underline how sport—like any human activity—is a moral activity that should seek first to build up human communities and celebrate the dignity of each person. Through personal growth and development, along with the moral desire to create a better, more just world, people of faith can engage sport as a means to cooperate with God's grace and assist in the growth of others and in the development of better communities. Fittingly, the book's conclusion engages sport through the lens of eschatology, or the theological study of the "last things." This chapter moves us into a perspective of hope, as we more deeply consider what the redemption of sport might look like on a personal, communal, and ecological level.

The uniqueness of this book is that it draws from both the world of sport and the discipline of theology to create a more comprehensive, overarching way to understand participation in sport. It touches on many subfields of theology that connect to sport: sporting histories; a theology of play and sacramental worldview; Christian anthropology and soteriology; Catholic moral thought on virtue and rivalry; and Catholic social teaching. Thus, we present an introduction into theology through sport, convinced that both are not only intellectual endeavors but can promote understanding, mercy, justice, fairness, love, hope, and spiritual flourishing for everyday living.

CHAPTER 1

From Saint Paul to Pope Francis

Sport in Catholic History

Love it or hate it, few would question that sport matters dearly in the twenty-first century. The more contested point concerns if and how sports have mattered in the twenty prior centuries of Christian history. Yet read the words of William Fitzstephen, a twelfth-century writer based in London:

> After dinner, all the young men of the city go out into the fields to play at the well-known game of football. The scholars belonging to the several schools have each their own ball, and the city tradesmen, according to their respective crafts, have theirs. The more aged men, the fathers of the players, and the wealthy citizens, come on horseback to see the contests of the young men, with whom, after their manner, they participate, their natural heat seeming to be aroused by the sight of so much agility, and by their participation in the amusements of unrestrained youth.[1]

Youth rushing outside to play sports after school. Club teams competing for a city championship. Parents living vicariously through their children's sporting endeavors. When one reads Fitzstephen's account from eight centuries ago, it seems that the modern sports-crazed society may not be as unprecedented as one thought.

The goal of this chapter is both audacious and necessary—namely to sketch out the most important contours of the Roman Catholic tradition's

---

1. Quoted in Carter, *Medieval Games*, 127.

historical engagement with sport. Whatever new vistas we hope to open in Catholic theological engagement with sport, we recognize that Catholicism is a tradition-based faith. At the same time, the Catholic and broader Christian church's attitudes and engagement with sport have dynamically evolved through time. Beginning with the biblical and patristic foundations of Christianity, this chapter synthesizes key developments, evolutions, and even revolutions in how Christians and especially Roman Catholics have engaged sport. The chapter concludes with five key theological lessons that can be drawn from this history

DO NOT RUN IN VAIN: BIBLICAL AND EARLY CHURCH PERSPECTIVES ON SPORT

What may be most striking about sport in the Bible is its near-complete absence from the canonical texts. Even as Greco-Roman sport served as what Aloys Koch calls a "vehicle for communion with the divine and for regulating humanity's relationship with God or the gods,"[2] the people of Israel did not comment much on it. To be sure, one can locate references to athletics and physical exertion in the Hebrew Bible, such as Jacob's famous wrestling match with an angel in Gen 32:25. But in a formal way, the Old Testament does not engage ancient sport in any sustained way. As we will argue, this biblical sports lacuna may have a silver lining, as it opens up a new day for Christian engagement with sport in the modern world.

The most explicit reference to sport in the Catholic Old Testament is not an auspicious one for would-be Christian athletes.[3] In 1 Macc 1:11, a group of young Jews decide to "make a covenant" with their new king, the Greek Antiochus IV Epiphanes, who had taken over the region in 175 BC. For the writer of Maccabees, this idolatrous "covenant" is signified by the construction of a new "gymnasium in Jerusalem" (1 Macc 1:14). To compete in the Greek gymnasium, Jewish male athletes underwent surgical procedures to remove the marks of circumcision, likely to assimilate better with Greek athletes who trained and competed in the nude.[4] Furious at this violation of Judaism's sacred covenant marker, the Jewish priest Mattathias and his sons, including Judas Maccabeus, launched a successful revolt against Antiochus, a rebellion which continues to be commemorated in the Jewish Hanukkah feast. This violent incident established a legacy that lingered

---

2. Ellis, *Games People Play*, 1.

3. Koch, "Biblical and Patristic Foundations," 82. The Roman Catholic canon includes seven books not found in Protestant canonical Scripture, including 1 and 2 Macc.

4. Crowther, *Sport in Ancient Times*, 75; Baker, *Sports in the Western World*, 26.

through the early Christian tradition: sport was often located at the tense intersection between Judeo-Christian religion and Greco-Roman culture, and for critics could easily become a vehicle for idolatry.

The New Testament's engagement with sport remains sparse, but trends more positive. Jesus offers no explicit commentary on sport in the four canonical Gospels. However, Saint Paul on multiple occasions invokes the motif of running as a metaphor of discipleship, most commonly in his repeated injunction to "not running in vain" (Phil 2:16; Gal 2:2). The most famous example of the running metaphor comes from 1 Cor 9:24–26, written to a Corinth community that hosted one of the four major athletic festivals of the ancient Greek world:[5]

> Do you not know that in a race the runners all compete, but only one receives the prize? Run in such a way that you may win it. Athletes exercise self-control in all things; they do it to receive a perishable wreath, but we an imperishable one. So I do not run aimlessly, nor do I box as though beating the air; but I punish my body and enslave it, so that after proclaiming to others I myself should not be disqualified.

Paul's purpose here and elsewhere (see for example Phil 2:16–27; 3:13–14; 2 Tim 2:5; 4:7) is not to praise sport in and of itself. Rather, Paul is using sport as a metaphor for discipleship, exhorting early Christians to exemplify Greek athletes' qualities of self-control, discipline, and perseverance.[6] Yet the cultural borrowing here also involved transformation. As the biblical scholar Victor Pfitzner points out, Paul's usage of the "athlete for Christ" metaphor subverted some of the stereotypical ancient associations with athletic honor by encouraging the Corinthians to embrace service to others rather than personal prestige.[7]

Following in the footsteps of Paul, several of the church fathers of the patristic period (AD 100–600) adopted this language of athlete for Christ.[8] On his way to martyrdom in Rome in the early second century, Saint Ignatius of Antioch, one of the first Christian bishops, commended his followers to "bear the infirmities of all, like a master athlete," and "like an athlete to

---

5. Baker, *Sports in the Western World*, 14. Corinth hosted the biannual "Isthmian games."

6. Paul's sporting metaphors were common in both the Greek and Hellenistic Jewish rhetorical parlance of the first century (Koch, "Biblical and Patristic Foundations," 88; Pfitzner, "Was St. Paul a Sports Enthusiast?," 91–92; Hoffman, *Good Game*, 42–43).

7. Pfitzner, "Was St. Paul a Sports Enthusiast?," 104.

8. For general commentary on this early church language, see Kelly, *Catholic Perspectives on Sports*, 99–106.

take blows yet win the fight."⁹ Ignatius helped establish the powerful Christian exemplar of the martyr-athlete, a model embodied by the young North African women Saint Perpetua and Saint Felicity of Carthage, among many others. Following in the footsteps of the martyrs, fourth- and fifth-century Christian monks adapted Paul's language of *askesis*, or "discipline," from which we take our modern word "athletics," to describe their own lives of rigorous asceticism. For example, the Western monastic forerunner Saint John Cassian (360–435) described how the monk as a "skilled athlete of Christ, like a lofty victor, wins out over his rebellious flesh," overcoming wrath, pride, and apathy as he "engages lawfully in the struggle for perfection."¹⁰ For his part, Saint John Chrysostom, the Greek Archbishop of Constantinople and renowned preacher, applied the metaphor to the broader education of lay youth, a theme that reappeared multiple times in the later tradition: "Raise up an Athlete for Christ! I do not mean by this, hold him back from wedlock and send him to desert regions to prepare him to assume the monastic life. . . . Raise up an athlete for Christ and teach him though he is living in the world to be reverent from his earliest youth."¹¹

Even as early church leaders embraced the Greek language of *askesis* and *agon* (contest) to describe the athlete of Christ, they were far less sanguine about the spectacle of the Roman *ludi* (games). If the Greeks had introduced violent Olympic sports such as *pankration*,¹² the Romans perfected the packaging of sports violence through gladiatorial games and chariot races. This in part reflected the Roman Empire's closer association of sport and exercise with military training, as well as its encouragement of sports spectacle as an outlet for potential social unrest.¹³ Despite (or perhaps because of) their wild popularity within the Roman Empire, the *ludi* drew harsh scrutiny from early Christian theologians. Around the year 200, Tertullian of Carthage, the irascible early Christian apologist, condemned the games in the longest ancient Christian treatise on sport. Tertullian attacked Roman games for their pagan overtones, arguing that "the entire apparatus

---

9. Ignatius of Antioch, "Letter to Polycarp," 96–97.
10. Cassian, *Institutes*, 128, 203, 221, 272.
11. Chrysostom, "Address on Vainglory," 95.
12. Akin to modern MMA or UFC, Greek pankratiasts engaged in no-holds-barred boxing/wrestling in which one could "trip, hack, break fingers, pull noses and ears, and even apply a stranglehold until tapped on the back, a sign that the opponent had given up" (Baker, *Sports in the Western World*, 20).
13. Crowther, *Sport in Ancient Times*, 92–93. By the year 300, upwards of 175 days on the Roman calendar included games and spectacles, including sixty-six days for chariot races and ten days for gladiatorial contests (Baker, *Sport in the Western World*, 31; Hoffman, *Good Game*, 31).

of the shows is based upon idolatry."[14] But he also raised critiques that might hit closer to home with the modern sports buff. Which fan has not experienced the feelings of "agitation," "rage," "bitterness," and "grief" that Tertullian highlights?[15] Or the ways in which sport-inspired passion and gambling can lead the fan into full-on fanaticism: "See the people coming to it already under strong emotion, already tumultuous, already passion-blind, already agitated about their bets."[16] He also castigated the gladiatorial games for disfiguring the human body, not to mention leading spectators to indulge in sinful pleasure of another's suffering and pain.[17] For Tertullian, genuine Christian identity entailed a countercultural stance against the transient pleasures of chariot races and gladiatorial contests: "Why, the rejection of these amusements is the chief sign to them that a man has adopted the Christian faith."[18] Although Tertullian's voice was the most strident, his critiques were shared by the vast majority of early Christian leaders. Across the Roman Empire, gladiators had to renounce their work to receive Christian baptism; Christian spectators at the games could be excommunicated from the Eucharist; and Christian emperors ultimately banned gladiatorial fights in the early fifth century.[19]

Even as many share Tertullian's and the early church's critiques of the gladiatorial games, modern readers are likely more suspicious of his seeming rejection of physical pleasure as such. This raises the specter of what theologians call "dualism," namely the tendency to strongly separate the bodily from the spiritual, typically to the denigration of the former. In Christianity, dualism was encouraged by the early tradition's embracing of streams of anti-material Platonic philosophy, the monastic idealization of celibacy, and an eschatological outlook that prized heavenly reward over earthly fulfillment. Such sentiments are clearly reflected in Tertullian's rhetorical question: "Can we not live without pleasure, who cannot but with pleasure die? For what is our wish but the apostle's, to leave the world, and be taken up into the fellowship of our Lord."[20] At the same time, one should

---

14. Tertullian of Carthage, *De Spectaculis*, ch. 4, para. 1. Tertullian extends this critique of the idolatrous nature of the Roman games in chapters 5–13 of his treatise.

15. Tertullian, *De Spectaculis*, ch. 15, paras. 3–4.

16. Tertullian, *De Spectaculis*, ch. 16, para. 1.

17. Tertullian, *De Spectaculis*, chs. 18–19. The third-century North African bishop Cyprian of Carthage's summation of the sin of gladiatorial spectating is even pithier: "Man is slaughtered that man may be gratified" (quoted in Baker, *Sports in the Western World*, 37).

18. Tertullian of Carthage, *De Spectaculis*, ch. 24, para. 1.

19. Baker, *Sports in the Western World*, 39.

20. Tertullian, *De Spectaculis*, ch. 28, para. 1.

not exaggerate the influence of this stream of Christian dualism. Following the Hebrew tradition going back to the creation narratives of Genesis, many early church fathers understood human beings as holistic creatures, "unified soul-bodies" rather than disembodied souls.[21] Countering the strongly dualistic gnostic Christians, Saint Irenaeus of Lyons, the second-century bishop and theologian, posited that the human body was "constitutive of human personhood."[22] This early Christian defense of the goodness of the body reflected deeper theological principles of incarnation, bodily resurrection, and the goodness of the created world, as we will explore further in chapters 2, 3, and 4.

Looking back on the biblical and patristic witness on sport, several summary conclusions emerge. First, the Bible is generally silent on sport, meaning that a modern Christian theology of sport is not predetermined by the biblical witness. Yet this silence is interrupted by the condemnation of idolatry in Maccabees and Paul's invoking of the athlete of Christ language to symbolize discipleship. The former theme is carried forward in early church criticisms of the Roman gladiatorial games, while early Christian monks and martyrs embraced the athlete of Christ metaphor with its connotations of both *agon* and *askesis*. And despite lingering currents of dualism, the biblical and early church tradition taught that the human person was a holistic unity of body, soul, and spirit. As we will see, this integral understanding of the human person undergirded a growing embrace of sport, leisure, and recreation in medieval Christian Europe.

MIRTH IN MODERATION: CHRISTIANITY AND SPORT IN THE MEDIEVAL AND EARLY MODERN PERIODS

If sport in the ancient Greco-Roman world was closely intertwined with pagan religion, it was largely desacralized in medieval Christianity. Sport played little role in the formal practice of the Christian religion in Europe, and Christian authorities largely made their peace with sport. At the same time, both popular and elite sports flourished in European society, leading theologians like Thomas Aquinas and late-medieval Humanist Catholics to advocate for what we call "mirth in moderation."

The Latin term *ludus*—used in the ancient world to describe Roman spectacle—came to encompass a much broader array of games, theater,

---

21. Koch, "Biblical and Patristic Foundations," 84, 91–93.
22. Kelly, *Catholic Perspectives on Sports*, 9.

recreation, and tournaments in medieval Europe.[23] This included throwing games such as bowls (later marbles); outdoor ball sports, including an early version of soccer known as *soule*, in which villages would compete to throw a ball into the rival village's parish church;[24] table games such as chess and backgammon; swimming and other water sports; and upper-class sports such as hunting, falconry, hawking, and jousting tournaments.[25]

This listing of medieval sports also demonstrates the integral connection between sport and war in feudal Europe. Reflecting the early church's nonviolent leanings, the medieval church initially opposed jousting, and formal church councils condemned tournaments on five separate occasions in the 1100s.[26] But as church authorities increasingly made peace with war via the Crusades, they also acquiesced to warlike sports. This rapprochement was facilitated by the large number of former knights who joined medieval monasteries, along with monastic reformers' growing emphases on rigorous physical discipline. For example, the aptly named Samson, Benedictine Abbot of Bury Saint Edmonds in twelfth-century England, was described as "extremely temperate and active and strong, and loved to go on horseback or on foot until age got the better of him."[27] Political authorities prized archery as a training ground for war, and tournaments became mock trials for Crusaders. In the fourteenth century, English kings went so far as to condemn soccer since "ball games and other diversions kept the peasantry from their archery practice."[28] Symbolically, the Catholic Church's embrace of violent sport culminated in 1471 with a jousting tournament hosted in none other than St. Peter's Square.[29]

At the village level, churches provided the space and time for sport. Sunday mornings were set aside for Mass, but Sunday afternoons were times for recreation. In this spirit, parish grounds served as sites for recreational soccer games and holy day stick-and-ball competitions that later evolved into field hockey.[30] Although men dominated upper-class sports like jousting and falconry, women participated in soccer as well as stool-ball, a game

---

23. Carter, *Medieval Games*, 17.
24. Guttmann, *Sports*, 64.
25. Reeves, *Pleasures and Pastimes*, 89–105; Carter, *Medieval Games*, 87–88.
26. Guttmann, *Sports*, 53.
27. Carter, *Medieval Games*, 58.
28. Carter, *Medieval Games*, 86; Baker, *Sports in the Western World*, 55.
29. Guttmann, *Sports*, 53.
30. Baker, *Sports in the Western World*, 45–47. Hoffman notes that this practice of hosting Sunday sport also brought in considerable revenue for local parishes (Hoffmann, *Good Game*, 62).

that later gave rise to cricket.³¹ For historian William Baker, nearly all modern sports have their roots in the "play of medieval peasants."³²

In the midst of this rising popular and elite participation in sport, medieval theologians adopted a guardedly positive attitude toward sport. In his magnum opus, the *Summa Theologiae*, Saint Thomas Aquinas posited that relaxation and rest were crucial aspects of human life that relieved the "weariness of the soul." Although Thomas argued that one can sin through "inordinate laughter and inordinate joy in excessive play," he also criticized "the man who is without mirth" for being "burdensome to others, since he is deaf to the moderate mirth of others."³³ Following Aristotle, Thomas argued that moderate play had an important place in the well-ordered human life. The virtue of *eutrapelia* (best translated as "pleasantness" or "judicious pleasure") should be cultivated through play and recreation.³⁴

By the fifteenth and sixteenth centuries, both Italian Catholic Humanists and Jesuits were embracing sport as an integral aspect of the education of youth. In Italy alone, more than eighty books were written on the topics of sport, play, and recreation between 1450 and 1650.³⁵ In one of these early works, Aeneas Sylvius Piccolomini, the Italian cardinal and future Pope Pius II, argued that boys require training in body, mind, and soul. Athletic "bodily contests" such as running, jumping, swimming, horsemanship, and archery can help produce "sturdiness of body," while also forming capable soldiers needed to "fight against the Turks."³⁶ Like Aquinas, Piccolomini saw play as a crucial part of a balanced human life, with school divided between work, sport, study, and recreation: "One should not always be intent on schooling and serious affairs, nor should huge tasks be imposed upon boys, for they will be crushed with exhaustion by such labors, and in any case if they feel overcome by irksome burdens they may be less receptive to learning."³⁷ Early Jesuits followed this trend by expanding the time for sport in their school curricula. Reducing in-class time to just over five hours, the Jesuits added an hour of sport after lunch, forty-five minutes of leisure time after other meals, and brief recreation periods between classes.³⁸ Michel de Montaigne, the seventeenth-century French Catholic philosopher, shared

---

31. Kelly, *Catholic Perspectives on Sports*, 35–36.
32. Baker, *Sports in the Western World*, 42.
33. Aquinas, *Summa Theologiae* II.II., Q.168.2–4.
34. Kelly, *Catholic Perspectives on Sports*, 110; Hoffman, *Good Game*, 63.
35. Hoffman, *Good Game*, 69.
36. Piccolomini, "Education of Boys," 141, 143.
37. Piccolomini, "Education of Boys," 143.
38. Kelly, *Catholic Perspectives on Sports*, 47.

the Jesuits' intertwining of pedagogy and play and encouraged students to engage in racing, wrestling, dancing, music, hunting, and horsemanship. For Montaigne, sport was part of the holistic formation of the human person: "We are not bringing up a soul; we are not bringing up a body; we are bringing up a man."[39]

Such positive Catholic humanist approbations of sport did not go unchallenged in the early modern Christian world. Although Martin Luther was a fan of fencing, bowling, and wrestling, and the Reformed founder John Calvin allowed for play on Sunday,[40] their Protestant Puritan successors in the Anglo-American world were not so generous. For the Puritans, the chief end of man was his "diligent pursuit of his calling in productive work," and sport and play were criticized as forms of "idleness."[41] The Puritans saw Sunday as a day of worship, not a day of rest or recreation, and the Catholic tradition of Sunday play fell victim to the rigorous spirit of Puritan devotion.[42] Versions of these Puritan attitudes soured official American Protestant viewpoints toward sport well into the nineteenth century.[43]

In summary, the medieval period saw a growing popular embrace of sport, including early forms of soccer and other stick-and-ball games, and elites encouraged militaristic sports like fencing, archery, and jousting. Sport did not have a formal religious function, but churches facilitated popular participation through offering their grounds for play on Sundays and holy days. Jesuits and other Catholic Humanists increasingly incorporated sport and play into their school curricula. And theologians such as Thomas Aquinas, Aeneas Piccolomini, and Michel de Montaigne argued that play and leisure were integral components of the virtuous life. We turn now to the modern period, an era when sport reached unprecedented heights of popularity within culture and church alike.

---

39. Quoted in Kelly, *Catholic Perspectives on Sports*, 45.

40. Hoffman, *Good Game*, 74–75; Baker, *Playing with God*, 15.

41. Hoffman, *Good Game*, 77. Harvey notes that the Puritans allowed for exercise, but even this was oriented toward improving the efficiency of work (Harvey, *Brief Theology of Sport*, 52).

42. Hoffman, *Good Game*, 84–85.

43. Grundy and Rader, *American Sports*, 9–14.

ELEVATING SPORT, REDEEMING HUMANITY: CATHOLICISM, THE PAPACY, AND SPORT IN THE MODERN WORLD

The golden age of sport—the period in which sport emerged as a modern cultural phenomenon—is typically dated to the latter half of the nineteenth century. In the midst of what Baker aptly calls a "leisure revolution,"[44] both Europeans and Americans had more time and money to dedicate to activities outside of work. Between 1850 and 1900, golf and tennis came to America; the Olympics restarted after a 1,400-year hiatus; the rules of modern soccer and hockey took shape; American football, basketball and volleyball were invented; and boxing and cycling took off. Many of these sports quickly became globalized. Under the aegis of British colonialism and American manifest destiny, soccer, baseball, basketball, and cricket entered Latin America, Asia, and Africa, where colonized peoples would soon make the games their own.[45] And as modern people flocked to playgrounds and parks, they also embraced spectator sports. For example, 22,000 fans watched the Harvard-Yale football game in 1890, and 20 million fans attended American baseball games in 1900.[46]

Not surprisingly, American Christians in the late nineteenth and early twentieth centuries also awoke to sport. After centuries of decrying the frivolity and idolatry of sport, Protestant ministers underwent a "great reversal" in their attitudes.[47] Most prominent was the Protestant "muscular Christian movement" led by figures such as the English clergymen Thomas Hughes and Charles Kingsley, and the American ministers Thomas Wentworth Higginson, Washington Gladden, and G. Stanley Hall. The muscular Christians argued that sport was the key path to building moral character and "carry[ing] the gospel to the body," in Hall's memorable phrase.[48] This linking of "spirituality to physical vigor" reflected a perceived crisis of masculinity in white, middle-class Victorian societies, tensions which are explored further in *Chariots of Fire*, the 1981 film about the life of Olympic runner and devout Evangelical Christian Eric Liddell.[49] Muscular Christianity directly shaped the rise of the Boy Scout movement and the YMCA (Young Men's Christian Association) in Britain and North America. YMCA

---

44. Baker, *Playing with God*, 23.
45. Guttmann, *Sports*, 167–79, 206–49.
46. Hoffman, *Good Game*, 99–100.
47. Hoffman, *Good Game*, 102.
48. Putney, *Muscular Christianity*, 1.
49. Grundy and Rader, *American Sports*, 26; Hoffman, *Good Game*, 119.

missionaries and other Protestant ministers introduced basketball to China in the 1890s, encouraged Japanese female athleticism, and brought soccer, cricket, and rugby to British Africa.[50] Longstanding bans on Sunday games fell away in the United States, and soon ministers would use sport as a "vehicle for evangelization" via groups like the Fellowship of Christian Athletes (FCA).[51]

Although not as prominent, parallel "muscular Catholic" movements emerged in the United States during this period. In the late nineteenth century, Jesuit colleges like Georgetown, Fordham, Santa Clara, and Xavier incorporated "field day games" and recreation hours as part of their curricula.[52] In the 1920s, Catholic campuses formalized this by embracing intercollegiate sports, including college basketball; Catholic colleges Holy Cross and Loyola Chicago would go on to win national championships in 1947 and 1963, respectively.[53] Most famously, Notre Dame football emerged in the 1920s as a national marker of Catholic identity. Led by chaplain Fr. John O'Hara, Notre Dame fused ethnicity, religion, and masculinity by encouraging visits to the Marian Grotto, team attendance at pregame Mass, and careful tabulation of students' and players' "Eucharistic receptions."[54] In the 1930s, Catholic youth sports culture took off in urban America with Bishop Bernard Sheil's establishment of the Catholic Youth Organization (CYO) in Chicago (see chapter 8). As the CYO spread across the country, the gym became an integral part of parish infrastructure, showing just how far the tradition had evolved from the time of the Maccabees.

In other areas, however, the Catholic tradition had not modernized. Most prominent here was the hyper-masculine, chauvinistic nature of early-twentieth-century Catholic sports movements. Typically, sports were envisioned as ways to reach young men, and Catholic authorities expressed deep anxieties over the impact of sports on women. For example, the German bishops roundly condemned the Nazis in the 1920s for their perceived sexualization of women's bodies, and the Vatican came out against women's

50. Guttmann, *Sports*, 206, 230, 241.

51. Meyer, "Historical Relationship," 65. William Baker notes that most early modern European communities never adopted a ban on Sunday sports, and Lutheran and Catholic immigrants brought these more tolerant "Continental Sunday" traditions to America (Baker, *Playing with God*, 148).

52. Putney, *Muscular Christianity*, 9; Kelly, *Catholic Perspectives on Sports*, 120–24. Decades later, Fordham football produced Vince Lombardi, one of the "Seven Blocks of Granite" who later became the legendary coach of the Green Bay Packers (Maraniss, *When Pride Still Mattered*, 58–59).

53. Gasaway, *Miracles on the Hardwood*, 15–16.

54. Massa, *Catholics and American Culture*, 199–204. See also Baker, *Playing with God*, 138–39.

public participation in track and field events due to perceived "masculinization" that would detract from women's natural roles as mothers.[55] Despite the patriarchal attitudes of the Catholic hierarchy, American Catholic women found manifold ways to engage in sport, reflecting the huge growth in organized women's sport in the early twentieth century.[56] Most famously, the 800-student, all-women's Immaculata College in Philadelphia became a national power in college basketball after World War II, and ultimately won the first three national championships in women's basketball between 1972 and 1974.[57]

The boom in modern Catholic sport spilled over beyond explicitly church circles, especially in Europe. Raised in a devout Catholic home and the product of French Jesuit schools, Pierre de Coubertin established the Olympic movement as a new kind of patriotic and humanist religion. Coubertin adopted the Olympic motto of *Citius, Altius, Fortius* ("Faster, Higher, Stronger") from a French Dominican rector of a school sports association, and he labeled the International Olympic Committee (IOC) as a "college of disinterested priests."[58] Later, IOC president Avery Brundage described Olympism as a "twentieth-century religion, a religion with universal appeal which incorporates all the basic values of other religions, a modern, exciting, virile, dynamic religion, attractive to the youth."[59] Whatever his movement's secularizing impulses, Coubertin convinced Pope Saint Pius X to host an exhibition of French, Belgian, and Italian gymnasts in 1906, and Pius X collaborated with Coubertin in an unsuccessful attempt to bring the Olympics to Rome in 1908.[60] As Olympism was taking root, Catholic national sports associations, along with the pan-European *Fédération internationale catholique d'éducation physique* (FICEP), arose across the continent. As in America, these associations looked to build patriotism and moral character, while also serving as a means of evangelizing youth and re-Christianizing increasingly secular societies.[61] In the meantime, French and Belgian missionaries brought their love of soccer to Africa, where the Catholic Marist priest Raphaël de la Kéthulle founded Congo's first sporting club, introduced soccer to the capital city of Léopoldville (later Kinshasa),

---

55. Vanysacker, "Attitude of the Holy See," 801–5.
56. Grundy and Rader, *American Sports*, 170–80.
57. Byrne, *O God of Players*, 1.
58. Baker, *Playing with God*, 120.
59. Baker, *Playing with God*, 123.
60. Baker, *Playing with God*, 121; Lixey, "Sport in the Magisterium of Pius XII," 104.
61. See Munoz and Tolleneer, *L'Église, Le Sport*.

and oversaw the construction of three soccer stadiums, including the largest in all of Africa in 1952.[62]

After the initial thawing of church-sport relations under Pope Pius X (reigned 1903–14), subsequent twentieth-century popes increasingly described sport as a critical point of intersection for the Catholic Church to engage in modern society. Pope Pius XI (r. 1922–39) was an accomplished mountaineer who wrote about the ways in which climbing brought him into closer contact with the spiritual realm.[63] During his long pontificate, Pope Pius XII (r. 1939–58) issued more than twenty statements on sport and emphasized how the discipline of sport can strengthen the body and "sharpen the senses," even as he critiqued the ways in which moderns and especially fascists had propagated a "cult of the body."[64] In essence, Pius XII saw the Catholic Church's role as opening sport to a broader transcendent horizon, rather than becoming an end in itself.[65] We will return to this theme at the end of the chapter.

Pope Saint John Paul II (r. 1978–2005) carried forward this emphasis on elevating sport within a spiritual horizon. Described as the "Pope of Athletes,"[66] John Paul II was an avid mountain-climber and issued over 120 discourses on sport during his twenty-seven-year pontificate.[67] More than his predecessors, he also embraced sport's role as a "cultural mediator" that could bring people together across racial, religious, and political divisions, contributing to what John Paul liked to call the "civilization of love" (see chapter 8).[68] For the Polish pope, sport's *telos* (end) was not simply to propagate itself, but rather to build human virtues of "dignity, freedom, and the integral development of man," while also contributing to the development of self-discipline and the "joy of life."[69] In this sense, the Catholic Church's approach to sport is "not an attitude of rejection or flight, but one of respect, esteem, even through correcting and elevating them: in a word, an attitude of redemption."[70] This approach of redemption—rather than wholesale acceptance—acknowledges that sport continues to be marked by shadows of

---

62. Van Reybrouck, *Congo*, 173–74.
63. Vanysacker, "Attitude of the Holy See," 799.
64. Pius XII, quoted in Feeney, *Catholic Perspective*, 31, 48.
65. Lixey, "Sport in the Magisterium of Pius XII," 109, 118.
66. Mazza, "Sport in the Magisterium," 123.
67. Vanysacker, "Attitude of the Holy See," 796.
68. Vanysacker, "Attitude of the Holy See," 125, 127–29.
69. John Paul II, quoted in Feeney, *Catholic Perspective*, 70, 72–73.
70. John Paul II, quoted in Feeney, *Catholic Perspective*, 69.

commercialism, nationalism, economic inequality, cheating, violence, and discrimination.[71]

Finally, Pope Benedict XVI and Pope Francis have continued this constructive magisterial engagement with modern sport. Benedict's unique contribution lay in his recognition of how sport is not simply a means to enjoy relaxing leisure, but also an important way for modern people to experience excitement and "escape from the wearisome enslavement of daily life."[72] In keeping with the overall theme of his pontificate, Pope Francis has strongly emphasized how sport can contribute to a culture of encounter, in light of sport's ability to unite people and build dialogue across borders of culture, language, race, religion, and ideology, which is presented more fully in chapter 8.[73] In 2018, Francis commissioned the Dicastery of Laity, Family and Life to issue the Vatican's most extensive magisterial teaching on sport, "Giving the Best of Yourself." This document reiterates several emerging themes in modern papal teaching on sport, such as sport's contribution to the virtuous life, sport's role in facilitating creative freedom exercised within limits, and sport's potential to "foster friendly relations between people of all classes, countries, and races."[74] At the same time, "Giving the Best of Yourself" notes the harmful features of modern sport, including a "winning at all costs" attitude, an obsession with profits, corruption, nationalism, and the violent and derogatory practices associated with "negative spectating."[75]

Overall, the late nineteenth and twentieth centuries saw an unprecedented boom in both sports participation and sports spectating around the world.[76] Overcoming their previous ambivalence or hostility, both Catholic and Protestant leaders propagated a muscular Christianity with a central place for sport and fitness in Christian life. Catholic popes engaged sport as

---

71. John Paul II, "Address of John Paul II," para. 8.

72. Benedict XVI, quoted in Clemens, "Sport in the Magisterium of Benedict XVI," 141.

73. Francis, "Address of Pope Francis to Members of the European Olympic Committee," para. 2.

74. Holy See Dicastery for Laity, Family and Life, "Giving the Best," §§1.1, 1.3, and 3.6. The quotation echoes *Gaudium et Spes*, §61, the most explicit Vatican II passage on sport in the modern world: "May this leisure be used properly to relax, to fortify the health of soul and body through spontaneous study and activity, through tourism which refines man's character and enriches him with understanding of others, through sports activity which helps to preserve equilibrium of spirit even in the community, and to establish fraternal relations among men of all conditions, nations and races."

75. Holy See Dicastery for Laity, Family and Life, "Giving the Best," §4.1.

76. For important Christian perspectives from the Global South, see Adogame et al., *Global Perspectives*.

one of the primary "signs of the times" in the modern world,[77] arguing that infusing sport with Christian virtue could elevate sport, enhance human dignity, and build a civilization of love.

CONCLUSION: FIVE THEOLOGICAL TAKEAWAYS FROM THE CATHOLIC TRADITION ON SPORT

Looking back on the broad sweep of the Catholic historical tradition on sport, what can we conclude? What areas emerge as especially fruitful contexts for contemporary theological engagement? Among many possibilities, we would highlight five key themes.

First, references to sport are sparse in the Bible and the early Christian tradition. On one hand, this is a serious lacuna, and for some Christians reinforces the relative theological insignificance of sports.[78] Yet there is also an opportunity here. Unlike highly contested contemporary issues such as sexuality or marriage, a Catholic theology of sport does not have to sort out a contested scriptural witness. The tradition is not wholly silent, nor is it overdetermined. In other words, there is ample space for a "new day" in theological engagement with sport, as this book sets out to offer.

Second, sport provides a new and fruitful way to engage a deeply incarnational "theology of the body." The phrase itself is typically associated with Catholic sexual teaching, and especially John Paul II's influential corpus of work.[79] But the Catholic tradition's incarnational understanding of the human person as a holistic body-spirit undergirds a positive appreciation for the central roles of sport, recreation, exercise, and play in youth education and human life more broadly. Sport offers one of the preeminent ways that modern people experience their bodies and engage the material world, yet it is also a primary means for the integral development of the human person's mind and spirit. We will examine these incarnational themes in more depth in chapters 3 and 4.

Third, sport throughout the tradition has offered powerful metaphors for Christian discipleship and the seeking of moral virtue. From Saint Paul and ancient Christian monks to the modern papacy, the discipline of sport has served as both a template and a vehicle for character development and

---

77. The language of "signs of the times" is from Vatican II, *Gaudium et Spes*, §4.

78. Due to biblical silence, the Protestant Reformer John Calvin classified sport and recreation as among the "adiaphora," or matters of indifference (Hoffman, *Good Game*, 75).

79. John Paul II, *Theology of the Body*; Wojtyla, *Love and Responsibility*.

moral formation. As will be examined more closely in chapter 7, this linking of sport and morality is not foolproof or without ambiguities. But theology must take seriously sport as one of the primary markers of identity in the modern world, and the church remains committed to raising up athletes for Christ here in the twenty-first century.

Fourth, the Catholic historical tradition reminds us that the dangers and shadows of sport are present in every age. If past Christians were too quick to condemn or trivialize sport, contemporary Christians may be overly inclined to uncritically celebrate it. Yet the dangers that Tertullian and others highlighted in ancient Rome—idolatry, spectacle, commercialism, and violence—remain very much present in the current era of ESPN, Reddit, and Bleacher Report. The church's ultimate purpose is to give glory to God by supporting the integral development of the human person and the salvation of souls. Sport has the potential to contribute to the personal and social mission of the church, yet it can also usher in negative forces of social division and exploitation, as we will examine in chapters 7 and 8.

In this spirit, then, theology's role is not just to celebrate sport, but also elevate it to a higher purpose. This is best facilitated when sport is neither seen as its own religion, *a la* Coubertin's Olympism, nor as a pillar in what Pope Pius XII called a "closed and intransigent nationalism,"[80] as was evident in Nazi Germany. At the same time, denigrating or dismissing sport is equally harmful, especially given the central role that sport plays in both modern culture and the individual lives of young people. Rather, the Catholic tradition sees sport as part of a sacramental worldview and as best located within a broadly transcendent, theistic understanding of the world. Like sacraments, sports are communal symbols that point beyond themselves to a transcendent reality, yet also help bring about that reality through embodied practice (see chapter 3). And one of the pressing theological tasks facing Christians and people of good will is how to facilitate sport's contributions to the civilization of love, human dignity, and the culture of encounter (see chapter 8). First, though, we need to go back to the beginning, namely to the spirit of play that marks the Catholic, Christian understanding of God as Creator.

---

80. Pius XII, quoted in Feeney, *Catholic Perspective*, 30.

CHAPTER 2

The Spirit of Play

The Heart of Sports and Religious Faith

THERE IS A LOOK that every athlete, coach, or sports fan has received from someone, which says: "You can't spend that much of your free time on sports, can you?" Whether it is attending games, following fantasy leagues, or listening to sports-talk radio, nonfans sometimes question sportspeople's in-depth dedication to fun and games. In today's sports-crazed day and age, there is some latitude shown to those who cannot get enough of their favorite sports, and yet fandom or unending sport participation can look out-of-touch, foolish, or immature to others.

As we demonstrated in chapter 1, Christians have participated in sport throughout history. This is because, at least in part, sport speaks deeply to the human condition and the human connection to God. Thus, from a theological point of view, we want to ask, "How is the Spirit of God at play within our human bodies and our communities?" Understanding more completely the heart of sport—that is, its spirit of play—can enrich the conviction that human beings are made in God's image and likeness.[1] While others may reprimand sportspeople for their dedication, those who choose to commit to sport find something dynamic within it.

This chapter studies the spirit of play in two sections. The first distinguishes between play and sport, examining the importance of play in sport and in society at large. We argue that the vitality of the spirit of play within sport appears to be absent or distorted in today's scientifically oriented

---

1. L. Johnson, *Revelatory Body*, 105–6.

world, or what philosopher Charles Taylor calls the modern world's "immanent frame."[2] The second section builds on the first and articulates three aspects of play that are fruitful for theological reflection: freedom, connectedness or unity, and transcendence. Unpacking how the spirit of play in sport demonstrates these aspects can enhance the thinking and experiences of those engaged in theology and sport. A brief conclusion reaffirms the importance of the spirit of play, especially in light of religious faith's praise of childhood.

THE SPIRIT OF PLAY: ESSENTIAL TO SPORT AND HUMAN LIVING

Sport is a derivative of play. Play is a basic human activity which appears across human cultures and the animal kingdom. Sport is experienced as universal in a globalized, media-fed world, but its role is not as foundational as that of play. American sport sociologist Jay Coakley describes sport as a set of competitive activities—whether involving rigorous physical exertion or complex physical skills—institutionalized by an organizational body where participants are motivated by enjoyment or external rewards.[3] Track and field, for instance, may seem as simple as running, jumping, and throwing, from a recreational standpoint, but sporting rules and standards of participation require governing bodies, penalties for rule-breakers, and the awarding of trophies and prize money. Sport can become highly organized and serious. Sport is a complex human phenomenon, engaging all levels of society and government while appealing to people of different ethnicities, ages, genders, and more. Participants include players, spectators, coaches and referees, along with more hidden roles like statisticians, mascots, and sporting goods salespeople. Sport is embedded in a globalized twenty-first century, playing a significant role in many people's lives.

Sport can lift the human spirit to its highest peak and send it to wallow in the worst of human messiness.[4] At its best, sport offers a number of physical and mental health benefits for participants. It can be a place of unfolding drama, acceptance, and friendship, providing mentors for young people and breaking barriers between ethnocultural groups. At its worst, sport can promote an obsession to win that dehumanizes participants, leading to cheating, drug and physical abuse, and deepening ethnic divides. It can become overcommercialized and a pawn in geopolitical disputes. The

---

2. Taylor, *Secular Age*, 539–93.
3. Coakley, *Sport in Society*, 20.
4. Hoven, "Recovering Spiritual Centers," 55–57.

moral ambiguity of sport requires a constant renewal of its play-spirit. Organizations like Project Play and Right to Play[5] highlight the need to harness the spirit of play in sport so that its many benefits may assist communities around the globe; these promote play as the heart of human re-creation and sport as a means to foster excellence in people.

A theology of play can help in this effort. Proponents of play in sport rightly highlight the potential benefits of sporting participation and the need to question negative youth sporting trends, like early specialization, heavy time and travel schedules, and lack of proper coaching. The dominance of these trends is often set by a hypercompetitive attitude that forces adult mentalities into youth sport. Simplifying sports and shaping them around the spirit of play can make them more accessible and inclusive for kids—and adults—today.

Outside of sport, research into play highlights the social costs of losing the spirit of play. Consider how the North American lifestyle is often oriented toward performance and work: people labor for long hours to become successful in a career and at school, which secures wealth, class standing, and a more comfortable living standard. An obsessive industriousness and subsequent demanding lifestyle become excessive to the point that people often boast when they are overworked and hyperbusy.[6] Hungering for an escape in free time, society's screen-obsessed world offers the constant buzz of smartphones with TikTok, Snapchat, and unlimited video streaming. Instead of doing things simply for their own sake—for instance, enjoying a good meal, glass of wine, or time spent with family and friends—people seek out instrumental purposes and subpurposes—that is, what will make them laugh, be entertained, or earn money on the side.

It is plain to see that modern culture has become overly serious, losing its ability for play and even limiting the ability to giggle or dwell in delight.[7] Wanting to be impressive and oriented toward success, people gear every minute toward their work goals. Philosopher and Catholic intellectual Michael Novak argued that the roots of this mentality lay with Marxism and the Protestant work ethic, two worldviews that leave little room for playfulness and delight.[8] The former privileges production and work; the latter is anchored in an individualistic Calvinistic doctrine that purges pleasure and

---

5. For more information on these organizations, see https://www.aspenprojectplay.org/ and https://www.righttoplay.ca/en-ca/.

6. Ramsay, *Reclaiming Leisure*, 56.

7. Ramsay, *Reclaiming Leisure*, 52.

8. Novak, *Joy of Sports*, 218–28.

delays enjoyment for the afterlife.[9] Others have claimed that a hypercapitalist, consumerist viewpoint drives a competitiveness that overwhelms human lives and zaps any real enjoyment. Whatever the cause, cultures that lose interest in the spirit of play risk becoming more flippant and self-indulgent in trivial distractions if they avoid more humanly satisfying forms of play.[10]

The importance of play is found in its simplicity in human experience and its complexity for human understanding.[11] Play is a free activity that is both serious and nonserious, which at the same time is absorbing and freeing.[12] Humans must freely choose to play, but in choosing it they lose themselves in it. In an act of free play, the act is performed for itself and not for anything beyond itself, as experienced in a game of hide-and-seek, dancing with others or alone, or swapping jokes or stories with someone. The simplicity of play is enjoyed for its innocence, absorption, enthusiasm, and delight. Its nonutilitarian essence counters our work-a-day world.

How do people reclaim this spirit of play? Twentieth-century Thomistic philosopher Josef Pieper questioned the loss of play as his German homeland rebuilt itself after World War II. He believed that the reconstruction required more than engineers and builders; creativity was needed to reconsider the vocation of human beings in modern society. This creative effort required leisure, which is not synonymous with idleness or laziness. Pieper promoted the ideal of leisure to break the ongoing cycle of ends and means of everyday life. Instead, he wanted people to make time to reflect on "humanity's spiritual self-understanding . . . the deep connection between leisure and spiritual freedom," according to one synopsis.[13] With the continued growth of a technological mindset in a computerized world, know-how and production can become the central values of life. Subsequently, spending leisure time in wonder and deep thinking can be viewed as a waste of time. But wasting time is exactly what we need! For Pieper, human beings become unhinged without leisure: increased work schedules and ongoing busyness stamp out the need for receptively seeing and savoring things as they are.[14] Reclaiming the spirit of play requires awakening the senses of awe and admiration toward all that is within the world.

Prior to Pieper speaking out against the loss of the spirit of play, Dutch cultural historian Johan Huizinga set out to explain the primary significance

---

9. Kretchmar and Watson, "Paradoxical Athlete," 28–29.
10. Ramsay, *Reclaiming Leisure*, 52.
11. Ramsay, *Reclaiming Leisure*, 51.
12. Huizinga, *Homo Ludens*, 3.
13. Kimball, *Experiments against Reality*, 343.
14. Kimball, *Experiments against Reality*, 346.

of play in human culture. In his classic text, *Homo Ludens*, Huizinga argued that researchers are wrong to look for an evolutionary purpose in play, as if to determine the goal of play. Instead, he proposed that play must first be understood for "its profoundly aesthetic quality."[15] Huizinga explained: "The fun of playing resists all analysis, all logical interpretation.... It cannot be reduced to any other mental category ... this fun-element characterizes the essence of play."[16] For him, play is a function of living and cannot be broken into smaller pieces; it is a first principle of human reality. Thus, recovering a full sense of the spirit of play uncovers a deep part of human nature. Unfortunately, modern people have an impulse to separate their serious world (that is, intellectual, mature, difficult, cultural) from play (that is, physical-emotional, infantile, easy, natural).[17] In contrast, Huizinga argued that play is a vital element that creates the very possibility of culture and thus precedes more serious things. While appearing to be utterly useless, it remains indispensably important. For him, play came before and made possible major intellectual and cultural activities, whether law, literature, or love. It is not mere foolishness. It allows for exploration, deep imaginative thought, fostering of friendship, and other capacities.[18] As Huizinga and others lament, aligning organizations and modern society according to efficiencies of technology and scientific thoroughness threaten to dampen the play instinct.[19]

A defense of play need not overrun other parts of life. People must still earn a living, clean their homes, and clip their nails even as we question an overly zealous work mentality driven by production, efficiency, and discipline. For philosopher G. K. Chesterton, one must both fully drink the intoxicating waters of play while being soberly alert to its limits. Chesterton believes Christians should revel in the pleasures of play and not become blind to the perils of play and the discontent in our world. Enjoying the world requires addressing inequalities in the world, including in sports. A realist seeking after truth, Chesterton accepts the bizarre nature of reality and holds Christians to a higher standard, where they must find "fiercer delight" in play and celebration and "fiercer discontent" against forms of injustice.[20] Here Chesterton keeps in check the potentially escapist nature of play through a passionate engagement in human living. As discussed

---

15. Huizinga, *Homo Ludens*, 2.
16. Huizinga, *Homo Ludens*, 3, 7.
17. Ramsay, *Reclaiming Leisure*, 52.
18. Kretchmar and Watson, "Paradoxical Athlete," 25.
19. Huizinga, *Homo Ludens*, 199.
20. Kretchmar and Watson, "Paradoxical Athlete," 29–31.

in chapter 1, medievalist Thomas Aquinas explains that playful activities provide refreshment, relaxation, and pleasantness for people, as described by the Aristotelian concept of *eutrapelia*.[21] He holds play in high esteem, comparing it to the contemplation of wisdom, where both are enjoyable and done for their own sake. In light of this thinking, Aquinas argues that someone might sin if they do not have a reasonable amount of play in their lives; similarly, they may also sin if play becomes excessive or escapist. In both Aquinas and Chesterton, the pleasure of play is prized and admired, though both philosophers call for balancing the spirit of play in their own ways.

A modern insight can help in furthering understanding of a Catholic theology of sport. Several decades ago, Protestant theologian Langdon Gilkey wrote about the distinguishing characteristics of Catholicism. Among his insights, he remarked that the Catholic religion manifests "a remarkable sense of humanity and grace in the communal life of Catholics," more than he believed he experienced as a Protestant in the middle of the twentieth century.[22] What he saw as more universally embodied in Catholicism is "the love of life, the appreciation of the body in the senses, of joy and celebration, the tolerance of the sinner, these natural, worldly, and 'human' virtues."[23] Thus, the spirit of play for Catholics is historically far removed from a strictly puritanical or spiritualist endeavor. Instead, Catholicism tends to emphasize God's presence in the world or God's nearness or immanence, whereas Protestantism typically leans toward emphasizing the absence of God from the world and God's distance from creation.[24] Protestantism will typically fear the risk of idolatry and superstition, whereas Catholicism tends to be more concerned with a world where God is only marginally present. While neither position is false and some Catholics today might identify more with Protestant tendencies (and vice versa), the slight distinction reveals how a Catholic theology of sport will lean toward grasping the pleasures of sport, questioning a lack of grace and joy, and embracing the possibility of God's presence in the sweat of it all.

THE SPIRIT OF PLAY: FREEDOM, CONNECTEDNESS, AND TRANSCENDENCE

Play is an integral part of human living, a fundamental element for human flourishing. It is not merely a distraction or a moment to recharge within a workaholic world. In fact, it is a natural part of evolution, present in the

---

21. Kelly, "Christians and Sport," 46–48.
22. Gilkey, *Catholicism Confronts Modernity*, 160.
23. Gilkey, *Catholicism Confronts Modernity*, 160.
24. Greeley, *Catholic Imagination*, 5.

animal kingdom, and foundational to the formation of human culture. Physical or mental benefits of free play aside, religious thinking appreciates its freeness, festivity, connectedness, and openness.[25] Play can be a reminder of humankind's origins and destiny, their communion with God and others. At its most basic level, play reminds us all that humans are spiritual, religious beings.

For something as important as play, one would think that the Bible would be a leading booster of it. Biblical scholar Luke Timothy Johnson notes that there are relatively sparse explicit references to play in the books in the Bible (similar to the lack of sporting examples, as stated in chapter 1).[26] The most common play activity in the Bible is the making of music, as when David played a harp for Israel's King Saul (1 Sam 16:16–17), followed by animals playing, like the instance of Ps 104 which recounts the playing of sea creatures (v. 26). Johnson notes that the most famous instance of play occurs in the book of Exodus, where the Israelites "ate and drank and rose up to play" before the golden calf at Mount Sinai (32:6). This negative instance of play can be countered by a positive image of earthly reconciliation, where a child plays unharmed near a cobra's den in Isaiah 11:8. Johnson explains that some play imagery is implicitly invoked in sex (Gen 26:8) and the delight sensed in God's act of creation (Prov 8:30–31). Nevertheless, for such a foundational experience, it is surprising that the Scriptures are not more forthcoming on the topic.[27] Whatever the allusive nature of biblical references to play, one should not simply dismiss the topic. Rather, if theology tries to make sense of what God is up to in the world, then for Johnson "the human activity of play must be regarded as potentially of the greatest significance for theological reflection."[28] If a spirit of play is integral in every culture, it is necessary for a deeper examination of sport.

This point is also made in the work of Huizinga. Paradoxically, play is serious and silly, linked to spiritual values and cultural importance. In truth, the two—play and seriousness—appear interchangeable and one-in-the-same, while remaining completely opposed to each other. Play wants to become more serious, while that which is most serious, like law and war, can become imagined as a form of play. Thus, one commentator notes that culture emerges, develops, and renews itself from this interplay of seriousness

---

25. Johnston, "How Might Theology of Play Inform?," 12.
26. L. Johnson, *Revelatory Body*, 86.
27. L. Johnson, *Revelatory Body*, 87.
28. L. Johnson, *Revelatory Body*, 87.

and play,[29] where this deeper reality begs for more careful theological reflection than the Bible puts forth.

The remainder of this section reviews what Johnson calls the three most striking aspects of play for theological thinking and presents them in light of further theological considerations and contemporary sporting examples. These major aspects can enrich thinking about play and also show the value of theological reflection.

Freedom

Luke Timothy Johnson notes first the theme of freedom for theological investigation: "the paradox that the human spirit experiences a distinctive and joyful freedom when constrained by rules to which the human has freely consented."[30] The freedom of play is confounding: people's freedom to enter into play is matched by their loss of freedom when absorbed in an activity. Two authors explain: "Being chosen by play, being captivated by play experiences, emphasizes the forfeiture of our freedom. We choose to play while, at the same time, expecting that play will return the favor and choose us."[31] Choosing to play is a moment of both action and receptivity. People embrace play and then must be embraced by play. The feigner, cheat, or spoilsport do not fully allow play to embrace them. Instead, the one who freely enters into play's delight lets it take control of their living.

Athletes know well the need to fully commit to play's embrace. Two basketball examples are instructive. Steve Kerr, head coach of the Golden State Warriors, has won multiple NBA championships as a coach and player. Kerr has marveled at the joy and childlike enthusiasm of his star point guard Stephen Curry. Curry's entering into and receiving from the game reveals a love for playing the sport. Subsequently, joy is one of the pillars of Kerr's coaching philosophy: "Joy causes you to focus on the journey; not just the end result. It fuels the fires of perseverance in the hard times. Joy enables you to play looser, with more freedom and aliveness, which ultimately means you're going to play with more creativity and tenacity."[32] In using words like "journey" and "perseverance," Kerr underlines the need to become wholly devoted in play. Such devotion is then reciprocated, where a player can relax safely under play's shield and play more freely and completely on the court.

---

29. Otterspeer, *In Praise of Ambiguity*, 54.
30. L. Johnson, *Revelatory Body*, 104.
31. Kretchmar and Watson, "Paradoxical Athlete," 24.
32. Freiberg and Freiberg, "4 Things," para. 5.

NBA All-Star Pascal Siakam explains how his playing style lost its freedom and thus choked out his abilities on the court. As a youngster in Cameroon, Siakam was sent to a junior seminary to become a Catholic priest, but he eventually became a basketball star at New Mexico State.[33] After winning an NBA title with the Toronto Raptors in 2019, he and his teammates were knocked out of the playoffs the following year. Reviewing the final game of the season, Siakam noted how he had lost his playful spirit: "I'm always somebody [who] has fun playing the game and I love this game and I don't (ever) want to be able to play the game without any joy."[34] Distractions and pressures within the sport moved him from what mattered most: enjoying the game. Siakam, like Kerr and Curry above, recognized the need to fully enter into the sport and give himself over to it, finding joy within his offering.

Sport psychologists often speak of finding flow within sport, where players are in their zone, locked-in, or can't miss. Flow theory underlines the enjoyment attained when people perform an activity for its own sake (i.e., autotelic) rather than for extrinsic rewards.[35] There is a difference between attaining pleasure and enjoyment: a pleasurable activity does not require extensive attention or personal investment, whereas enjoyment is found typically when people's attention is fully given and they experience growth in that area. Fully and freely entering into an activity allows the enjoyment received to be greater than the pleasure amassed. In freely choosing to play—whatever form of play is chosen—play enhances the quality of life.

Play also reveals an important moral quality of human freedom, where there can be different depths to freedom.[36] If one is free to play tennis, one might get lucky enough to make a perfect shot and take a point from a superior opponent. However, this is not much of an accomplishment. The real growth in freedom would be to sacrifice one's time and dedicate one's talents to the sport, improving to the point where one can consistently hit the ball well and win important rallies. Honing skills and developing as a player allows an athlete to enter into the game more freely and more effortlessly. Constraining oneself by the rules of the game and a coach's instruction produces a richer freedom and internal enjoyment. This reality within playing a sport affirms the moral quality of human freedom; one can be more or less free. Further, play is also acknowledged for its role in moral growth

---

33. Siakam, "Taking a Chance on the Unknown."

34. Ganter, "Raptors' Pascal Siakam," para. 5.

35. Kelly, "Flow, Sport, and Spiritual Traditions," 49. Flow theory was established by Mihaly Czikszentmihalyi.

36. Pinckaers, "Freedom for Excellence," 59.

and human independence. Play's exploratory nature releases oneself from pressures of felt need; it introduces one to new activities for their own sake and pleasure; and it enticingly shifts an individual into more sophisticated forms of play that move one from animal intelligence to specifically human reasoning.[37] In both moral growth and the ability to find greater freedom, play serves an indispensable role.

The power of play is captured in the novel *Indian Horse*, by Richard Wagamese. A young Ojibwe boy, Saul Indian Horse, was taken from his family in the 1950s to a government-sponsored, church-run residential school. As Saul fights for survival in the harshest of school environments, he finds hope in learning how to ice skate. After shoveling the snow off the outdoor skating rink at the break of dawn, Saul skated around the surface and, at least momentarily, felt free of the tragedy of the residential school: "As I laced on the skates my fingers actually trembled. Not from the cold but from the knowledge that freedom was imminent, that flight was at hand. I floated out onto a snow-white stage in a soliloquy of grace and motion. I loved it. Every time I skated I felt as though I had created the act. It was pure and new and startling."[38] Play's exploratory and moral qualities gave Saul hope. "Every time, I would envision the move and then make it happen. I reached out with all the love in my heart and let it carry me deeper into the mystery."[39] For Saul, the mystery was the unseen world made by the Creator and told to him by his grandmother. Experiencing greater freedom on the ice enabled him to reach out beyond himself and find hope in his tragic situation.

The spirit of play—its freeness and total absorption—mirrors important Christian beliefs about creation. Just as Saul experienced freeness in his absorption in play, similarly it is believed that God the Creator created the universe out of wisdom, love, and delight (Prov 8:30–31), playing it into existence.[40] The *Catechism of the Catholic Church* states how the universe "proceeds from God's free will" because God "wanted to make his creatures share in his being, wisdom, and goodness."[41] All of creation is invited to share in this play event. In a world upheld and sustained continually by the Creator, creatures utterly depend on their Maker and celebrate God's "wisdom and freedom" and "joy and confidence."[42] This divine playfulness openly invites all to a freely given communion with God and all creation. A

---

37. MacIntyre, *Dependent Rational Animals*, 85.
38. Wagamese, *Indian Horse*, 64.
39. Wagamese, *Indian Horse*, 66.
40. H. Rahner, *Man at Play*, 12.
41. *Catechism of the Catholic Church*, 295.
42. *Catechism of the Catholic Church*, 301.

more complex understanding of play helps comprehend a central Christian doctrine, and the structured freedom within play reveals something deeper about Christian belief.

Connectedness

The second aspect of play that requires deeper theological reflection is connectedness: "play provides a place where we can observe the interplay between the individual body and other bodies that emphasizes the coordination (even in competition) among them in the making of a greater 'body.'"[43] Studies into human and animal play underline the social dynamics of play, where children's rough-housing or lovers' flirtatious touches make possible deeper connections. In play, a richer unity is often possible in an embodied way through both cooperation and even competition, improving bodily awareness within and among human beings. Today many people long for connection in an era aptly described as the "lonely century."[44] Play draws us physically and emotionally together quite unlike anything else.

The experience of feeling connected or strongly unified to a teammate or opponent during sport participation is common yet still remarkable. Bonds built through playing and practicing together unite people, whether on a local recreational team or at the top levels of international play. In preparation for the 1980 Winter Olympics in Lake Placid, New York, Father David Bauer—whose famous Boston Bruins brother, Bobby, helped build the Bauer Hockey equipment company—addressed the Canadian Olympic hockey team with the idea that the unity felt in sport was a major marker in a sporting life:

> Realizing that, as you are taking to the ice with 20 others, you all have one common goal of playing together that is beautiful, uplifting and satisfying. It is a noble quest to represent that team and share together in whatever the results of that contest may be. I recall, on a few occasions, how deep the agony was of sharing a defeat together [and] how much joy we shared in a victory—how each felt his own contribution to the victory. We win together, and as a team, we suffer defeats and setbacks. The unity of endeavour, the unity of spirit, is strong.[45]

---

43. L. Johnson, *Revelatory Body*, 104–5.
44. Hertz, *Lonely Century*, 6.
45. Bauer, "Olympic Speech," 1.

Bauer added that the ability to play and practice together produces teams that are more tenacious to play against. He concluded his reflection with a prayer: "Father, unify our team as we play together."[46] Bauer extols the spiritual value of unity, where through cooperation individual efforts produce something humanly and divinely satisfying. From a tactical standpoint, the sum is greater than its parts; from a human perspective, coming together as a team changes individuals in a real way. This is an experience of God's grace working within human experience (as we will explore further in the next chapter).

Play within sport is often competitive, promoting intense athletic performances that seek victory in a contest. This head-to-head nature of sport, where some claim that competition has only a destructive element to its functioning, can become dangerous to the development of persons.[47] However, this mentality overlooks the cooperative elements of sport within a competitive environment: agreement among parties to play by rules, respect shown to opponents, hosting games and welcoming one's opponent to a field or court, improving skills through co-striving for excellence, and sharing social signs of respect (e.g., a customary handshake, gift exchange, or even a shared meal at a tournament). Hypercompetitiveness stemming from a winning-at-all costs mentality, whether expressed through cheating, drug use, or bending the rules of the game, forsakes the pledge to play the game as it is agreed upon. These issues block players' abilities to connect with one another and their opponents (see more in chapter 7).

Problems within sports that twist the spirit of play must be critically and carefully named, exposed, and framed. Sport sociology has a critical role in this regard. Research into the ethics of sport, like the bribing of referees or the marginalization of female athletes, highlights fundamental injustices within the sporting world. To learn about historical or structural problems can be difficult for sports fans, where the findings reveal injustices that seemingly diminish sport's magical qualities and unifying capacities. On the other hand, such critical sociological analysis runs the risk of propagating a view of sport that frames issues through a victim-perpetrator binary framework that only names victims and the accused.[48] Using this lens alone to examine sport overlooks the complexities of human living and the paradoxical nature of truth, especially as found in the spirit of play. Feeling and seeing how sport brings together human persons—enabling their cooperation and making them a larger body or team—is also an important element for a

---

46. Bauer, "Olympic Speech," 1.

47. Kohn, *No Contest*, 2. See examples of this concern in L. Johnson, *Revelatory Body*, 100–104.

48. Center for Action and Contemplation, "My Story."

proper understanding of sport's social impact. A religious stance that opens the human spirit to the created world pushes back against the modern tendency to trust only in oneself, what one can empirically verify, and doubt anything beyond oneself.[49] An inclusive religious viewpoint enables people to see new possibilities, to draw together that which seems separate, and to trust in a God who seemingly made the world with many ambiguities.

This deeper sense of connection and unity through play requires human reflection. Players often recognize that through their playing experiences they have gained many friends—and perhaps that a majority of their friendships come from sporting participation. Jesse Owens, four-time 1936 Olympic Champion and symbol of African-American pride, memorably commented: "Friendships born on the fields of athletic strife are the real gold of competition. Awards become corroded; friends gather no dust."[50] Reflecting on sporting experiences brings to light the power of play instead of viewing sport as little more than an escape from reality. In the complex activity of sport, participants have the opportunity to understand all that is human in a self-revealing mirror.[51] Thus, grasping the foundational unity among human persons is perhaps no more evident than in the moment of play.

The deep communion desired by religious persons is captured well in the playful spirit of worship, especially as loneliness grows amidst an individualizing, technologically-driven society. For Catholics, unity with others is made visible when people enter the church at baptism: they become incorporated into the body of Christ and, according to the *Catechism*, all "natural or human limits of nations, cultures, races, and sexes" are transcended.[52] In the act of worship, the spirit of play is evident; however, this might surprise some faithful. Many see worship at Mass as too scripted and the antithesis of play, but they miss what is right before their eyes: the priest is dressed in an alb and stole, celebratory music is played, and particular rules for the order of prayer are followed. This is a playful, imaginative setting. Whereas people often seek out sources of entertainment to avoid life's troubles, events of worship are moments to acknowledge one's deepest concerns and with an open spirit recognize that God's playful grace is capable of reshaping one's life and circumstances. Further, in this playful setting, participants are reminded how rigid divisions of class, race, political ideology, and gender are not of God's reign. Play thus has a vital role in connecting worshipers, especially as moralists and pragmatists question religious worship as

49. Lane, "Reconstructing Faith for a New Century," 160, 172.
50. Yerkovich, "WE," 215.
51. Bauer, "Philosophy of Sport," 2.
52. *Catechism of the Catholic Church*, 1267.

something that is merely theatrical or even trivial.[53] In the playful spirit of worship, religious believers are purified from spiritualisms that separate the soul from the human body, that privatize Christian faith, or that lack the courage to face life as it is.[54] Becoming part of a larger reality (i.e., the body of Christ)[55] seems only possible with the help of the playful Spirit given from God the Creator.

Transcendence

Third, Johnson describes his final aspect of play for theological reflection: "play is a readily available example of the experience of transcendence, when, even momentarily, an individual has the sense of being both in one's own body and present in the bodies of others."[56] Whereas the second aspect of play focuses on connection with others, this third dynamic shifts the emphasis toward sensing something beyond that which can be seen or measured—that is, can one feel both in her body and be present in the bodies of others?

Another story from *Indian Horse* describes this sense of transcendence—of being both in our body and in others' bodies—when Saul plays his first game of ice hockey with other boys:

> There was a collision at the blue line and the puck squirted free. It spun like a small planet in a universe of white. Everyone reacted at the same time. I could hear the clomp of their blades. But I pushed hard, evenly, and I was at full speed in three strides. I scooped the puck onto my stick and cradled it as I pumped with my other arm. . . . I was flying, skating as fast as I could go, and then time slowed to a crawl. I could hear my breath, the yells of the other boys behind me, feel the pump of the blood in my chest, see the eyes of the goalie squinting in concentration.[57]

Feeling alive in his first game action, Saul sensed the other boys around him, including a connection with the opposing goalie who stood between him and the goal. Just as the puck seemed like a planet within the solar system, Saul felt part of something much bigger than a trivial match with schoolmates.

---

53. Guardini, *Church and the Catholic*, 171.

54. Lane, *Foundations for a Social Theology*, 167.

55. Lane, *Foundations for a Social Theology*, 158. See 1 Cor 10:16; 12:27; Eph 4:12; Rom 7:4.

56. L. Johnson, *Revelatory Body*, 105.

57. Wagamese, *Indian Horse*, 69–70.

In the modern world, many people reasonably accept the apparent limits of nature as set by scientifically based thinking.[58] The problem with this naturalist position is that people have experiences that point beyond their own self-interest and, in the case of play and its unitive aspect, nudge them toward considering the interconnectedness of all things in the universe. We explore this in more depth in chapter 3, but for now it is important to note that the experience of play can bring human lives together in a remarkable way. Anyone playing on a good-spirited team knows how teammates begin to anticipate their teammates' next move on the field of play. Players will speak about their team functioning like a "well-oiled machine," but the synergism produced is more than mechanical. Before a coach yells instructions to her point guard coming up the court, the player does precisely what the coach was thinking about. The coach finds it difficult to put this connection into words. These actions are more than efficiencies in sport; they reveal a deeper connection shared among players and coaches who spend endless hours together. Play can transcend individualistic portraits of life, where even sworn enemies or members of rival political parties or ethnic groups can rise up and connect at a deeply human level. The bodily experience of transcendence in play says that fulfillment requires moving outside of oneself.

This striving beyond oneself reflects an experience told by Serena Williams, arguably the greatest tennis player ever. Raised as a Jehovah's Witness, Williams spoke about a silent prayer she offered during play at her sixth Australian Open championship in 2015: she felt "down and out" in the final match, but prayed for strength.[59] In that moment, she believed that God pulled her through to victory. Williams rarely speaks about her faith publicly, but the experience flowed out naturally during her acceptance speech at center court. Amid the struggle to defeat Maria Sharapova, another human determined to earn victory, the challenge and depth of the moment grasped Williams, and she was put in touch with something greater.

Johnson's three aspects of play for theological reflection—freedom, connectedness, and transcendence—lead to important insights. One commentator summarizes how leisure enables the spirit of play: it "alerts us not to our power over reality but to our ultimate dependence on initiatives beyond our control.... [It] is both an openness to reality and an affirmation of mystery, of 'not being able to grasp' that which one beholds."[60] Entering into the play-spirit offers people the freedom to become open and receptive to

---

58. Taylor, *Secular Age*, 20.
59. Winston, "Serena Williams' Secret Weapon," para. 5.
60. Kimball, *Experiments against Reality*, 346.

reality for what it is, instead of only manipulating it. They sense an ultimate interdependence with all humans and a transcendent Being, where finding delight in a moment (e.g., playing catch or shooting hoops with friends) is possible because the universe is upheld by God or some larger cosmic rules of justice.[61] To fully enter into the delightful serious-nonseriousness nature of play—where one gives oneself completely over to the silliness of play—theologian Hugo Rahner believes that wholehearted frivolity is required: "That our Creator had originally endowed us with a different and more finely attuned relation between the body and soul than that which we now possess, and that our task is now to regain it, in suffering and in seriousness of purpose, to regain it though in doing so our lives are rent asunder."[62] Fully embracing the spirit of play is not a childish act, but an apparent act of faith that upsets our assumptions and requires a turn toward the Creator.

CONCLUSION: PLAY AS SYMBOLIC AND CONFOUNDING

An understanding of the symbolic complexity of play is necessary for a Catholic theology of sport, especially when play is dismissed as naivety. In contrast, we conclude that today's distinction between childhood and adulthood is distorted. For instance, Huizinga saw play as a sacred action as he inverted the relationship between play and seriousness. When life is viewed as something similar to playing a game, one creates seriousness through play and begins to resemble the action of God the Creator.[63] Thus, Huizinga's complex, symbolic thinking about play challenges technological thinking that assumes that the immediate function of an action or thing is its only meaning. Such flat thinking makes life absurd. Instead of being understood through a causal or evolutionary mindset, play should be grasped as childlike (not as childish actions), enabling human beings to laugh, delight, or feel a sense of enchantment.[64]

It should not be surprising that religious traditions often cherish childhood. Instances of this abound in Christianity: the celebration of the birth of Jesus at Christmas, the abundance of medieval artwork of the infant Jesus, and Jesus' own willingness to let the children come to him (Matt 19:14). The Gospels engage in symbolic thinking about children: Jesus claims that people cannot enter the kingdom of God unless they are born again (John 3:1–8),

---

61. H. Rahner, *Man at Play*, 7.
62. H. Rahner, *Man at Play*, 7–8.
63. Otterspeer, *Reading Huizinga*, 56.
64. Otterspeer, *Reading Huizinga*, 56.

asks for childlike abandonment to God's providential care (Matt 6:25–33), and rebukes those who would harm a child (Matt 18:6).[65] It is unsurprising then that one scholar argued that religion is a form of play because play is the "symbol and interpreter of freedom."[66] A spirit of play enables an escape from the trappings of the self and allows for embracing beauty, rest, unity, and truth; a stale, legal obedience in religion entangles people in harshness, superstition, or self-righteousness. Play's aspects of freedom, connectedness, and transcendence resonate with religious life at its best.

Play is vital for human living but can easily be misconstrued. While Catholicism has been generally consistent in its positive praise of play, including sports and pleasure,[67] figures like Aquinas, Chesterton, and Augustine—who called for careful weighing of pleasures because we are what we love—do not seek an earthly paradise by fleeing into a play world. Today, this escapism might be seen in athletic lives that lack balance and are consumed by sports, or in the unending play of video games or e-sports. Having no life outside of sports, in fact, would betray much of the paradoxical truth captured in a spirit of play. To this end, Rahner reminds us that the person at play is a "grave-merry" sort.[68] To be able to fall under play's spell is to fuse together two opposed elements in a religious unity, where existence is both joyful and sorrowful, a comedy and a tragedy, because human freedom involves peril. Rahner adds: "there is no play that has not something profoundly serious at the bottom of it, and even when children play, they come . . . under the spell of absolute obligation and under the shadow of the possibility that the game may be lost." The delight and pleasure of play run the risk of vanishing; tragedy and injustice remain present inside and outside of sports.

Play remains a confounding reality. It appeals to the aesthetic and symbolic dimensions of sports, while paradoxically it does not dismiss practical demands of struggle, performance, and achievement on the field of play.[69] The spirit of play within sports entails rethinking the world around us, where it becomes possible to find God in all things through a sacramental worldview.[70] We turn to this topic in the next chapter.

---

65. *Catechism of the Catholic Church*, 305.
66. Bushnell, *Play and Work*, 22.
67. Kretchmar and Watson, "Paradoxical Athlete," 28.
68. H. Rahner, *Man at Play*, 27.
69. Hoffman, "Whatever Happened to Play?," 24.
70. L. Johnson, *Revelatory Body*, 105–6.

CHAPTER 3

Seeing What Is There

Sports, Transcendence, and Sacramental Perspective

Author Daniel James Brown's marvelous book *The Boys in the Boat* tells the true story of collegiate and Olympic rower Joe Rantz. From hardscrabble, working-class roots in Washington state, Joe put himself through college at the University of Washington, where he joined the rowing team. Later, he was part of the 1936 Olympic eight-man crew that stunned the world by taking gold at "Hitler's Olympics" in Berlin. When Joe described to Brown his experiences for *The Boys in the Boat*, it was not learning to row, the long hours of training under gray skies, the many victories or defeats, or even the Olympics that moved Joe to tears:

> It was when he tried to talk about "the boat" that his words began to falter and tears welled up in his eyes . . . watching Joe struggle for composure over and over, I realized that "the boat" was something more than just the shell or its crew. To Joe, it encompassed but transcended both—it was mysterious and almost beyond definition. It was a shared experience—a singular thing that unfolded in a golden sliver of time long ago, when nine good-hearted young men strove together, pulled together as one, gave everything they had for one another, bound together forever by pride, respect, and love. Joe was crying, at least in part, for the loss of that vanished moment but much more, I think, for the sheer beauty of it.[1]

---

1. Brown, *Boys in the Boat*, 2.

Most people can relate to Joe's attempts to articulate powerful realities beyond their ability to express. This chapter views these experiences through a Catholic theological lens by explicitly developing a sacramental perspective of sport. This perspective is based in the Catholic doctrine that all of creation has the capacity to mediate God's presence.

Building on the spirit of play introduced in chapter 2, the first section of this chapter explains Charles Taylor's concept of an "immanent frame" that constitutes the modern, Western understanding of the world, and then contrasts two ways of living within this frame. One view sees sports and life "closed" to transcendence; the other view is "open" to transcendence. This contrast highlights the problem of an immanent worldview closed to transcendence. Our solution is to offer a sacramental perspective that is open to transcendence. The second section presents the theology undergirding a sacramental perspective and identifies five sacramental principles that are operative in all facets of life and especially evident in sport. These sacramental principles are then explained and exemplified in a sporting context in each of the remaining sections.

A SACRAMENTAL PERSPECTIVE IN AN IMMANENT FRAME

Imagine a runner is asked, "How was your run today?" She could respond by saying, "It was great. In 23:01, I ran 3.1 miles; my cadence was 179 steps per minute; I spent 86 percent of my time at lactate threshold, with an average heart rate of 157 beats per minute." Alternatively, the runner could explain, "It was a joyful run. It really opened my soul and gave me a chance to savor God's grace today." Broadly speaking, these two descriptions illustrate contrasting worldviews described by Charles Taylor in his landmark book, *A Secular Age*.

Prior to the eighteenth-century Enlightenment, most people presumed an integral connection between the spiritual and the material dimensions of the universe. In Western Christian culture, there was a purpose "higher than" human flourishing that was the goal of human life, and there was a "beyond" within the natural and scientifically empirical world.[2] In this context, one did not choose to see God's transcendence: it was as obvious and taken for granted as the effects of gravity today. According to Taylor, today's Western worldview is different and is understood from within an "immanent frame."[3] In his usage, "immanent" means "enclosed"; in other

---

2. Taylor, *Secular Age*, 20.
3. Taylor, *Secular Age*, 539–93.

words, one understands the universe to be "enclosed" as if it were in a box. This box is characterized by the implicit presumption that humans live in "a world entirely within a natural (as opposed to supernatural) order."[4] In this frame, only what can be empirically measured has ultimate meaning. This exclusively rational frame of reference is not "usually, or even mainly a set of *beliefs*"; rather it is the existential "context in which we develop our beliefs."[5] Commenting on Taylor, James K. A. Smith emphasizes that we all inhabit this immanent frame "*even if we believe in transcendence*. . . . The question isn't *whether* we inhabit the immanent frame, but *how*."[6] This is the key: according to Taylor, within this given frame of the world, each person can choose a "take," or worldview. Some live within this metaphorical box as if it were "closed" to God's transcendence, while others inhabit this frame as if it were "open" to this transcendence.

"Transcendence" is an important term to understand because it is used in both "closed" and "open" perspectives, but with different meanings. Within a closed perspective, it usually means "beyond" what had been previously accomplished.[7] God is not recognized in this view, though many idols based on political, economic, or personal views vie for allegiance. In contrast, in an open perspective, such as a Catholic worldview alluded to in chapter 2, there is something "more" or "beyond" the physically empirical. In this view, transcendence invites one to recognize God's presence "within" or "through" the material of the world. An analogy helps describe this worldview. Imagine being outside an enormous open-air stadium on game day. One can hear the excitement inside but cannot understand its cause and meaning from outside the stadium. One can walk around the stadium, or peer through the gate, recognizing something important is going on inside, but if one is closed to entering "within"—transcending into a view from inside the stadium—one is left frustrated as to the cause and meaning of what is going on. This is analogous to transcendence in an open, religious worldview: one transcends within or "through" the stadium turnstile—the

---

4. Smith, *How (Not) to Be Secular*, 141.

5. Taylor, *Secular Age*, 549 (italics original).

6. Smith, *How (Not) to Be Secular*, 93 (italics original).

7. In a closed immanent frame, transcendence can also denote a separation from the material that leaves the physical world behind. This hard separation between the natural and supernatural (*Secular Age*, 547–48) interprets a "miracle" as anything that violates the laws of physics. This view ironically is shared by "materialists and Christian fundamentalists" (547), though the former use it as a justification denying religious claims of transcendence, while fundamentalists use it as a basis for religious faith. Catholicism rejects the either/or of this distinction. One could say the material and transcendent coordinate, not contradict.

experience of the material world—to recognize what has been there all along: God's grace.[8]

This distinction is important because most people find friendships, personal growth, and amazing athletic feats in sports significant in today's immanent frame. However, "closed" compared to "open" worldviews lead to different conclusions about what these experiences mean and where that meaning comes from. For example, the previous responses to the question "How was your run?" exemplify these two perspectives of the universe from within today's immanent frame. The first response illustrates a closed perspective because it exclusively communicates empirical information about a run. The second response presents a perspective open to the possibility that there could be something "more" to the physical experience. This exaggerated contrast highlights Taylor's point: there are two perspectives on a run or any experience, both from within the same immanent frame—one closed from, the other open to, God's transcendence in the universe. The distinction here should not obscure the important fact that people can find forms of meaning in life within a worldview closed to God's transcendence. Joy, personal significance, friendship, and "flow experiences"[9] can all be experienced through sports within a closed frame, but they do not point to anything beyond themselves. Such perceptions can be explained by psychology, sociology, or another narrative that describes human experience. Many potential explanations proliferate within today's closed frame, but these cannot fully respond to humankind's deepest questions and desires. The person seeking a meaningful account for compelling experiences in sports from within a closed frame is stuck like the sports fan trapped outside the stadium in the analogy above. Instead of entering the stadium and opening the lid of the immanent frame to a perspective of creation that is open to the potential of divine transcendence, one either despairs or settles for partial explanations for what is going on in the stadium.[10]

The problem with the closed view that dominates contemporary Western culture is that it limits human understanding of the world. There is fundamentally no meaning beyond oneself; one's desires become the center of meaning and value. What is "true" or "right" often becomes what the most powerful person wants it to be. What is "really real" can be measured,

---

8. Another analogy: the person could enter the stadium, not understand the rules, and think people are just screaming their heads off. However, by entering into the fan experience (learning rules, supporting a team, etc.), one can begin to understand the game and the reason for the excitement. Two people can look at the same world but see it through different lenses. Which lens is ultimately more satisfying and explanatory?

9. Czikszentmihalyi, *Flow*, 4; Kelly, "Youth Sport and Spirituality," 138–44.

10. Taylor, *Secular Age*, 768.

commodified, and monetized. Given this, many people today, including many claiming belief in God, functionally accept and perpetuate this default worldview to determine the value of everything they encounter, including the significance of sport. As a result, sports have become functional, typified by excessive focus on measurables such as winning, statistical achievement, and betting lines, and their worth explained solely in utilitarian terms; for example, good for one's physical health, social bonds, or increasing income. This understanding distorts sports and diminishes those who participate in, coach, and view them.

The solution to the limitations of the closed frame described above is to live within the immanent frame as if it is open to a transcendent view of the world.[11] The spirit of play explained in chapter 2 is an example of openness to transcendence within sports and life. The claim here in chapter 3 is that play and sports can fill an important role in helping one embrace a perspective that is open to God's transcendence in a contemporary context. Theologian Richard Gaillardetz cites Taylor when he writes that, "even within this immanent frame we can detect a lurking sense of transcendence present in ordinary human engagements . . . for many today, sport remains a sphere of human engagement in which the transcendent, or what Christians simply call grace, is encountered."[12] A perspective open to God's transcendence roots one's meaning and value in something outside of oneself, and unites individuals across boundaries of time and culture. Olympic rower Joe Rantz, whose story was cited at the outset of this chapter, did not break down in tears or struggle to describe the "boys in the boat" because of the time it took to cross the finish line or the number of victories they won. Such reductive, functional explanations cut off an essential perspective of the world that fully accounts for profound human experiences. As important as empirical data is, there needs to be a worldview that also includes an openness to God's transcendent grace in a delightful run or experiences with loyal teammates.

In Catholicism, a "sacramental" worldview resolves the limitations of a closed immanent frame. This worldview or perspective overcomes the limitations of a closed immanent frame by recognizing the transcendent within and beneath human experiences. For example, in sports, human skill, agility, determination, courage, integrity, forgiveness, mercy, teamwork, and community—all of what is most human—can point to God in whose image humans are created. From a sacramental worldview, all experiences in sport and life offer profound opportunities to reflect on God's presence, and so

---

11. Smith, *How (Not) to Be Secular*, 93; Taylor, *Secular Age*, 544–56.
12. Gaillardetz, "For the Love," 155–56.

one must seek to recognize this presence and interpret what these experiences mean.

CONCISE THEOLOGY OF A SACRAMENTAL WORLDVIEW

Though *sacramental* may recall images of the seven ritual sacraments of the Catholic Church, a sacramental worldview precedes and is the foundation for those liturgical rites. This worldview—or perspective—begins with creation and is most clearly evident in the Incarnation of Jesus Christ. As stated in chapter 2, the world exists because God freely created and sustains it as artistically depicted in the biblical book of Genesis. In the first creation account, God looked at all of creation and "saw that it was good" (Gen 1:25). God next created humankind in God's own image, and the Genesis writer then amplifies God's initial evaluation: "God looked at everything he had made, and found it *very* good" (Gen 1:31).[13] God's initial judgment, that creation, including humankind, is very good, is affirmed when God became part of creation through the Incarnation of Jesus Christ. "Incarnation" roughly means "becoming flesh," so Jesus as the Incarnation expresses "God becoming flesh in the person of Jesus." In essence, the Incarnation demonstrates the great dignity of being a creature.[14] Jesus makes explicit the potential of all material creation to reveal God's desire to draw humanity to Godself. It is through his physical, created humanity that Jesus demonstrates his full divinity; thus, through his humanity, Jesus offers salvation. He is the basis for a sacramental perspective.

The Incarnation demonstrates that all creation can mediate God's presence, which is also known as grace.[15] The power of God's grace "does not destroy nature but grows from within nature."[16] Humans have the choice to recognize and respond to this grace. When one embraces God's grace, the result transforms the person, and through the person, potentially, transforms the world. The key is that God does not change; humans do. The awareness of God changes, and one's response to this new awareness

---

13. Himes, *Doing the Truth*, 26.

14. Himes, *Mystery of Faith*, 22–23.

15. Lawler, *Symbol & Sacrament*, 53–58. God's presence is technically "uncreated" grace because it is God present in what God created and sustains. The human response to "uncreated grace" is called "created" or "sanctifying grace." The transition point from "uncreated" to "created" grace is the human response.

16. Lane, *Experience of God*, 28.

changes the person. God does not change humans without their cooperation, their "yes."

The *Catechism of the Catholic Church* explains that creation and human culture can function as signs and symbols mediating God's grace.[17] As both body and spirit, humans "express and perceive spiritual realities through physical signs and symbols" both with one another and in relationship with God.[18] The "material cosmos is so presented to [humankind's] intelligence that [humankind] can read there traces of its Creator... and symbolize both [God's] greatness and [God's] nearness."[19] Within a sacramental worldview "spiritual realities" and "God's greatness and nearness" are not foreign to human experience, but are drawn from human experience.

Sports are sacramental when they open the closed lid of today's immanent frame and prompt recognition of God's grace in creation. To avoid confusion with the seven ritual sacraments in Catholicism, awareness of graced moments in sports and everyday experiences may be better understood as theologically similar to what the *Catechism* calls "sacramentals." "Sacramentals do not confer the grace of the Holy Spirit in the way that the [seven ritual] sacraments do, but by the Church's prayer, they prepare us to receive grace and dispose us to cooperate with it. . . . 'There is scarcely any proper use of material things which cannot be thus directed toward the sanctification of [humankind] and the praise of God.'"[20] To the extent sports awaken, remind, and sustain awareness of God's presence, they can "prepare us to receive grace and dispose us to cooperate with it" and so be sacramental encounters.

A sacramental worldview is an attitude and way to encounter sports and all of life. Recall from chapter 2 that theologian Hugo Rahner explained that creation is like an act of play for God. God did not need to create the world; it was an act analogous to human freedom, expression, and recreation (literally, "re-creation").[21] Unlike God, humans "toil" (Gen 3:17) and are limited by many factors, such as time and the finitude of the physical body. If Rahner is right, when humans step away from their purposeful toil and play freely, without an objective beyond the game itself, they more closely resemble the God who freely created them than they do when they labor in their work.

---

17. *Catechism of the Catholic Church*, 1145 and 1149.

18. *Catechism of the Catholic Church*, 1146.

19. *Catechism of the Catholic Church*, 1147.

20. *Catechism of the Catholic Church*, 1670; the *Catechism* here cites *Sacrosanctum Concilium*, 61.

21. H. Rahner, *Man at Play*, 15–17.

Learning to see sports and the world from a sacramental perspective is a spiritual habit that takes training and practice, something athletes are familiar with. Training minds, bodies, and spirits requires focus on the fundamental principles. The remaining five sections of this chapter each identify a sacramental principle[22] and illustrate it through sports examples to further explain what it means to bring a Catholic sacramental lens to a theology of sport.

1. All experience is mediated.
2. Whatever humanizes divinizes.
3. God is always present in and through the world.
4. What is always and everywhere true must be recognized somewhere at some time.
5. God works through human experience.

1. All experience is mediated.

A sacramental worldview, and subsequently ritual sacraments and "sacramentals," necessitates realizing that no one encounters anything in the world—a person, event, or idea—in a "direct" way: all experiences in the world are mediated.[23] For example, consider an initial sensory experience like catching a ball. This act is mediated through one's nerve endings in the hand through the central nervous system and interpreted by the brain to mean "ball there, hold on." Additionally, all experiences must be mediated through symbols. Language provides symbols—words—to mediate and interpret experience and perception of the world. To understand the prior example, the written words "ball" and "hold" are understood and interpreted by the reader based on long-prior education. Theologian Michael Lawler explains that all experiences of the world are mediated through symbols, which give meaning to the experience. In Lawler's words, "We do not know any reality directly and immediately, but only indirectly through the mediation of one or more ... symbol systems."[24] Humans symbolize and interpret life's events and sensations through the language of gestures, words, images, and actions for communication and meaning.

22. In various works Himes summarizes "sacramental principles" (e.g., "Living Conversation," 232; *Mystery of Faith*, 13; "Finding God," 12).

23. Lawler, *Symbol & Sacrament*, "Chapter 1: Prophetic Symbol," 5–28; pp. 11 and 16 relate most directly here.

24. Lawler, *Symbol & Sacrament*, 16.

Taylor explores words as mediators in *A Secular Age*. "The highest things, things to do with the infinite, with God, with our deepest feelings, can only be made objects of thought and consideration for us through expression in symbols."[25] The language of poetry, he contends, is "world-making"; "through creating symbols it establishes new meanings."[26] Taylor uses the example of "spirit." Without the word "spirit" we would still have "wind" and "breath," but neither of these terms begin to capture what the word "spirit" does. In his words, "spirit enters our world through language; its manifestation depends on speech."[27] The reality of what is expressed, always a potential, must be stated to be brought into full existence. Symbols and words are needed to express what is perceived as reality.

A powerful example of language mediating meaning comes from Helen Keller's autobiography *The Story of My Life*. Deaf and blind since she was nineteen months old, Helen did not understand her physical and emotional sensations because she lacked a language system to interpret them. Her moment of insight came at age seven when she realized her teacher's representative imprints on her hand as water ran over it denoted the feeling she was experiencing. She writes:

> I stood still, my whole attention fixed upon the motions of her [teacher's] fingers. Suddenly I felt a misty consciousness as of something forgotten—a thrill of returning thought; and somehow the mystery of language was revealed to me. I knew then that w-a-t-e-r meant the wonderful cool something that was flowing over my hand. The living word awakened my soul, gave it light, hope, set it free! . . . As we returned to the house every object which I touched seemed to quiver with life. That was because I saw everything with that strange, new sight that had come to me.[28]

Helen had had many encounters with water before that realization, but she lacked a language system to understand the sensory experiences. She did not understand the "cool something" because she lacked a meaning system to mediate what water is and does. In short, symbols are the only way to comprehend oneself and understand relationships with others and the world—no experience is intelligible without symbolizing.

The explanation above related to language demonstrates the potential confusion between "signs" and "symbols." First, words like "ball" or "hold"

---

25. Taylor, *Secular Age*, 756.
26. Taylor, *Secular Age*, 756.
27. Taylor, *Secular Age*, 756.
28. Keller, *Story of My Life*, 23–24.

are typically single-dimensional, communicating one-to-one, known, objective abstractions.[29] A yellow flag means "rule violation" and an old English "D" denotes the Detroit Tigers. These are usually signs that point to a single known referent: each meaning is clear, and there is no depth or mystery. Other words can transition between being more signatory or symbolic. For instance, "water," in the example with Helen Keller, is more ambiguous. On one hand, "w-a-t-e-r" means the chemical compound identified by its component formula, H2O. However, water can have deep constellations of meanings related to rebirth, cleansing, and life itself, and so the term "water" can also serve as a symbol with infinite depth of meaning.

Words as symbols communicate important realities such as *courage, pain, love, justice,* or *curiosity* that are not empirical and yet are essential for full human living (one cannot empirically measure units of courage). These and many other powerful word-symbols are neither visible nor physical, but they are veritable and true. Lawler explains that "the human mind can never get to the bottom of a symbol and be done with it."[30] For instance, the words "I love you," or, for an athlete, "You made the team," raise as many questions as they answer. One can witness and experience these realities, but never fully grasp or explain them in their own lives, much less in the lives of others. Part of being human is to decide what these realities mean; symbolic words and actions mediate as best they can these meanings and their importance.

Context, intention, and a willingness to comprehend each play roles in differentiating between sign and symbol. To understand the symbol, one must enter into it and be willing to "see" beneath the concrete entry point to obtain deeper understanding. For example, is the number 42 in Major League Baseball just a number between 41 and 43? Or does it represent deeper significance in Jackie Robinson's integration of the league? His jersey number, 42, has been retired as a symbol and doorway to an infinite depth of meanings surrounding racial injustice, equal opportunity, the nation Americans aspire to develop, and courage and perseverance in the face of bigotry. MLB could never fully express the meaning of retiring Jackie Robinson's number 42. There is always much more than the physical or observable in symbols; it is never "just" a game, nor is it ever "just" a symbol.

A sacramental worldview asserts that all creation and humanity itself have the potential to mediate and point to the One that creates and sustains the world. All human experience is mediated and then interpreted. An unmediated experience is unintelligible and thus meaningless. One does

---

29. Lawler, *Symbol & Sacrament*, 18–19.
30. Lawler, *Symbol & Sacrament*, 21.

not encounter God's objective self, but only mediately through the world created and sustained by God. The entire universe, including humankind, is graced and therefore has the potential to symbolize—reveal and point toward—the Divine Creator. In the Christian view, the world as graced and transcendent has profound implications for how one interprets sport and experiences within sports.

2. Whatever humanizes divinizes.

The second sacramental principle is the most succinct: whatever humanizes divinizes.[31] Whatever is most authentically human points to the Creator in whose image humans are created.

From this perspective, any experience in life that celebrates the best of humanity, makes one more human and humane, and offers a momentary glimpse of transcendence, is an experience of God mediated through the created world and therefore potentially sacramental. However, the claims "sport is a religious phenomenon"[32] or that "sports are religious" need to be carefully reviewed and explained because they are often understood within worldviews closed to God's transcendence. The result is a generally functionalist and utilitarian approach to religion and the phenomenon of religiosity, which is a valuable contribution to understanding the relationship between sport and religious faith. This understanding is incomplete, though, when it distorts questions of human meaning or misrepresents God and religious faith within today's immanent frame. Thus, this sacramental principle opens the world to a perspective that coordinates with human experiences in sports and life.

This sacramental principle also provides a check on quasi-religious interpretations of sport for what are ultimately commercial purposes. The things of the world manifest God but are not God; to insist otherwise is to raise a new idol today. As noted in the introduction, many have suggested that sports have become the new "civic" religion or equate sports to religion.[33] For example, NFL quarterback and future Hall of Famer Tom Brady co-founded The Religion of Sports, a media company based on the claim that "Sports *are* religion."[34] Brady and many others have recognized that A) sports often profoundly impact peoples' lives, and B) sports have an

---

31. Himes, "Living Conversation," 233. See also Himes, "Boston College 150th Anniversary Mass."

32. Bain-Selbo and Sapp, *Understanding Sport*, 137.

33. Novak, *Joy of Sports*, xvi; Ellis, *Games People Play*, 108–13.

34. Religion of Sports, "Religion of Sports | The Space Between," 0:34.

accessible spiritual or transcendent dimension that seems to address deep human desires and needs in ways similar to religion and religious practice. A reasonable, popular, and erroneous conclusion is that sports are therefore religion.

However, something is clearly going on at the intersection of sports and religious faith. The theological anthropology outlined in chapter 4 and this sacramental principle begin to provide an explanation. Sports are profoundly human and anything that is truly human can mediate and be an experience of God. Sports are a particularly effective channel of God's grace in contemporary culture for many reasons. Sports illuminate incredible human generosity and self-gift as well as dehumanization and alienation. This juxtaposition of love and sin is part of the human drama amplified by the inherent disappointments and excitement, new beginnings, dramatic endings, and redemption stories that follow cyclical patterns within contests, seasons, and careers. The drama of sports is also relatively easy to understand; there is a contest with clear rules—even the "unwritten rules" are well understood—and there are obvious benchmarks in winning and losing, as well as measures for individual success. Lastly, sports are almost universally accessible and engaging in themselves for athletes and spectators alike. At their best, sports help people be more human, and because whatever humanizes divinizes, they can point to God in real ways. But sports are not religion.

3. God is always present in and through the world.

Is God more present during a basketball game, Catholic Mass, or chemistry class? It is a trick question because God is equally—and fully—present in all those experiences. What is the difference? One is usually more aware of God's presence during a religious ritual such as a Mass. While it is always and everywhere true that God is present, God may be more recognizable at some times and in some places because people are attuned to God's presence in those places and times.[35] By analogy, consider the clothes you are wearing or the air you are breathing: most people most of the time are unconscious of these important elements. It is similar with God. People are unaware of God's presence because they are accustomed to it or take the superficial nature of the world for granted; one does not call it to attention because one is busy, uninterested, or unfamiliar.

Whatever breaks through these often-overlapping human states of busyness, disinterest, or unfamiliarity to call attention to important realities

---

35. Himes, *Doing the Truth*, 107.

has the potential to be a sign or mediator of God in the world; it can be sacramental.[36] All facets of life have this potential sacramental dimension, but sacramental encounters in sports are particularly vivid and accessible. In sports, human consciousness is occasionally rocked by moments where one cannot help but say "wow."[37] For example, start with the question: "What in your sports experience has made you say 'wow?'" In other words, what sports events and experiences have been beautiful, challenging, powerful, memorable, or deeply moving?

Some might cite awe-inducing individual performances such as those by Olympic sprinter Usain Bolt or Olympic swimmer Michael Phelps; others the excellence of an athlete in a team sport such as basketball's LeBron James or soccer's Lionel Messi and Megan Rapinoe; for others it is the stunning skill of snowboarder Shaun White; the artistic grace of figure skater Anna Shcherbakova; the combination of power and agility of gymnast Simone Biles; or Alex Hannold's meticulous concentration during his free solo climb of El Capitan. Sports fans might also reference the determination of Julie Moss at the finish line of the 1982 Iron Man Triathlon or the integrity of professional golfer Brian Davis at Hilton Head in 2010. The public feats of these athletes and countless others like them become reference points celebrating some of the best attributes of humankind.

Notably, when sharing memorable and moving experiences in sports, conversation often quickly moves beyond iconic athletes and moments to intimate personal recollections with sports: consider Olympic rower Joe Rantz trying to express the significance of the "boys in the boat." Often, no one besides the person was aware of the moment: a high school women's basketball player remembers being subbed out and catching her breath, feeling a sense of rightness in the world; a runner describes running on a spring morning, the grass thick with frost; a powerlifter tries to explain the significance of setting a personal record for a deadlift. It might be watching a child play a sport, at any level, whether it was a great play or simply a routine game where one is momentarily overwhelmed with parental love for reasons that cannot be explained. It could be three generations of baseball fans, grandfather, son, and grandsons, sitting in the bleachers all wearing ballcaps matching that of the home club. Sometimes it is a composite memory of supporting a specific team over years of fandom as a family.

In our courses and conversations, students and friends almost universally report that the community, as well as friendships made in the context of sports, are among their most treasured memories. For example, becoming

---

36. Himes, *Doing the Truth*, 108; Lawler, *Symbol & Sacrament*, 47.
37. O'Malley, *Wow Factor*, ix–x.

friends with a once-bitter rival; getting to know teammates after games or practices; the stories and jokes that pass the time on bus rides; or waiting before competition in a tournament. It could be shooting hoops with a sibling or friend, or "having a catch" with a parent as exemplified in the film *Field of Dreams*. A neighbor once described his youthful memory: "It was the best thing, just playing football with my friends on the playground 'til dark."

The human propensity to ignore the potential to see God in life generally and sporting experiences specifically challenges this sacramental principle that God is present in and through the world. Specifically, people are often unaware they are operating within a closed immanent framework that blocks transcendence in the world. From this view, everything can be explained; whatever cannot be explained is not real and so is invalid. As a result, one's capacity for wonder and openness to grace atrophies into indifference or cynicism. People do not see God's grace because they do not look for it. People also overlook the sacramental potential in loss and even suffering. It is easy to forget—or ignore—that these painful experiences have the potential to be reminders of grace, something thoroughly addressed in chapter 5.

4. What is always and everywhere true must be recognized somewhere at some time.

The fourth sacramental principle is that what is always and everywhere true must be recognized somewhere at some time.[38] An illustration of this sacramental principle might be senior night for a high school athlete. Typically, on senior night, the team and coaching staff affirm and celebrate the seniors with words of praise, a hug or handshake, and perhaps a memento representative of the team that season. The respect and love have always been there, but they had not been explicitly stated and symbolically embodied. Through ritual presentation, these truths move from ephemeral abstractions to memorable realities.

There is an infusion and proliferation of meaning when something is explicitly celebrated. God works through these moments because God works through human actions when one implicitly recognizes the need for overt symbolism to mediate the deepest realities of oneself and one's communities. People can never fully express their gratitude to coaching mentors, love for loyal teammates, grief at an injury, or sadness at the close of a career. There simply is no other way to communicate these truths, and they cannot be left unacknowledged, all the while recognizing that whatever

38. Himes, *Mystery of Faith*, 13.

is said will be incomplete.[39] These ritual expressions, however inadequate, both reveal who the person was created to be and point towards God's grace operative in the person's life—recall that what humanizes divinizes. There is no magic formula, which misunderstands both God and sacraments. From a sacramental perspective, when God's grace, which is always there, is acknowledged it becomes present to the extent that the community has these truths brought to their attention and is invited to respond to them. In this celebration they are experiencing what senior night symbolically mediates: the respect and love of the team for the senior members that has been present all along.

Consider this rough analogy using the Lombardi Super Bowl Trophy presentation. One could imagine that it would make more sense for the exhausted winning team to retreat to the locker room for the needed treatments, a healthy meal, and then proceed to get a good night's sleep. However, there is an instinctive need to affirm and celebrate the winning team's accomplishments. Were a team to skip the trophy presentation (and later parade!), they would still be Super Bowl champions, but it would not be publicly affirmed and in a spiritual sense made "real." Humans need symbols and rites to make real and evident what is most important and meaningful. The cold fact of an event becomes endowed with significance that is mediated in its expression. The abstract and unreal is made present and real through the symbolic words and actions of a ritual, whether a senior-night celebration or Lombardi Trophy presentation. For both the Super Bowl-winning football player and the senior-night athlete, the ritual ceremonies are meaningful to the extent that they represent the dedication, sacrifice, and camaraderie necessary for the achievement.

Another example of this sacramental principle is the phenomenon of sports memorabilia that represent and celebrate what is always and everywhere true. Most athletes and fans have items that represent experiences and people whose significance could never be fully expressed. The correlation between sports memorabilia and sacred relics has become cliché, but no less valid.[40] Through a sacramental lens these mementos symbolize experiences that mediate encounters with and awareness of God's presence. The item itself serves to communicate the significance of the experience. As such, it has sacramental potential for those willing to see the connection between the experience the item represents and God's grace. In this way, a memento of that high school team or a Super Bowl ring becomes a tangible signifier of all that cannot be put into words by the one who earned it. The memento

---

39. Himes, *Doing the Truth*, 84–85.
40. Bain-Selbo and Sapp, *Understanding Sport*, 35.

is a symbol of an experience (e.g., senior season or Super Bowl-winning team) that itself represents an even deeper cloud of meanings. The tactile "realness" of sports memorabilia, which embodies the experience and thus expresses the significance, appeals to the human desire for meaning.

Significance is not imposed on these experiences or mementos from an outside experience. Magical thinking imagines an extrinsic power working through the item or experience to manipulate the person from without. A sacramental worldview recognizes God's grace intrinsic in the world; this connection with God transforms the person from within. In this way the sports experiences or mementos can remain empty and meaningless for individuals without interest or connection to the experiences celebrated. For instance, an outside observer can watch a senior-night celebration or Lombardi Trophy presentation ceremony with detachment; the ritual has no connection to deeper meaning for her, and so is neither symbolic nor "real."[41] Similarly, years later someone may find the photo in an album, or a collector might buy a Super Bowl ring at an auction, but neither the photo nor the ring would have the depth of shared communal meaning that it did for the one who originally earned the keepsake.

5. God works through human experience.

This final sacramental principle, that God works through human experience, synthesizes two related facets of a Catholic worldview. First, symbolic human actions do what they represent. Second, consistently expressing beliefs strengthens commitment to the values being expressed. This synthesis draws on the previous four sacramental principles and previews the theological anthropology that is the subject of the next chapter.

The Vatican II Council, in the Constitution on Sacred Liturgy, explains that sacraments are signs that instruct; they presuppose faith, at least an unconscious openness to transcendence, which they "nourish, strengthen, and express."[42] Theologically speaking, humans are created in God's image to be loving and creative; they exist to receive and respond to God through this love. Love necessitates relationship and community, which requires personal integrity, unity with others, and the world, which includes human history and culture as well as the natural environment. Physical bodies are where humans encounter God's love, and so bodies are a place of spiritual expression, sanctification, and self-giving love. From a sacramental

---

41. Lawler, *Symbol & Sacrament*, 53, 57–58.
42. *Sacrosanctum Concilium*, n59.

worldview, God exists within and through all these relationships, thus they can potentially mediate God's grace.

The *Catechism* describes the seven ritual sacraments as "efficacious signs of grace"[43] that "confer the grace that they signify."[44] In other words, in a sacramental worldview, symbolic human actions do what they represent.[45] For example, the Sacrament of Reconciliation (or confession) is an efficacious sign—doing what it represents—in manifesting the grace of God's love and forgiveness.[46] God's action is signified in the sacramental experience; the human action itself does not bestow grace as if God is being conjured. A sacramental perspective is not magical. By expressing this abstraction, the ritual sacrament mediates and celebrates the reality of God's love through the created world, what the *Catechism* calls the "sacramental economy,"[47] to become present to and "bear fruit in" the person encountering God with the "required dispositions."[48] Over time, coherently expressing fundamental beliefs enhances understanding of, and commitment to, the truths being expressed. Two insights for a sacramental worldview are important here. First, symbolic human actions do what they represent. Second, expressing values ritually enhances commitment to the truths being expressed. Together, these insights substantiate the sacramental principle that God works through human experience.

These insights are relevant because what humans do with their bodies, ritually and habitually, over time forms them as individuals and as a community. Further, symbolic human actions do what they represent, and consistently expressing values ritually enhances commitment to the truths being expressed. Individually, these practices form one's deepest self and personal character. Communally, these actions can enhance the unity to which humans were created to contribute. Humans are most themselves as individuals within a community characterized by giving and receiving love. When members of a team are open to this nonscientific but very real unity, even if it is only intuitive, actions that signify this unity further build this unity. Specifically, the expression of a team builds a team. An example is a team linking arms to take the field. Consider common images of a basketball or volleyball team's bench during the end of a close game where the players hold hands or put arms over one another's shoulders. Another common

---

43. *Catechism of the Catholic Church*, 1131.
44. *Catechism of the Catholic Church*, 1127.
45. Himes, *Doing the Truth*, 107.
46. Lawler, *Symbol & Sacrament*, 35.
47. *Catechism of the Catholic Church*, 1076.
48. *Catechism of the Catholic Church*, 1131.

example might be a team breaking a huddle with everyone's hand in the middle and a collective "team" chanted in unison as everybody withdraws their hand and returns to the sideline or game. Team dinners, apparel, training sessions, meetings, and myriad other activities can function to represent and build team unity when everyone "buys in" and recognizes, perhaps preconsciously, the significance of joining together in these symbolic actions. These expressions transform people on multiple levels—the unconscious, conscious, spiritual, and cognitive—at the same time over time. Thus, in a worldview open to transcendence, God can be truly present through what can only be called "team spirit." Given this, it is necessary to clarify that sports are not the equivalent of the seven Catholic ritual sacraments. Nevertheless, sports are part of a sacramental worldview, perhaps even a privileged part of that worldview given their sociocultural importance, and so potentially important signs of God's grace, especially for those disposed to enter more deeply into lived experiences as encounters with God.

Regrettably, sports also exemplify what happens when individuals and communities neglect, inadequately mediate, or inconsistently embody the values expressed through symbolic actions and words. Examples include a team espousing a slogan of "unity" as they break a time-out huddle that is divided by unaddressed conflict, or a coach that constantly preaches "commitment" but is always looking for a better deal for himself and displays casual disregard for his players' well-being. Such co-opting of the symbolic words destroys the potential symbolic meaning as well as the reality of the team community. In these instances, the team and coach are going through the motions as if the symbols substitute for the authentic commitment which the symbols are intended to represent and make real. The symbolic words are emptied of meaning and authentic connection and are manipulated to control others. The relationships of the team become utilitarian for each individual's own purposes, be they social, commercial, or political. People distort relationships and their expression when they are seen as a means to one's own end.[49] If a team diminishes, inadequately understands, or inconsistently embodies foundational life-giving truths, the team becomes disconnected from them and susceptible to individual delusions or social fads that tell members who they are and what is important.

There is an analogy between sports teams and churches here that should be noted. If a community neither recognizes nor lives its guiding truths, they diminish; the community they substantiate unravels while other implicit selfish values become dominant. The guiding truths become

---

49. Lawler, *Symbol & Sacrament*, 57–58 presents a theological explanation for this in terms of Catholic ritual sacraments.

obscured by self-centered desires. The community's words and symbols become rote practices performed because they are what has always been done; they no longer effectively mediate between eternal truths and lived choices. When the truths are lost or misunderstood, the community becomes unmoored and unfocused; the individuals lose commitment, interest, and ultimately faith in what the community stands for, be it a team or church.

CONCLUSION

A sacramental worldview asserts that God's transcendence is present in and through the world. There is not a graced (transcendent) world and a natural (scientific) world. There is one natural world that mediates grace. Catholicism incorporates both perspectives to interpret human experiences. These experiences can be breathtaking and tear-inducing. This chapter opened with an excerpt from the outset of *The Boys in the Boat*, the story of collegiate and Olympic rower Joe Rantz. Later the book includes a chapter titled "Touching the Divine," which includes a rowing mentor's insight shared with Joe that applies to rowing, but which like so much in sports is actually about all of life:

> "What mattered more than how hard a man rowed was how well everything he did in the boat harmonized with what the other fellows were doing. And a man couldn't harmonize with his crewmates unless he opened his heart to them. He had to care about his crew. It wasn't just the rowing but his crewmates that he had to give himself up to, even if it meant getting his feelings hurt..." [The mentor] "reminded [Joe] that he'd already learned to row past pain, past exhaustion, past the voice that told him it couldn't be done." He then said something that Joe remembered for the rest of his life: "When you really start trusting those boys, you will feel a power at work within you that is far beyond anything you've ever imagined. Sometimes, you will feel as if you have rowed right off the planet and are rowing among the stars."[50]

While neither Joe nor his mentor may have used the term "sacrament," they seem to be trying to articulate an encounter with God's transcendence in sport as described in this chapter. The language exhorting Joe to "give himself up to" and "feel a power at work within you" echoes more explicit theological language that Catholicism uses in describing the encounter between God and humans. As beautiful as the symbolic language is—"rowing

50. Brown, *Boys in the Boat*, 234–35.

among the stars"—it still seems inadequate, as all symbols fall short. It is not that different words are needed; a different view of the world is needed to be the basis for words about transcendence. Ultimately, people receive God's mediated grace to the extent they are willing to recognize it in the world—grace is never forced upon them. If one knows how to recognize God in the world and looks for God through sports, one is more likely to recognize God's presence. To understand what this divine presence means more explicitly for human persons, we turn to the topic of Christian anthropology in the next chapter.

CHAPTER 4

The Human Team

God, Anthropology, and Sports

"I WAS BORN TO be a point guard, but not a very good one" is the first line in Pat Conroy's prologue to *My Losing Season*, his memoir of his 1966–67 basketball season playing for The Citadel. He continues:

> There was a time in my life when I walked through the world known to myself and others as an athlete. It was part of my own definition of who I was and certainly the part I most respected. ... I was a basketball player, pure and simple, and the majesty of that sweet sport defined and shaped my growing up. I cannot explain what the sport of basketball meant to me, but I have missed it more than anything else in my life since it issued me my walking papers and released me to live out my life as a voyeur and fan. I was never a very good player, but the sport allowed me to glimpse into the kind of man I was capable of becoming.[1]

Conroy's beautiful prose voices what many of us have felt: I was born to be an athlete; I find myself in sports; sports help me be the person I was created to be. What do these feelings signify? What does it mean to find oneself in sports or that sports help one be the person they were created to be? To be fair, in the passage above, Conroy is neither explicitly attempting to explain who he is nor suggesting he literally was born to be only a point guard. However, he is a best-selling writer whose fiction and memoir illuminate the story of why he is who he is. It is incomplete, of course; no one can

---

1. Conroy, *My Losing Season*, 1.

definitively answer who they are. In *My Losing Season's* almost 400 pages, Conroy in fact does attempt to explain what basketball and that one season meant for his entire life.

This chapter directly addresses the fundamental questions that Conroy was essentially responding to in his memoir: Who am I? Why am I here? What should I do?

While there are many contemporary narratives that address these questions, we use Christian theology as the basis for our response and explain how this relates to the human love of sports.

A CHRISTIAN THEOLOGICAL ANTHROPOLOGY FOR SPORTS

What is it that people love about sports? The list will undoubtedly be long, and though there will be unique elements based on each person, many are likely shared among athletes and observers, such as the peak experiences[2] of an athlete in competition; the camaraderie among teammates, competitors, and fans; the satisfaction of an achieved goal or skill perfected, even if only momentarily. However, why do humans repeatedly seek and value these experiences? What is it behind, beneath, or within the sporting experience that makes someone say, as Conroy does, that a sport was so important to him he could not explain it, and yet it compelled him to write an entire book about it? We, the authors of this book, propose that it is because sports are profoundly human; they can magnify what is best about being human in ways experiential, understandable, and tantalizingly repeatable. Yet, because sports are so human, they also have the potential to mirror human frailty and sin, which offer a backdrop for dramas of atonement and redemption, which are similarly human traits. All of this raises the questions: What does it mean to be human? And what might this have to do with sports?

An anthropology is needed. Broadly speaking, an anthropology defines what it means to be human. However, every anthropology is based on core beliefs and fundamental values. Sometimes called a "center of meaning and value," these core beliefs consciously or unconsciously guide one's life choices and understanding of oneself and the world. For example, Bert Mandelbaum, an orthopedic surgeon who served as team physician for the US Men's Soccer National Team, draws on evolutionary biology to suggest what it means to be human and how this relates to the affinity for sports.[3] In

---

2. What Mihalyi Czikszentmihalyi calls "flow experiences" and Abraham Maslow names "peak experiences" of transcendence.

3. Mandelbaum, "You Were Born to Be an Athlete." He is also the author of *The*

his short article titled "You Were Born to Be an Athlete," he claims physical traits such as speed, strength, and endurance are an "evolutionary birthright bestowed upon our early human ancestors."[4] His thesis is that "when we start to think of ourselves as born athletes and built to survive, we're in a much better position to overcome the toughest challenges that life can throw at us."[5] While this summary skates over deep psychological and biological claims, his view represents those that see human enjoyment of sports exclusively as part of the human evolutionary legacy. Mandelbaum's evolutionary biological perspective speculates that because human life today rarely includes the original challenges bodies developed to respond to, people are drawn to sports to develop physical attributes that were once needed for survival. We see this perspective as insufficient. The implied anthropology remains in a closed immanent frame and fundamentally denies the sacramental worldview presented in the previous chapter. In contrast with this common view, the Catholic worldview sees both the world and the human person as infused with God's grace. A theological anthropology is therefore needed.

A Christian theological anthropology defines what it means to be human based explicitly on beliefs about God and God's role in the world expressed in the doctrines of the Trinity, incarnation, and sin. This does not contradict the scientific theory of evolution, but rather demonstrates the complementarity of modern science and contemporary Catholicism. Scientific thinking identifies *what happened*; theological thinking helps understand *what it means*. The difference is in perspective, which is important because Christians trying to live a graced life encounter life's events differently than those with other worldviews. For example, Christians need guidance to realize how God's grace operates in and through the world, while also responding to the "signs of the times" in a science-oriented modern age.[6] A Christian anthropology lays out a framework for this. Sports strongly suggest there is transcendence in the world, but as demonstrated in the preceding chapter, a worldview and language are often lacking to articulate and interpret what this sensed transcendence means. An authentic Christian anthropology does at least three things relative to sports: it offers a way to understand oneself in relationship with God and sports; it gives a basis of human identity and meaning outside of sports or any other potential idol

---

Win Within.

4. Mandelbaum, "You Were Born to Be an Athlete," para. 3. Note the anthropology; to be human means "to be an athlete."

5. Mandelbaum, "You Were Born to Be an Athlete," para. 6.

6. Vatican II, *Gaudium et Spes*, §4.

vying for central allegiance; and it provides means to justifiably evaluate sports and the role of sports in contemporary life.

We formulate our theological anthropology drawing on the insight of twentieth-century Catholic Flemish moral theologian Louis Janssens, who constructed a theological anthropology he labels "the human person integrally and adequately considered" (HPIAC).[7] HPIAC is the inspiration for, but distinct from, the eight dimensions of a Christian anthropology that we formulate below.

1. Humans are created in God's image and likeness.
2. Humans are relational and creative.
3. Humans are restless and filled with yearning.
4. Humans are embodied and corporeal realities.
5. Humans are limited, dependent, and endowed with innate dignity.
6. Humans are created male and female.
7. Humans exist to receive and respond to God.
8. Humans are created good, but susceptible to the allure of sin.

What follows is our explanation of these anthropological dimensions drawn from Janssens's work and their relevance for a Catholic theology of sports.

1. Humans are created in God's image and likeness.

The foundation for Catholic anthropology is found early in the book of Genesis: humans are created in God's likeness and image (1:27). Thus, to understand what it means to be human, one must look at what the biblical tradition reveals about God. Throughout the Bible, God is a God of creation and relationship. This does not, however, define God. Theologian Michael Himes writes that "the first and most important thing to know in theology is that whatever you think of when you hear the word 'God' is not God."[8] Himes posits that God is an "absolute mystery" that eludes human understanding, quickly qualifying that he means "mystery" in a way that defies an answer but always invites further exploration. God is the "absolute mystery

---

7. Janssens, "Artificial Insemination," 3–29. His work is based on the official commentary on *Gaudium et Spes* (Vatican Council, *Schema constitutionis pastoralis de ecclesia in mundo huius temporis*, 2:9). We are indebted to Todd Salzman for directing us to Janssens's work. See Salzman and Lawler, *Introduction*, ch. 5.

8. Himes, *Doing the Truth*, 9.

which grounds and supports all that exists."[9] Therefore, "God" is not a name, a person, or even class of being.[10]

A quandary is immediately evident: If God is absolute mystery, then how does one even do theology—namely talk about God? All talk about God pushes the limits of human language and understanding, but it is not impossible to speak of God.[11] Descriptive language in metaphors and images can provide insight into God's revealed identity. For example, in Scripture, God is described as a rock (Ps 78:35), breath (Isa 59:19), flame (Exod 3:2–3), truth (John 1:14), beauty (Ps 50:2), and a widow looking for her lost coin (Luke 15:8–10). These images all point to true attributes of God, but none are fully correct and even collectively are far from complete. So, what does one do? Himes proposes there is a "least wrong" image of God that gets closer than anything else in our attempt to functionally image God in a meaningful way.[12] For this, Himes turns to the First Letter of John in the New Testament where the evangelist states that "God is love" (4:8, 16). The original Greek of the text specifies that God is *agape*, which is love that is fully other-centered, seeking nothing in return; it is pure "self-gift." The full mystery that is God is unknown, but if one views God as self-giving love, one will have a proximate understanding of who and what God is.

In other words, God can be imaged as a relationship among people. Though perhaps unusual, this aligns with an image of God that is fundamental in the Bible, Christian tradition, and Catholic practice. Himes points out that the ancient Nicene Creed (the great statement of Christian faith valid for over two billion Christians today), as well as the practice of beginning prayer with the Sign of the Cross, both profess belief in a God who is Father, Son, and Holy Spirit. This is the doctrine of the Trinity: one God imaged in the relationship of three persons, and foundational to Christianity. Saint Augustine explained the Trinity as the "Lover" (Father), the "Beloved" (Son), and the "Love shared between them" (Holy Spirit).[13] God therefore is a continual mutual outpouring of self-gift that unites the lover and beloved. In this light, Himes interprets Matt 18:20, "For where two or three are gathered together in my name, there am I in the midst of them," as meaning, "where two or three come together in genuine *agape*, true mutual self-gift, there I am." The Trinitarian God is therefore present wherever self-giving

---

9. Himes, *Doing the Truth*, 9.

10. *Catechism of the Catholic Church* describes God as "pure spirit," 370.

11. Himes, *Doing the Truth*, 84.

12. Himes, *Doing the Truth*, 9–10; Himes, "Living Conversation," 227; Himes, *Mystery of Faith*, 7.

13. Himes, summarizing Augustine, in *Doing the Truth*, 17; Himes, *Mystery of Faith*, 8; Himes, "Finding God," 10.

love is present in the world. This returns to the original image of God from John's First Letter: God is love (4:8, 16). And the Trinity, God as self-giving love, is fully embodied in the person of Jesus of Nazareth, which is the doctrine of the incarnation.

2. Humans are relational and creative.

Jesus as God's incarnation reveals important truths about humanity.[14] Jesus teaches about and demonstrates the kingdom of God, which is God's reign or influence in the world. Further, his incarnation affirms humans are created in God's image (Gen 1:27) and created "very good" (Gen 1:31). Humankind is so good that God decides to become human in all things except sin (Heb 4:15). God does not call people to be anything they are not—they are called to be fully human because in being fully human they fulfill the image in which God created them. The more one accepts his destiny to be who he was created to be, the more like God he becomes. God created out of love, and so humans are at their most human, most who they are created to be, when their *agape* love is the basis for creating and nurturing healthy relationships with oneself, other individuals, communities, the material world, and God.

Jesus shows humanity who and what God intended humankind to be through his actions and preaching. Jesus' "greatest commandment" recorded in all three Synoptic Gospels is, "You shall love the Lord, your God, with all your heart, with all your soul, and with all your mind. This is the greatest and the first commandment. The second is like it: You shall love your neighbor as yourself" (Matt 22:37–39; Mark 12:30–31; Luke 10:25–28). Initially, it seems two commandments are given, love God and love your neighbor, but a *third* commandment is understood: love oneself. One must fully accept and love oneself to be able to give of that self and then fully accept another person.[15] Today, this triple commandment for relationship further implies relationship with the created world, which is the context for loving God, neighbor, and self.[16]

Sports are fundamentally relational. Athletes learn from family members, friends, coaches, and mentors; they have teammates, training partners, competitors, and sometimes spectators. Even the most solitary athlete such

---

14. Himes, *Mystery of Faith*, 20.
15. Salzman and Lawler, *Introduction*, 114.
16. Pope Francis's encyclical *Laudato Si'* is a recent and prominent statement emphasizing the fundamental human relationship with the created world, and the created world as the context for relationships with God, others, and self (e.g., n12).

as a mountain climber or ultramarathoner relies on the experiences of others in the sport. Quite simply, without relationships there are no sports—and no humankind. The quality of relationships is the primary determining factor for successful experiences in all sports in large part because relationships necessitate personal and communal responsibility. For sports, these responsibilities include taking care of oneself, teammates and competitors, officials, sometimes spectators, and the environments, both natural and social, that sustain the sport. Athletes and advocates need to take care of one another and the sport itself in the present so future generations can enjoy it. Because human dignity is based on being created in God's image, everyone has the responsibility to ensure this dignity and subsequently that all human "rights are recognized, respected, co-ordinated, defended and promoted."[17] The very term "sportsmanship" implies responsibility for the game that itself is a human creation.[18] The responsibility for others inherent in sports reflects the larger responsibility that humankind has for one another and the environment that is evident in Catholic ethical and social teaching, which are introduced in chapters 7 and 8, respectively.

In addition to being relational, sports are delightfully creative. Chapter 2 introduces the connection between God's self-giving love playfully creating the material world, and human play and sports. At their best, sports are spontaneously creative, and each athlete is constantly creating a movement or sequence that is utterly unique to her or him in the moment no matter how many times it has been practiced earlier or previously executed by other athletes. This is true whether it is a ten-year-old with friends on a patch of grass or a professional athlete in Olympic competition. The tension in sports between structure and creativity, the "plan" and improvisation, reflects these human tensions in all aspects of human life. Too little creativity bores and stifles, while too much results in chaos and confusion. Sports invite and amplify human creativity and ingenuity, yet within parameters and boundaries of rules, physical limitations, and sometimes team goals. Recall the theology of play in chapter 2: human play reflects the free and communal nature of God. Further, a sacramental worldview as explained in chapter 3 is open to God's presence experienced in self-giving relationships. These first two dimensions of our theological anthropology make explicit the basis for our claims about play and a sacramental worldview in those chapters.

---

17. John XXIII, *Pacem in Terris*, §60.

18. Though "sportspersonship" is gender inclusive and our intent here, it reads awkwardly. "Sportsmanship" is still commonly used, and no alternative term fits our meaning.

3. Humans are restless and filled with yearning.

Humans, in their deepest selves, are restless, incomplete, and filled with a hunger for more. Humans seek not only the goods of life, food, shelter, and knowledge, but also meaning and purpose, which in turn is the basis of human spirituality. Given that humans are created in God's image and likeness, the *Catechism of the Catholic Church's* description of God as "pure spirit" illuminates each person's deepest self, the soul.[19] The glossary of the *Catechism* defines the soul as, "The spiritual principle of human beings. The soul is the subject of human consciousness and freedom; soul and body together form one unique human nature. Each human soul is individual and immortal, immediately created by God."[20] Each person's deepest self thus reflects the transcendent and spiritual reality of the Creator in whose image he or she is created. As Saint Augustine writes, "You made us for yourself, and our hearts are restless until they rest in you."[21] Theologian Ronald Rolheiser explains that spirituality is based on human desire embedded deep within the heart of each person: "What we do with our longings, both in terms of handling the pain and hope they bring us, that is our spirituality."[22] These desires and resultant spirituality are fundamental to being human.

Relationships and transcendence are intrinsic components of spirituality. When one has a healthy self-love and life-giving relationships with other people, and cares for the natural environment of the earth, God, who is least-wrongly imaged as relationship, vivifies those relationships. From a sacramental perspective, these connections transcend the materiality of the world. Explicitly deepening one's relationship with God through intentional practices such as prayer and worship enhances one's spirituality that is a component of all relationships. These connections "within" experience and the world are integrative and unitive. For example, the link between human relationships and care for the earth is evident, as in Pope Francis's *Laudato Si'*; friendships viewed within a frame open to God's transcendence become places of spiritual encounter, and "wow" moments in sports are recognized as the spiritual experiences they are. Humans are created for relationships and transcendence; in fact, these two human experiences become united within a Catholic anthropological worldview. A healthy spirituality moves

---

19. *Catechism of the Catholic Church*, 370.
20. *Catechism of the Catholic Church*, 900. The glossary entry cites the *Catechism*, 363, 366, 1703. The remainder of the entry states: "The soul does not die with the body, from which it is separated by death, and with which it will be reunited in the final resurrection."
21. Augustine, *Confessions*, 1.1.
22. Rolheiser, *Holy Longing*, 5.

people to be more who they are created to be—relational and creative—which leads them closer to God.

Spirituality can also manifest in selfishness, which distorts one's view of the world, moves one to be less than he was created to be, and leads to fear, deceit, and violence. No other creature will ever be more or less than it is. William O'Malley writes, "Rocks will never be more or less flinty; carrots will never be more or less vegetable; cows will never be more or less bovine."[23] Humans, however, created in the image of God, who is free, have free will to be more or less than they were created to be. When humans are less than they were created to be, they are inhuman and behave inhumanely as they dehumanize themselves and others. The fundamental spiritual question is not whether one is restless and filled with yearning, but whether one's response to these desires will be life-giving or dehumanizing.

Sports therefore are spiritual to the extent they are an expression of, and arena for, human desires. Will spiritual hunger drive the athlete in healthy and life-giving ways, or move her to harm herself and those around her? Athletes know this hunger well. There are stories of college football coaches so driven to win that they take time out from postgame locker room celebrations of a national championship to call high school recruits, unable to savor the moment with the current team. Individual athletes seek a personal record ("PR"), a perfect jumpshot, and moments of "self-forgetting" that Mihalyi Czikszentmihalyi calls "flow."[24] For athletes it is the consummation of grace, speed, power, and control that epitomize the best of one's capacities. For spectators, there is a desire to witness; by witnessing, they participate in beautiful and powerful moments of human ability, spirit, and kinship.[25] Sports are a prominent response to the innate human hunger for meaning and purpose but should never be seen as an end, or *telos*, in themselves, as recent popes have argued, something summarized in chapter 1.

4. Humans are embodied and corporeal realities.

Related to inherent desire and spirituality is the fact that humans are embodied corporeal realities. The classical duality of spirit-body needs to be overcome to better see the intrinsic corporeality of being human. There is a dialectical tension between the duality of spirit-body and humans *being* as opposed to *having* bodies. The fruit of this tension recognizes the spiritual

---

23. O'Malley, *God*, 1.

24. Czikszentmihalyi, *Flow*, 64. He describes it as a "loss of self-consciousness."

25. This insight is at the heart of the Nike footwear advertising campaign featuring LeBron James and the slogan, "We are all witnesses."

importance in the physicality of human existence, and the possibility of the body as a locus of grace, spiritual awareness, and sanctification.[26] This does not deny or denigrate the human spirit, but rather recognizes that what happens to human bodies matters to one's very self. It is both/and instead of either/or when addressing human bodies and spirits: Christians should neither idolize the physical body in what Richard Gaillardetz calls the "Dionysian tendency," nor should they disparage the body like ancient Gnostics.[27] Further, people experience the world mediated through their five senses, which are corporeal. Similarly, people express themselves through their bodies; as explained in chapter 3, bodies symbolize individual people to the outside world. Bodies are the place of encounter with the created world, others, and God.[28] If Hugo Rahner is right that God, in addition to being creative, loving, and free, is also playful, then humans are embodying in a unique way the freedom and playfulness of their Creator-God when playing a sport that is "meaningful but not necessary."[29] In this view, sports are an expression and experience of being created by God, and perhaps a notable encounter with God who playfully and freely created humans.

The corporeal dimension of being human matters for all experience and value questions. Individuals' bodies and others' bodies are to be recognized, cared for, and respected as temples of the Holy Spirit. Such a view resists performance-enhancing drugs, unhealthy dietary regimes, dangerous overtraining, and genetic manipulations. Further, human embodiment demonstrates that humans are people of time and place; culture, context, and history all matter.[30] This does not justify relativism, but rather points out the obvious reality that, for instance, football is vastly different at various levels, from Pop Warner to high school to the NFL, and neither the players nor the games themselves should be treated in the same way.

The human desire for meaning and coherence in the world is at least as much spiritual as intellectual. This desire is affective and lived. It is a mistake to see spirituality, and by extension prayer, as primarily cognitive. Instead of seeing the desire for coherence in the world as an academic subject to be understood, spirituality and prayer are affective and behavioral. Relationships are initiated by felt emotions: one is drawn to another person;[31] reason deciphers these emotions; and relationships then grow beyond both

---

26. Janssens, "Artificial Insemination," 5–6.
27. Gaillardetz, "For the Love," 160–61.
28. Janssens, "Artificial Insemination," 6.
29. H. Rahner, *Man at Play*, 11. See also chapter 2 of this book.
30. Janssens, "Artificial Insemination," 9.
31. Smith, *Desiring the Kingdom*, 25–26.

emotion and reason to include a spiritual component. It is similar with God. A relationship with God is based on what one intuits and then does. This truism is articulated variously in the Catholic tradition: theology is "faith seeking understanding"; in other words, there is a sense that something is true and then one seeks to explain why it is so. Also, "orthopraxis precedes orthodoxy," which means roughly that right practice or choices precede right thinking. For example, athletes are accurately taught the fundamentals of their sport and then learn why this is. Coaches do not explain the mechanics of a jump shot; they teach the athlete the skill and then maybe later the athlete will understand the kinesiology and physics of an effective shot. Corporeal practices and habits, whether related to sports, schoolwork, relationships, or religion, form people into the humans they become.

5. Humans are limited, dependent, and endowed with innate dignity.

Physical bodies remind everyone at times of their limitations. They also point to responsibilities toward others' bodies and the created world, which all bodies inhabit. Specifically, humans are dependent and limited, while also endowed with innate dignity.[32] As dependent and limited, no one created himself or herself; one's purpose or meaning is to be discovered, not created; and everyone will die. Human innate dignity means each person is not an object or means to an end; one is both infinitely unique and fundamentally equal to other persons, regardless of gender, sexual orientation, age (including the unborn), perceived race, ability, education, nationality, or economic status.[33]

Human limitations are readily evident to every athlete and spectator: athletes lose a step (or more), strike out, miss putts, drop the ball, and find it more difficult to get out of bed the next day. Kobe Bryant, LeBron James, and Michael Jordan each missed more game-winning shots than they made;[34] Babe Ruth struck out 1,330 times;[35] and locally known athletes slow down, mess up, and lose unexpectedly. Sports force every athlete to recognize his or her limitations. Athletes suffer injuries and lose playing time to more talented teammates. Michael Novak analogizes losing in sports with death.[36] Innate human dignity and the fact that each person is unique and

32. Janssens, "Artificial Insemination," 5.
33. Janssens, "Artificial Insemination," 5 and 9.
34. Zhang, "Who Has the Most Game Winners," paras. 14, 17, 18, 22, and 23.
35. Kauffman, "Babe Ruth," para. 3.
36. Novak, *Joy of Sports*, 47.

fundamentally equal would at first seem irrelevant or antithetical to the competitive, meritocratic nature of sports. Yet it is these anthropological truths that cry out for fair play and equal opportunity and likewise resist the cynical commodification and abuse of sports and individual athletes.

6. Humans are created male and female.

An important yet contentious part of Christian anthropology relates to sexuality. Often "male and female" has been interpreted in a rigid, dualistic fashion that neglects the fundamental unity within creation. These dualisms and dichotomies spawn sexism that, to quote theologian Elizabeth Johnson, "classifies human beings, prescribes certain roles and denies certain rights to them on the basis of physical characteristics . . . sexism considers women essentially less worthy as human beings than men and sets up powerful forces to keep women in their proper 'place.'"[37] Sexism is evident in two related ways. First, sexism is sedimented in social, political, economic, and ecclesial structures that condition women and men to see females as subordinate to males.[38] Those elements related to females are placed under the control of their opposite, male-related counterpart. Such a stark view of created reality is a one-sided, androcentric perspective adopted by a patriarchal culture that has contributed to the Western emphasis on individualism, autonomy, and domination.[39] Second, sexism is embedded in patterns of thinking that establish the "humanity of male human beings as normative for all."[40] This rigidity of thought often presumes a male-dominant approach to gender that associates women with what is *below* (e.g., matter, feelings, body, and immanence) and men with what is *above* (e.g., spirit, intellect, self, and transcendence).[41] These structures and thought patterns perpetuate and substantiate one another, establishing a cycle that must be recognized and cared enough about to then change. One of the gifts of sport is its ability to value bodily experiences and consequently emphasize the radical unity between the body and spirit, female and male. Bodily experiences within sport highlight the interrelatedness within the human self.

Instead of giving priority to the male, as is often assumed from the creation of Adam (Gen 2:7), John Paul II stresses that the first man is only defined

---

37. E. Johnson, *Consider Jesus*, 99.
38. Sexism has significant corollaries with racism.
39. Lane, *Foundations for a Social Theology*, 97.
40. E. Johnson, *Consider Jesus*, 100.
41. Lane, "Christian Feminism," 666.

as male *after* the creation of the first woman.[42] In Gal 3:28, Paul concludes a baptismal, creedal statement with the belief that there is no longer "male or female, for all of you are one in Christ Jesus." Further, as the *Catechism* teaches, the person's incorporation into the body of Christ at baptism transcends all "natural or human limits of nations, cultures, races, and sexes."[43] Elsewhere, the *Catechism* affirms that through the Holy Spirit all are baptized into the one body, and there remains no room for "*sinful inequalities.*"[44]

Modern sport has often accentuated a sexist viewpoint, where women initially had many restrictions on their sporting participation. These restrictions have been reduced in many ways today, as was evident in the equal numbers of women and men participating at the Tokyo 2020 Olympics, and sports like track and field and curling that have mixed-gender events. These underline the mutuality of the genders, as supported by much medical and psychological scientific evidence that attests to the fact that "all human beings embody both male and female experiences, qualities and characteristics in different degrees."[45] Theologian Jennifer Bader clarifies:

> While most (although by no means all) people consider themselves male or female depending on which genitalia they possess ... the scientific, bodily reality of sex is much more complex and involves chromosomes, hormones, brain structure and chemistry, and the like, that vary from person to person. In fact, hormonally, there seems to be more of a *spectrum* than a *dichotomous division* in which a given individual falls into one of the two categories "male" and "female."[46]

It is incorrect to define the human being according to a rigidly formatted male/female blueprint (i.e., one that supports preexisting stereotypes) or an androgynous framework that picks from only the supposed best masculine and feminine qualities, which can just as easily support stereotypes.[47] Instead, Dermot Lane argues for distinguishing between male and female without rigidly dividing the two in order to avoid "destroying the organic,

---

42 In *Theology of the Body*, Pope John Paul II writes that the first man (i.e., *adam*) is "defined as a 'male' ('*is*) only after the creation of the first woman" (*Theology of the Body*, 35). For the pope, this symbolically means that common humanity goes before sexual difference.

43. *Catechism of the Catholic Church*, 1267.

44. *Catechism of the Catholic Church*, 1938 (italics original).

45. Lane, *Keeping Hope Alive*, 30.

46. Bader, "Engaging the Struggle," 103 (italics original).

47. Lane, "Equality of All in Christ," 79.

inclusive and unified character of reality itself."[48] In other words, male and female must be seen in relation to one another. The overpromotion of male athletics by sports media and its viewers limits opportunities for women and leaves little room for mutuality among the genders. Rising above ingrained prejudices against both men and women can enable a vision of mutuality between the genders that forges new forms of freedom, trust, and mutuality in human relationships.[49]

7. Humans exist to receive and respond to God.

Why do humans exist? Humans exist to receive and respond to God.[50] Twentieth-century theologian Karl Rahner explains this as a "supernatural existential," which means humans are created to transcend their limited horizon to life with God in an unlimited horizon. God's presence and offer is experienced as grace. William Dych explains that humans experience this grace as "self-presence, freedom, and transcendence." In other words, part of what it means to be human is to yearn for transcendence while experiencing oneself as a limited being within a time and place. As receivers of grace and hearers of God's word, humans are called to be in relationship with God within their context or "particularities of all history."[51] This offer of life with God, God's grace, is why humans exist; it is offered to everyone and is the foundation and horizon for all human experience. Everything that is truly human can be a "channel of grace," a mediation of one's relationship to the transcendent God within a specific time and community.[52] "Being present to the moment" or "doing small things in a great way" captures an essence of this theological insight.

Created thusly, humans are attracted by transcendence manifest in what is beautiful, true, and good, the ineffable experiences that make one say "Wow." Humans intuit transcendence and grace in all facets of life, perhaps particularly in sports. Incredible feats of strength, perseverance, and agility are easily recognized, as well as inspiring selfless behavior in and around athletic endeavors. Because humans are created to receive and

48. Lane, *Foundations for a Social Theology*, 99. Lane refers to Saiving, "Androgynous Life," 16.

49. Lane, "Christian Feminism," 667.

50. Carr, "Starting with the Human," 18; see also K. Rahner, *Foundations*, 24–25.

51. Dych, "Theology in a New Key," 13; see also K. Rahner, *Foundations*, 20–23.

52. Dych, "Theology in a New Key," 14. A page earlier, he is more specific: "The God who came to be known through the history of the Jewish and Christian peoples can also be known through the history of all people, however different their way of conceptualizing and expressing this knowledge might be."

respond to God, they experience and express this recognition in a variety of ways related to their cultural context. All human endeavors are potentially graced and carry latent transcendence. In short, to the extent humans are drawn to and recognize transcendence in all areas of life, they are "perceivers of grace" and hearers of God's word.[53]

8. Humans are created good, but susceptible to the allure of sin.

The word "sin" in Hebrew is *hatta*, which means "to miss the mark" or target. The more humans accept their destiny to be who they were created to be—loving and creative—the more like God they become. To sin, then, is to fall short of that goal; this diminishes one's humanity. The great temptation is to reject one's humanity, and deny the humanity of others, both of which "miss the mark," which results in dehumanization and alienation.[54] Sin is often understood as individual acts, which the *Catechism* confirms.[55] However, the *Catechism* also defines "original sin"[56] and explains "structures of sin."[57] These realities are not identical, though it can be helpful to understand them in tandem. Some explanation is necessary, and analogies may be helpful.

Original sin is the disharmony experienced within oneself, in one's intimate relationships, in larger communities, between humans and the natural world, and ultimately between humans and God.[58] The ancient Genesis writers, the early Christians, and even the theologians who first defined original sin in 1547 at the Council of Trent viewed the individual person as

---

53. K. Rahner, *Foundations*, 50–51; see also Carr, "Starting with the Human," 17–18.

54. Himes, *Doing the Truth*, 25. He interprets Gen 3:5 as Adam and Eve demonstrating this unfortunate temptation to deny their humanity. The temptation for humankind is, "Don't believe what you've been told earlier in Genesis, you're not like God at all, you're human and therefore worthless. But do this, and you'll be like God!"

55. *Catechism of the Catholic Church*, 1868. "Sin is a personal act." Catholicism delineates types of sin into mortal and venial categories varying in degree based on what is done or omitted, and to what extent the individual had full knowledge and consent to the sin (*Catechism*, 1854–64). Venial sins weaken love and lead one away from God but don't break one's relationship with God. Mortal sins destroy the relationship with God. A sporting analogy may illustrate the difference in gravity and consequence: a venial sin is an error that sets one back from the goal of a game, while a mortal sin results in disqualification from the game.

56. *Catechism of the Catholic Church*, 388–90. Original sin is not the same as concupiscence, which is the propensity for human desires to unreflectively lead toward sin. God's grace and virtuous living help humans overcome this default behavior.

57. *Catechism of the Catholic Church*, 1869.

58. *Catechism of the Catholic Church*, 396–401, esp. 400.

part of a corporate reality intrinsically connected to the larger community of humankind. This is dramatically different from the highly individualistic conception of a person dominant in Western culture today.[59] These earlier communities perceived that what happened to an individual necessarily impacted the entire community and its descendants—either for good or ill. Sin was a collective responsibility recognized in a way mostly lost in modern Western culture. A contemporary sports analogy demonstrates the ancient mindset: in a football game, when an offensive tackle is called for holding, the entire team is penalized—the whole team loses ten yards from the spot of the foul. The doctrine of original sin insists that everyone experiences the impact of original sin, *and everyone is accountable for original sin*. This seems odd in today's hyperindividualistic world. People resent being held accountable for what they perceive they did not do. However, consider the linebacker on the sideline: he is held just as accountable as the tackle who committed the penalty. That is like original sin: though attributable to Adam and Eve, everyone is accountable. The point is that no one person today is guilty of causing original sin, while everyone is responsible for its effects.

Original sin is the context for individual and structural sins. Today, each person is born into a world marred by individual sins that over generations have established sinful structures and dynamics that dehumanize and alienate people from themselves, others, God, and creation. Every person is born into this world harmed by these sinful structures; these systems impact individuals and communities by conditioning human experiences, thinking, and interpretations of events. Racism, classism, androcentrism, sexism, and consumerism are examples of these pervasive inherited structures that impact human life. These dynamics do not remain outside of individuals. They are internalized from society and culture, making them part of each person and community.[60] A last football analogy might illustrate the collective impact of structural sin. Imagine the offensive tackle called for the penalty is part of an undisciplined team. Irresponsibility has been ingrained at all levels of the program, so much so that it is not recognized by those within the program. The individual contributions, the "personal sins" in this analogy, such as penalties, mistakes, and faulty execution, reflect and perpetuate the much deeper malaise conditioned into the habits and attitudes in the program. Being on this team means being socialized into accepting this unhealthy culture and its particular manifestations as normal, just "the way things are."

---

59. Nor is this individualistic concept of the human person universal across the modern world. More communal and relational understandings of the human person remain common across Africa and significant parts of Asia and Latin America.

60. Loewe, *College Student's Introduction to Christology*, 162.

Individual and structural sins are therefore inherently connected. Moral theologian James Keenan explains that individual and structural sins are "pervasive, deceptive, and elusive."[61] Keenan defines sin as a "failure to bother to love,"[62] and he divides sin into two categories: sins out of weakness and sins out of strength. Sins out of weakness are those times where people recognize their flaws, struggle with them, and confess in varying ways that they "screwed up." These are real sins, but they are not mortal sins for the very reason that they are struggled with. On the flip side, sins from weakness can be too easily excused by claiming "I'm essentially good," which is true—as this dimension of theological anthropology explains. Unfortunately, people hear "essentially good" but not "susceptible to sin," and by "susceptible" we mean "powerfully drawn to sin in ways people often choose to ignore." Further, sins out of weakness are almost always "individual," and so by focusing on them one overlooks, consciously or not, the structural sins that cultivate widespread dehumanization and promote further individual sins. Thus, a danger with these sins of weakness is that people can recognize them and even confess them but not delve further into their causes, as well as other, deeper sins they do not confront.

Individual sins out of weakness can obscure the sins that come from strength, which are the mortal peril for most people and communities. Keenan describes sins from strength as human complacency about one's goodness which leads to a failure to love.[63] Instead of struggling with one's sinfulness and succumbing, which is a sin of weakness, these sins are casually overlooked because one is comfortable with where one is. People do not bother to look, and so they claim, as did the goats in chapter 25 of Matthew's Gospel, something like, "Gosh, I had no idea that this was going on."[64] That is the point: the person did not know because he did not care to know; he did not bother to love; and the consequences are devastating for communities and individuals. This delusion is the basis for widespread alienation and dehumanization, and the reason sin is pervasive, deceptive, and elusive.

---

61. Keenan, *Moral Wisdom*, 42.
62. Keenan, *Moral Wisdom*, 42.
63. Keenan, *Moral Wisdom*, 42–44.

64. Matt 25:31–46. This passage depicting the final judgment is unique to Matthew's Gospel. Jesus is portrayed as a shepherd separating the "righteous" sheep who ministered to the "least brothers" from the "accursed" goats who ignored them. The punchline comes when both sheep and goats deny ever realizing that Jesus was hungry, thirsty, a stranger, naked, ill, or imprisoned. Jesus lauds the sheep because they bothered to love, even though they did not recognize him. Jesus then responds to the accursed goats, "What you did not do for one these least ones, you did not do for me." The complacent goats did not bother to look for ways to love others in meaningful ways.

Sports can help illustrate Keenan's description of sin, whether from "weakness" or "strength" and a failure to bother. Generally, coaches and teammates appreciate athletes who acknowledge their flaws in training and competition. Such humble self-awareness ideally leads to efforts to correct the flaw. Sometimes an athlete improves in this area, but sometimes not. By analogy, Basketball Hall of Famer Shaquille O'Neal was notorious for poor free-throw shooting (52.7 percent for his career).[65] Shaq's free-throw shooting often "missed the mark" and was a weakness for him as a basketball player; he was aware of it and struggled with it.[66] Realistically, Shaq's coaches and teammates probably did not appreciate his free-throw shooting, but these struggles became, if not endearing, at least accepted as part of his game. The danger is that when everyone, including the athlete himself, focuses on his valiant struggle to make a free throw but frequently misses (sin from weakness), they overlook other perhaps more influential flaws in the player's game that he is complacent about (sin from strength).

Conversely, coaches and teammates dislike athletes who are oblivious to their weaknesses in training or competition. This frustration is amplified when the athlete refuses to even acknowledge the areas that need to be improved, especially when they are areas that might easily improve with a little care and attention. The self-satisfied complacency that communicates, "Nah, I'm good," is an instance of not bothering to develop one's God-given abilities. If one has a responsibility to at least attempt to develop the talents one is blessed with, then to reject this responsibility is an instance that makes one less than one could be. It is a diminishment or dehumanization of oneself. It also alienates the athlete from herself, her teammates, and God. This is an example of Keenan's sinning from strength. This pervasive attitude of not bothering to care is sinful and has catastrophic consequences for teams and individuals, as well as communities far beyond sports.

RELEVANCE AND REFLECTION

Why does a theological anthropology matter for sports? It matters for sports for the same reasons it matters for any human endeavor. When one asks, "Who am I? Why am I here? What should I do? What is right (or wrong?),"

---

65. Bleacher Report, "NBA's Top 10 All-Time Worst Free-Throw Shooters," para. 33. Shaq missed "over 5,317 free throws in his career." If he had shot just 70 percent, his career scoring average would have increased by 1.61 points.

66. We are using instances of "missing the mark" within sports to illustrate sins from weakness and strength in the everyday world. The intent is not to imply that missing a free throw is sinful in life off the court.

the response reveals an implicit anthropology. An anthropology rooted in the Trinity and incarnation is the foundation for all Christian life, including sports. First, a Catholic anthropology is the basis of understanding oneself, others, the material world, and God. Second, an explicitly theological anthropology illuminates the reality based on the incarnation that anything that is fully and wonderfully human, such as sports, can profoundly point to and embody an experience of God's grace. This is the basis of a sacramental worldview explained in the previous chapter. Third, considering the first two points, a theological anthropology provides a comprehensive basis for "right" and "wrong" in human behaviors.

An oversimplification of Catholic ethics, but a reasonable starting point—which will be developed in chapter 7—is the assertion that something is "right" to the extent it allows individuals and communities to be who they were created to be by God (namely loving and creative), and something is "wrong" to the extent that it inhibits this fulfillment and flourishing. For example, it is an unfortunate reality that oftentimes people are valued exclusively for what they do and what they own; the respect and dignity afforded them reflects what they can do for others or take for themselves from others. The individualistic self becomes the greatest good. Right or wrong becomes irrelevant; the only questions that matter are "Can I do it?" and "What's in it for me?" Narcissism is embraced, and greed becomes an essential economic good; exploitation of the marginalized and the environment are justified with cynical appeals to "individual freedom." These disvalues that corrupt contemporary culture are just as corrosive to sports at all levels.

A well-developed theological anthropology also critiques and corrects the current unreflective default implicit anthropology. A Catholic anthropology expresses a vision of human dignity that is in stark contrast to what the contemporary world—of which sports are a part—often says is valuable about a person. For example, angst about diminished athletic performance increases when an athlete's entire self-value is wrapped up in her identity as an athlete, and this anxiety is further amplified by a "survival of the fittest" sports mentality that values athletes as commodities directly related to their athletic ability; when this ability is diminished, they are forgotten about. In this atmosphere, injuries and declining performance are terrifying and a cause of deep spiritual distress. Similarly, many people spend countless hours and time pursuing material success, including athletic achievements, to cover their fear that they are not good enough, they are not valuable enough, and they are not worthy to be loved as they are, created in the image and likeness of God. Human greed is based in the fear that one will never be valuable in who he or she is; personal arrogance or diminishment of others is an attempt to cover the insecurity that one is not sufficient as one is, created with inherent dignity by God. These negative approaches to life and sports corrode a person from the inside and inevitably result in sinful alienation and dehumanization.

CONCLUSION

The theological anthropology outlined above insists that humans neither create themselves nor endow the universe with meaning: there is a Creator and Ultimate Reality that is recognized as God.

Sports sometimes confuse this. Instead of recognizing sports as a mediation to God among many possibilities, there is the temptation to make sports an end in itself or idol. An idol limits God's grace instead of opening a person to the limitless experience of God. Sports, like human beings, are essentially good, but are susceptible to corruptions that dehumanize and alienate. To the extent sports reflect the humans that organize, compete in, and watch them, they offer a unique opportunity to examine the best and worst of humankind's potential.

Sports can also mediate experiences of loss and suffering. As Pat Conroy concludes in *My Losing Season*:

> Sports books are always about winning because winning is far more pleasurable and exhilarating to read about than losing. Winning is wonderful in every aspect, but the darker music of loss resonates on deeper, richer planes. I think about all the games of that faraway year that played such a part in shaping me, and it is the losses that stand out because they still make their approach with all their capacities to wound intact. Winning makes you think you'll always get the girl, land the job, deposit the million-dollar check, win the promotion, and you grow accustomed to a life of answered prayers. . . . Loss is a fiercer, more uncompromising teacher, coldhearted but clear-eyed in its understanding that life is more dilemma than game, and more trial than free pass.[67]

Suffering and loss are part of human existence and Christian theological anthropology. The Christian response to loss is the subject of the next chapter.

---

67. Conroy, *My Losing Season*, 14.

CHAPTER 5

Sports Can Hurt

The Problem of Suffering and Loss in Sports

PEOPLE ENJOY SPORTS BECAUSE they include entertaining drama and experiences of joy in the camaraderie of friendship, physical exertion, personal achievement, and spiritual growth. However, sports also involve losing games, not meeting personal goals, decreased playing time, getting cut from a team, and painful injuries and rehabilitation; they can include self-doubt, anxiety, or depression based on athletic performance or team dynamics; there can be conflict with rival competitors, teammates, coaches, or among fans; and abuse and violence can be perpetrated within sports settings. Sports can hurt physically, emotionally, and spiritually, and so raise profound questions about how one understands loss, suffering, disappointment, and even death.

For example, a former student we will call Michael tells the story of being recruited to play basketball for an elite high school program.[1] After playing on the varsity team for his freshman and sophomore years, he and everyone else anticipated him becoming the star during his junior and senior years, with colleges certainly recruiting him. Unfortunately, during an early scrimmage before his junior season, he severely injured his knee. Looking back, he admits he had no idea the path his life would take from that point forward. His journey is not so much a "basketball story" but a life

---

1. "Michael's story" is inspired by an experience of a former student, but we also draw from the experiences of many others to create a composite character.

story, one with features many people will recognize. It is ultimately a story of new awareness that starts from personal pain and loss.

Similarly, another former student we are calling Maya was told at the outset of summer conditioning before her senior year of high school that she would not be on the varsity volleyball team in the fall, so if she came to the summer sessions, she would need to participate with the junior varsity and reserve teams.[2] A successful volleyball player, she and her family were devastated. It was too late to transfer to play elsewhere, and so, like Michael's, her experience is one of losing something she had been working towards for many years.

As explained in chapter 3, there are joyful "wow" moments that can prompt reflection on the cause and significance of the experience. These encounters can remind of and point to God's presence for those with a sacramental perspective. Similarly, sorrow and loss can be experiences of God's grace. This can be difficult to understand, so in this chapter we delve deeply into theology and human suffering to demonstrate that God can be encountered in these powerful if painful experiences.

This chapter first addresses the sources of suffering and then proceeds to explain Jesus' paschal mystery, which is the basis of the Christian response to suffering. It is a pattern or cycle of death to new life that plays out in one's life, but consistent with our thesis throughout this book, the cycle is particularly evident in sports. Though within this broad paschal cycle individual experiences will be different, we will share Maya's and Michael's stories to illustrate the recognizable pattern, highlight personal insights, and demonstrate theological points. The chapter also offers examples of athletes and fans responding to the intrinsic human need for meaning in life, and proposes entering into the paschal mystery, especially in response to suffering and death. The chapter closes by offering the Eucharist as the key to living the paschal mystery in sports and all of life.

WHERE DOES SUFFERING COME FROM?

When Michael was first injured, he says: "It didn't hit me. I mean, people get injured all the time. I'd been banged up before. It wasn't a big deal." It was not until the night before surgery that he began to recognize the significance of his injury. "The doctor said I'd be out for six months, maybe, which was all of my junior year of basketball. At the time that seemed like forever, a whole season." Michael remembers his dawning frustration and beginning to ask, "Why? Why did this happen to me?" When Maya was told she would

2. "Maya's story" is a composite of numerous former students' experiences.

not be on the varsity team, her initial response was shock, and then anger. She wanted to know, too, why she was cut. "Why is this happening?" she remembers asking. Their questions in the face of injury and loss are ones that have haunted humankind since writing developed. The Bible's book of Job is an eloquent presentation of humanity's desire to understand the "why" of suffering: Why does suffering happen to me (or my loved ones), and why is there even suffering at all?

When facing suffering in sports or life, one must identify the cause as much as possible, always knowing one may never explain it completely. For example, when an athlete is injured, the initial physical pain or numbness of the injury confirm that something in the body has been lost or disrupted. Where there had been a healthy body, there is now painful physical disfunction and disintegration. This experience can be fear-inducing. In a very real sense, the athlete's world can come undone as fundamental questions demand answers: "Why did this happen to me?" and maybe "Where is God in this?" A person can respond in ways that further disintegrate one's spirit, such as, "Everything sucks. Nothing matters. I don't matter." At this point the physical pain caused by the initial injury is at least equaled by the ensuing emotional and spiritual suffering.

Injuries are not the only cause of emotional and spiritual suffering in sports. When someone loses games, competes poorly, loses playing time, or does not make the team, a part of that person disintegrates or dies, the part that had a vision of herself as successful and therefore valuable because of her success in that sport.[3] When one experiences injury or disappointment one grieves because what had been expected—a successful experience—does not occur. The contradiction between the expected outcome and reality is scary because it calls into question all default suppositions and the expectations based on those suppositions. This was Maya's experience. She was a healthy athlete and very successful with her club volleyball team, aspiring to train with her friends on her school team and to contribute in whatever role was needed to help her team succeed in her senior year. When she got the email from the coach telling her she would not make the team, she says: "I cried for a week. I'm glad it was summer, so I didn't have to see anyone. I was miserable."

Maya's story is notable because of its ambiguity. On one hand, the initial cause of suffering can simply be the result of being human and contingent. Bodies deteriorate, tire, and will quit functioning. Injuries, losses in competition, falling short of a long-worked for goal, deterioration of skills and stamina, or getting superseded by more talented athletes are all part of

---

3. Rolheiser, *Holy Longing*, 153–57.

human limitedness. This does not make the suffering any less, but it does frame necessary theological reflection on suffering in sports and, by extension, all facets of life. Perhaps Maya was simply not good enough in the view of the volleyball staff. However, what to this day upsets her is that "I was never told why I was cut. No explanation was given, even though I'd asked. It was like I was banished or something."

In this way, human sin can also contribute to the suffering. For instance, though there's nothing inherently sinful about an injury, it can be a result of dirty play, abusive or careless coaching, or a sporting climate that distorts the significance of competitive achievement so much that it causes athletes to harm themselves in their pursuit of athletic success. Not making a team, as in Maya's case, or losing playing time can be less clear. When the evaluation process is fair, transparent, and communicated clearly, this can be an experience of human finitude, which is painful enough. However, sometimes a coach plays favorites, or the rationale is never explained, which initiates distrust and anger. In the case of even making a team, one must also question if the process is truly fair when the youth and high school sports scene is dominated by a "pay-to-play mentality" that costs families thousands of dollars a year, thus initiating a cycle of differentiation based on family income so some players have access to the best coaches and facilities, while others are painfully left behind—something addressed in chapter 8.

It is critical to acknowledge the impact of a setback by naming what has been lost.[4] It is not just "a starting position," "playing time," or "a professional contract," but *what the death of these possibilities represented to athletes in their sense of self and value as a human being*.[5] Sometimes the causes of these experiences are relatively obvious, as in the case of injury or competitive disappointment in the stories above. Causes of suffering can also be frustratingly mysterious, whether resulting from random happenstance, as in the case of a freak injury, or inexplicable evil, such as when people dehumanize themselves and others. Nevertheless, while identifying the causes of suffering is essential, the causes do not explain the meaning of suffering. In other words, the question is not even about the factual cause of suffering but rather why there is heartache, pain, and loss in the first place.

---

4. Rolheiser, *Holy Longing*, 148.
5. Ellis, *Games People Play*, 194.

SUFFERING AND LOSS IN SPORTS: THE PASCHAL MYSTERY AS A RESPONSE

For the biblical writers through to the present day, this question raises a well-known conundrum: if God loves humankind, and if God is all-powerful, then logically humankind should not suffer pain because an all-powerful God who loves humankind should stop the causes of suffering. To sketch a brief response to what is called the problem of "theodicy," a short review of theological anthropology from the previous chapter is necessary. God is a mystery but can be least-wrongly thought of as self-giving love (1 John 4:8).[6] Humans are made in God's image and likeness, and the purpose of human life is to fulfill the image in which humans were created, which is to use free will to be loving and creative (Gen 1:27). Evil is the rejection of this purpose and the misuse of freedom.[7] All explanations of evil are fundamentally incomplete and frustrating because, by definition, evil is what should not be.[8] This rejection of human purpose is evident in alienation from oneself, others, and God—which is sin. Humans both die and sin. Genesis 3 artistically depicts the theological connection between these two realities, both experiences of closure and rupture. While evil is inexplicable, sin is rooted in despair of one's creation in God's image.[9] God created humans infinitely valuable, but despair insists that humans are worthless, deficient, and meaningless, and this despair is the root of fear that is the basis for human suffering. There are, and throughout history have been, many responses to suffering, such as anger, apathy, and fear, as well as compassion and mercy. The Christian and Catholic response is God's love, which is most fully present in the incarnation, Jesus Christ.

Specifically, the suffering, death, and resurrection of Jesus Christ is at the heart of the Catholic response to pain and death. In Catholic theology, this sequence of Jesus' life-death-new life is known as the paschal mystery and is the culmination of his ministry dedicated to his Father's kingdom, the kingdom of God. Jesus' ministry heralding God's kingdom includes his preaching to crowds, wondrous deeds, and testimony to his disciples. His ministry of preaching and living the kingdom of God cannot be separated from the event of his resurrection, the culmination of his paschal mystery, which demonstrates that death embraced out of love is transformed to new,

---

6. Himes, *Doing the Truth*, 9–10; Himes, "Living Conversation," 227; Himes, *Mystery of Faith*, 7.

7. *Catechism of the Catholic Church*, 386–87.

8. Himes, *Doing the Truth*, 70. *Catechism of the Catholic Church*, 385, quotes Saint Augustine: "I sought whence evil comes and there was no solution."

9. Himes, *Doing the Truth*, 69.

resurrected life.[10] Jesus, in John's Gospel, reminds his disciples that "unless a grain of wheat falls to the ground and dies, it remains just a grain of wheat; but if it dies, it produces much fruit" (John 12:24). Jesus' paschal mystery invites people into, and unites them with, this foundational Christian conviction. This means that when countered with God's transcendent and self-giving love, suffering can precipitate experiences of new, transformed life, which is a deep Christian insight that must be approached very carefully.

It is crucial to understand that we are not justifying or excusing suffering. Suffering is neither inherently beneficial, nor can it ever be excused as "God's will" or "serving a purpose."[11] Elizabeth Johnson explains: "What happens at the cross [during Jesus' crucifixion] and consequently at all other suffering moments is that God, who is the absolute foe of evil, enters into compassionate solidarity with the suffering one in order to save. . . . The evil of this world, with all its power, is weaker than God, the compassionate One who enters into solidarity with the sufferer and ultimately saves."[12] The Catholic tradition denies that suffering can be explained fully, while simultaneously asserting that God's compassionate love revealed in Jesus' paschal mystery overcomes suffering and death.[13] The response to suffering in life, which includes sports, is to therefore enter into the vision and story of Jesus Christ and the paschal mystery.

Jesus' story and the paschal mystery undergird the symbolic gesture of the sign of the cross and image of the crucifix. For example, the sign of the cross and crucifix are often present in sporting events as athletes cross themselves or wear a crucifix on a chain or featured on a tattoo. The sign of the cross conveys the short prayer, "In the name of the Father, Son, and Holy Spirit," which explicitly echoes the rite of Christian baptism. Baptism is a ritual expression of one's desire to unite with God through Jesus' life, death, and resurrection—the paschal mystery.[14] Consider the ritual symbols of adult baptism: one is submerged underwater and ritually enters into Christ's death to then emerge, dripping wet, reborn into new life with Christ.[15] At their fullest, the sign of the cross and crucifix are reminders of God's response to human suffering evident in Jesus' ministry, death, and

10. Rolheiser, *Holy Longing*, 146.

11. E. Johnson, *Consider Jesus*, 125.

12. E. Johnson, *Consider Jesus*, 125. Johnson cites Edward Schillebeeckx in this passage.

13. *Catechism of the Catholic Church*, 404, 411.

14. Ellis, *Games People Play*, 191, cites Novak, *Joy of Sports*, 21, 47–48, for noting a connection between Eucharist, Baptism, and sports.

15. Full immersion for baptism most effectively symbolizes entering into Jesus' death and transformed life; were one to stay underwater, one would literally die.

resurrection. When athletes, or anyone, make the sign of the cross or adorn themselves with a crucifix, they are conveying theologically their desire to enter into and live Jesus' paschal mystery to which these expressions point.

The Paschal Mystery & "Terminal" vs. "Personal" Death

After Michael's injury and surgery, he remembers his junior year of high school as a dark and frustrating time. He was the "star basketball player" who could not play basketball; he could not even go to class because of all the stairs in his high school. He would sit in an empty school room from 8:30 a.m until 2:30 p.m. each day, sometimes doing homework, sometimes watching movies, and then would hobble to the gym to watch his teammates practice every afternoon. The frustration and despair became consuming; even getting up in the morning was a struggle. He explains: "Growing up, basketball was who I was. When I was injured, my whole identity . . . just gone." He was on crutches for months, relishing the pain of physical therapy because "at least it made me feel alive. Usually, I felt like I didn't have a purpose." He was in a bad place, ailing from depression and a sense of worthlessness. "I'd ask myself 'what's the point of being around?'" Though he did not recognize it at the time, Michael's injury and subsequent rehabilitation was a process of entering into Jesus' story and vision of life-death-new life, which is the paschal mystery.

To enter the paschal mystery, it is important to distinguish between "terminal" and "personal" death. Theologian Ronald Rolheiser suggests terminal death is easy to understand.[16] Terminal death is when one's heart stops beating, and earthly life and potential are ended. Jesus' terminal death on a cross ended his earthly life. However, the paschal mystery asserts that the tomb and death could not hold him,[17] and he was raised three days later. Jesus' terminal death was a "paschal" experience because his death was transformed by God into new life. This follows the paschal pattern initiated by God's liberation of the Israelites from bondage and death during the first Passover recounted in the biblical book of Exodus. Christians and Catholics unite their lives with Jesus by living out the kingdom of God and entering into the vision and story of his paschal mystery. At its heart, this is what Christianity is: humans unifying themselves with God through his son Jesus.

This paschal logic of death to new life is not only relevant for terminal death: each person can also realize paschal experiences in the endings she or

---

16. Rolheiser, *Holy Longing*, 146. The entirety of Rolheiser's "Chapter 7: A Spirituality of the Paschal Mystery" is foundational for this section.

17. Himes, *Mystery of Faith*, 35.

he experiences daily.[18] To clarify this, we build on Rolheiser's idea of a "paschal death" to interpret ended relationships, surrendering beliefs that one had been comfortable with, or other internal disintegrations as "personal deaths."[19] For example, Michael entered a process of personal death when he injured his knee. His image of himself as capable of anything, a powerful high school athlete, with an unfettered horizon of successes, came crashing down. It was not just a hurt leg; he lost his central narrative that organized his life, was the basis of his identity and important friendships, and carried his future hopes. He entered a process of dying to what he held dear. These losses are very real and feel like deaths inside oneself, though they are not directly terminal because one's heart keeps on beating and earthly life continues. Personal deaths are fear-inducing because they are emotionally and spiritually painful. They also foreshadow an individual's terminal death when one separates from what is known on Earth. In this way, "personal deaths" amplify fear and suffering. Deaths, both terminal and personal, are disintegrations of oneself, and fear of these deaths is the fundamental cause of suffering. These painful personal death experiences initiate either "resuscitated life" or "resurrected life," which invites important elaboration.[20]

Resuscitated life is when one's life carries on much as it was before the personal death experience. For example, one continues on after an injury or traumatic event similarly to the way one lived before the event; there is no change or new awareness in the individual related to whatever caused the suffering and disintegration. In contrast, Rolheiser affirms that what we term "personal" deaths can lead to a new, transformed way of being because "while ending one kind of life, [the personal death] opens the person undergoing it to receive a deeper and richer form of life."[21] He calls these occurrences experiences of resurrected life. In Catholic theology this does not replace the resurrected life believed to await after terminal death, but it foreshadows and even prepares for this eventual full unity with God. Jesus' paschal grammar of life-death-transformed life is something humans encounter constantly, whether they recognize it or not. This unity with God through Jesus and his paschal mystery is a dynamic process of ongoing conversion, an ever-new awareness of oneself and God in the world experienced in continually richer and fuller ways of being than what had been experienced before.

18. Rolheiser, *Holy Longing*, 148.

19. Rolheiser, *Holy Longing*, 148. "Personal death" is our innovation. We avoid "spiritual death" because of its traditional meaning in Catholicism, a person's soul in a state of mortal sin and so not united with God. This meaning is unsuitable here.

20. Rolheiser, *Holy Longing*, 146. Accepting God's grace transforms death in all its forms to resurrected life.

21. Rolheiser, *Holy Longing*, 146.

Maya and Michael faced the painful choice described by Rolheiser: they could either embrace the paschal mystery, including the personal deaths of much of what they had known, or they could cling to what they knew of their former lives before his injury and her not making the team.[22] Despite their Catholic upbringing, Michael and Maya had only the vaguest notion of the paschal mystery. Michael certainly could not connect it to his severe knee injury, and Maya had no idea what Jesus' resurrection might have to do with her miserable summer before her senior year of high school. At the time, both just wanted to know, "Why did this happen to me?" This most human of questions, if approached honestly, can lead to deeper unity with God through entering into the paschal mystery of Jesus.

INTUITING THE PASCHAL MYSTERY

God's love incarnated in Jesus Christ does not "explain" suffering, but "frames" it in a way that transforms suffering into new life through the paschal mystery. We propose that sports explicitly be seen as a component of spiritual training and immersion into paschal living because loss and disappointment are inherent risks in sports. We present Jesus' paschal mystery using examples from sports because they offer a rich opportunity to demonstrate this paschal logic. Instead of avoiding reflection on loss, sports offer a comparatively safe opportunity to discuss suffering. It is "safe" because as important as sports are, losing games, not making teams, and physical injuries pale in comparison to other causes of suffering in the world: tragic accidents, natural disasters, abuse, social injustice, violence, and genocide.

Michael's and Maya's experiences are illustrative of the paschal mystery. Michael's rehabilitation of his knee went poorly. Physical therapy did not bring back his explosive quickness. Even jogging was painful. Doctors were confounded. Eventually, he learned he would never be able to play basketball again in high school, much less college. His anguished tears and pounding fists, while temporarily cathartic, did not change the reality he had to face. Before his senior year of high school, he was at a crossroads and recognized that something had to change.

Maya's summer was similarly one of anxiety and frustration. She did not know what to expect when the volleyball season started in the fall. She describes an experience a few days before classes started as "when I realized that I needed to make the most of my senior year and I couldn't do that

---

22. Franciscan priest and spiritual writer Richard Rohr summarizes their situation: "If we do not transform our pain, we will most assuredly transmit it—usually to those closest to us." Rohr, "Transforming Pain," para. 2.

feeling sorry for myself or running away from volleyball." Both Michael and Maya were at a key moment in their living of the paschal mystery. They were at the juncture after their personal deaths where they needed to decide if they would move ahead in their senior years with resuscitated life or resurrected life.

Over time resuscitated living intensifies fear and anger in the face of loss, or one devolves into despair because there is no alternative beyond just carrying on after the personal deaths experienced. For Michael, if he did not recognize the death of his previous image of himself, he would short-circuit into despair because it was apparent that he would not fully recover. He could have fearfully clung to his previous vision of himself, perhaps this image motivating him to continue his attempt to fully return from his injury. This may seem like a laudable choice, committing to return, but it is based in fear of losing what is most valuable to him and then anger that it may be lost. Regrettably, there would be no transformative growth, and this choice does not consider what happens if the setback is too great to overcome, as was true in Michael's case.[23] Maya had just been angry. She was angry with the varsity coach and even her former teammates, some of whom she felt were ignoring her that summer.

Maya, like Michael, had no understanding of the paschal mystery at this point in her life. She explains her transformation as one of necessity. "I couldn't live my senior year like that, moping around, no way. My dad just told me to pick myself up and dust myself off, so that's what I tried to do." She became a youth coach for her volleyball club and continued to play for her club team. She made a point to congratulate the volleyball team on their success, even attending a few games, something that was not easy. "I'd always prayed, but before it was just like talking at God, I guess. For the first time I really found myself praying about things that were difficult for me, but it wasn't just about stuff I wanted, but about my perspective in life and the type of person I was. I didn't want to be an angry person, so that's what I prayed for."

For Michael, Catholicism had not been a large part of his life. "A once in a while type of deal," he explained. "Y'know, Christmas, Easter." However, as Michael tells the story, he was sitting in his same empty room at school when he was prompted by a random intercom announcement to the entire student body to take a moment and pray if they felt the need.

---

23. Transformative growth through the paschal mystery *may* include attempting to recover from a loss; however, resurrected life after a personal death is not the equivalent of "fighting to come back" or "returning" from a setback. New life through the paschal mystery is experienced as a deeper, richer understanding of oneself and one's place in the world in relationship with others, creation, and God.

> So, I turned off the screen of my computer and just sat there. Eyes closed, head down, and took a deep breath. I decided to pray, something I hadn't done in many years. Crossing myself in the name of the Father, Son, and Holy Spirit I felt something I can't explain, even now. A feeling of calm, real calm. It felt as if someone was telling me, "It is going to be okay," but I didn't hear anything, if that makes sense. From that moment on I started taking time out of my day to talk to God. Just telling him how I was doing and asking how he was. I stopped pitying myself. Things didn't change overnight, it took months, and although I wasn't able to play basketball like I had been doing all my life, I was able to reconnect with old friends and make a bunch of new relationships with people I hadn't known. Somewhere along the way I found a small part of myself.

Michael still needed to come to grips with the fact that he would never play basketball at the level he thought he would when he was sixteen years old, and many other things changed, but over time he found his life blossoming. His senior year he got involved in his school and larger community in ways that he never would have been able to do had he been playing basketball. Looking back, he encapsulates his experience: "Something was guiding me, I can't explain it."

Both Michael and Maya intuited a choice different from resuscitated life. They chose a Christian response to pain and loss. For them, the alternative was right in front of them, but they were initially blind to it, much like Jesus' disciples in the Gospels.[24] Christians unite their lives with the paschal mystery by living as members of Christ's body within his church today.[25] Jesus gives a primary condition for Christian living: "Whoever wishes to come after me must deny himself, take up his cross, and follow me. For whoever wishes to save his life will lose it, but whoever loses his life for my sake and that of the gospel will save it. What profit is there for one to gain the whole world and forfeit his life?" (Mark 8:34–36). God then blessed Jesus' final act of self-giving ministry, death on a cross, with new life. All people are invited to say "yes" to Jesus' ministry, vindicated by God through the resurrection, and unite their destiny with Jesus' paschal mystery. Christians are free to reject responding to the world with fear or anger because death has been

---

24. Mark's Gospel especially is filled with instances where Jesus' disciples blindly misunderstand his teaching (e.g., James and John in Mark 10:35–45). Immediately following this passage (10:46–52), Mark presents a blind man, Bartimaeus, desiring to see. At some level, the two passages should be interpreted together.

25. Vatican II, *Lumen Gentium*, 8.

overcome through Jesus. In this worldview, how one faces terminal and personal death is transformed, and thus how one embraces life is changed.

ENTERING THE PASCHAL MYSTERY

Many people intuit the paschal cycle and functionally embrace it to the extent they experience new life after suffering and loss, but they misunderstand why this is so and what this means for living. This was basically Maya's and Michael's experience before learning more fully about Catholic theology. Athletes we have talked to have described deep personal deaths that they healed from only after preconsciously following the grammar of Jesus' paschal cycle. This is a good thing, but also a lost opportunity if they do not reflect upon the spiritual and religious significance of these personal resurrection experiences, such as why this paschal grammar exists and what it might mean for their future, which surely will include more personal deaths as well as terminal death. Explicitly embracing the paschal grammar of personal suffering as a result of sports experiences opens one to fuller immersion into Jesus' paschal mystery, which is the dynamic of all growth and transformation. It is important to note the paschal mystery is not equivalent to the well-meaning human wisdom asserting that "every new beginning comes from another beginning's end."[26] The accumulation of these types of saccharine, greeting-card-wisdom sayings does not constitute a coherent worldview that can respond to the sufferings humans encounter.

To move beyond a superficial understanding of the paschal mystery, one must intentionally enter into it. Jesus' own transformation from death to new life in the paschal mystery is the paradigm for those who unite themselves to God through Jesus' ministry, death, and resurrection. Rolheiser identifies five components of Jesus' paschal cycle. He explains that each component is part of a "single process" and "needs to be understood in relation to the others to make sense of the paschal mystery."[27] His description is the basis of what follows[28]:

1. Good Friday: Jesus' death on the cross; "the loss of life—real death."
2. Easter Sunday: Jesus is raised by God to new life; "the reception of new life."

---

26. This aphorism is attributed to Lucious Annaeus Seneca the Younger and incorporated in the rock band Semisonic's 1998 hit song "Closing Time." The statement, "Everything happens for a reason" is similarly insufficient to address suffering in the world.
27. Rolheiser, *Holy Longing*, 147.
28. Rolheiser, *Holy Longing*, 147–48.

3. *The Forty Days*: The period between Easter Sunday and Ascension: "a time for readjustment to the new and for grieving the old."

4. *Ascension*: Jesus ascends to heaven; "letting go of the old and letting it bless you, the refusal to cling."

5. *Pentecost*: The Holy Spirit descends on Jesus' disciples; "the reception of new spirit for the new life that one is already living."

Maya and Michael's experiences illustrate each step of the paschal process.

1. *Good Friday: Jesus' death.* They needed to acknowledge their personal deaths. It was not Michael's injury or Maya not making the team, but the end of their images of themselves as successful athletes. They also needed to surrender a worldview that saw athletic success as the key determinant of their meaning and value.

2. *Easter Sunday: Jesus raised.* Michael and Maya needed to recognize where they were invited to new life in the form of transformed ways of seeing themselves and the world. This new view opened them to experiences and opportunities previously unimaginable.

3. *The Forty Days: Time to grieve and adjust.* They needed time to adjust to their new reality. Michael described months of coming to grips with the fact that his injury would not heal like he hoped, while Maya had a summer to grieve her surrendered dream of playing high school volleyball.

4. *Ascension: Do not cling, let go, be blessed by the past.* Both tried for a while to cling to what they had known, their previous worldviews and self-image. However, Rolheiser explains that past experiences, both good and bad, are part of each person, and so one must calmly let them go as opposed to angrily tossing them aside or idolizing them. To do this, Maya and Michael needed to see their past, including their past selves and the dreams those past selves had, as personal ancestors whose wisdom, however painfully earned, sustains them in their lives now.

5. *Pentecost: Accept God's Spirit for life now.* Lastly, both Maya and Michael needed to celebrate and be open to the lives they were now leading. Rolheiser writes: "Some of the happiest people in the whole world are seventy years old, and some of the unhappiest are that age. The difference is not who has kept himself or herself the slimmest and most youthful-looking, but in Pentecost."[29] Jesus' disciples received the Holy

---

29. Rolheiser, *Holy Longing*, 149.

Spirit on Pentecost, which freed them to be who they were in the context they were in.[30] Maya and Michael participated in Pentecost when they accepted God's Spirit in the new life they were currently living.

If the Catholic worldview is operative and not just nominal, the physical and spiritual pain in life is not any less, but there is a path toward resurrected life through the paschal mystery. The choices one makes in response to suffering both reveal and form one's worldview. One may at first fear or hesitate about letting go of a prior self-image, but God through Jesus assures that death has been overcome by God's love and that new life awaits. Only when a person chooses the paschal logic that rejects fear and anger will one be able to choose the blessing of new life experienced as a deeper, richer understanding of oneself and one's place in the world. This is an experience of living by faith and not by sight (2 Cor 5:7).

The significance of the paschal mystery in sports and life thus raises an important claim: suffering and loss can potentially mediate encounters with God. How is this possible? This claim necessitates a mature spiritual understanding of suffering and the paschal mystery because it can easily be misconstrued or distorted. It also recalls the Catholic sacramental worldview outlined in chapter 3. Christians frequently overlook the fact that Jesus died a failure. Betrayed by a friend, abandoned by his disciples, Jesus was tortured to death at the request of his religious and cultural leaders because of his commitment to the kingdom of God, where the meek inherit the earth, which had not happened in his lifetime, has not happened since, and does not look close to happening now. Jesus did not die a winner by any stretch of the imagination.[31] The God of the crucified Christ is a God of the marginalized, the suffering, and the losers. Sacramental experiences are powerful encounters with God, and these can be ordeals of spiritual suffering, personal death, and resurrection. These experiences can crack through the superficial shells that people create for themselves and thus open them to see themselves as they truly are. In this light, a distressing event such as an injury or not making a team can initiate a new understanding of oneself in relation to others, the world, and God.

A number of important cautions about entering the paschal mystery are needed. The paschal mystery is not about naively lighting a candle and singing "Kumbaya." This is real pain and suffering, and it cannot be ignored; one must go through it, and there are significant challenges. First, no one can know what new, resurrected life looks like. One may want to tell God her or his vision of resurrected life, but that is not how it works. Faith is

30. Acts 2:1–3.
31. Himes, *Doing the Truth*, 74; Ellis, *Games People Play*, 224.

needed, which is evidenced by an openness to God's grace working in ways one may not welcome or understand. For example, after a personal death, new life might include never playing one's beloved sport in the same way again, like Michael experienced; it might mean forging new friendships while letting go of long-held relationships; it may indeed be successfully coming back the next year and achieving competitive success. Second, it is important to understand that one does not seek death in a Christian worldview. Though Saint Paul, with the paschal mystery in mind, rhetorically asks "Where, O death, is your victory? Where, O death, is your sting?" (1 Cor 15:55), reasonable Christians do not diminish the significance of death, either terminal or personal. The paschal mystery is not about ignoring death, but rather it is about uniting oneself with God through Jesus' vision and story to overcome fear of death and so live fully. Third, a healthy grieving process as experienced by Michael and Maya is essential to living the paschal mystery. This invites gradual adjustment to new resurrected life and resistance to the anger and despair that accompanies suffering and loss. It can be neither rushed nor omitted. The paschal cycle does not call on one to forget the past, including relationships, nor does it mean one forgets dreams, pretends the pain of lost expectations and transformed worldview does not hurt, or imagines that loss and grief do not change oneself. It does mean one embraces this transformation as a part of life in Christ, and this ongoing process of conversion takes a lifetime.

LIVING THE PASCHAL MYSTERY

Sports are prominent public forums today that mediate meaning from life's events, not just those directly related to sports. Athletes, fans, and coaches express their faith through sports by making the sign of the cross before competition or pointing to the sky at key moments. There is prayer before, during, and after events by all involved. Many memorialize loved ones' names or initials on their apparel or in tattoos. At least sixteen American college football stadiums include "memorial" in their official name.[32] Some dedicate seasons or careers to deceased loved ones. For example, after former US Men's National Soccer Team captain Clint Dempsey scored the winning goal against Ghana during the 2014 World Cup, he pointed his index fingers to the sky in memory of his sister who died of a brain aneurysm and a close friend who died from an accidental gunshot.[33] There is also a proliferation of memorial services, often impromptu, at the deaths of

32. HERO Sports, "Do You Know?," para. 1.
33. Alleyne, "Secret Heartbreak."

athletes, for instance NBA player Kobe Bryant in 2020, or MLB pitcher Jose Fernandez in 2017. Also, fans are increasingly buried bearing mementos of their beloved team, and some fans can be buried in a coffin painted in the colors of their favorite soccer team. FC Barcelona reportedly included plans for space to inter 30,000 urns of fans' ashes in their refurbished Camp Nou, while England's Burnley FC donated £30,000 to create space near their home stadium for fans to spread the ashes of their loved ones. English football club Aston Villa hosts a "Holte Enders in the Sky" tribute at the end of each season where fans memorialize their deceased loved ones in a service hosted by the team's chaplain.[34]

In response to suffering and death, these sports rituals and expressions are hopeful but rudimentary attempts to break free of the immanent frame and grapple with loss in a general, accessible, and contemporarily acceptable way. The problem is that the reality of death and suffering require more than this. These ritual actions accompanying sport are significant, but modern sport was neither intended to wrestle with deep existential questions nor meant to be a primary carrier of meaning in death or joy. However, even those disinterested or unfamiliar with religious traditions resist claiming life is meaningless, leading to the question of "Why is there meaning?" and "Where does this meaning come from?" As explained in chapter 3, these questions point to what Charles Taylor calls "transcendence" in existence.[35] Death, suffering, and joy thus take place in a universe that has meaning, and people instinctively begin to ritualize these events, often in ways not fully understood. Without intentionally connecting these gestures to a larger matrix of human meaning, these expressions point to, but never achieve their potential to fully ritualize, an encounter with God that is latent within experiences of suffering and loss.

In Catholicism, the ritual sacrament of the Eucharist makes present the connection between God incarnated in Jesus, manifest in the paschal mystery, and embodied in daily life decisions. The Eucharist presents God's self-giving love in Jesus that is the heart of the paschal mystery, and it serves as the center of the matrix of human meaning through which one understands all of life's experiences.[36] Once one begins to interpret life in view of the Eucharist, all of life's experiences can be formative as they invite one deeper into the Christian vision and story. Humans unite with God through Jesus in the sacramental celebration of the Eucharist, which in turn guides

---

34. Lewis, "Sport after Death."
35. Taylor, *Secular Age*, 542.
36. Irwin, *Models of the Eucharist*, 142.

and forms them for daily living.[37] In this way, the Eucharist is the "source and summit" of Catholic life.[38] Jesus' paschal mystery celebrated in the Eucharist is the intersection between "understanding" one's life and "forming" oneself for that life. Within this worldview, sports can be an important place to comprehend the significance of living the Christian vision, while simultaneously a prominent place to deepen one's integration into Christ's paschal story. Sports afford this because they are profoundly human and are perhaps at times contemporary "liminal experiences" where one is particularly aware of how close God is to humankind.

People can live virtuous lives or intuit life's paschal grammar without explicitly recognizing God's role in these choices. However, Christians are called to consciously model their lives on Jesus' life and ministry, making moral choices that reflect their faith in God to further God's kingdom on Earth. This is the basis of Catholic morality and virtue as well as Catholic social teaching, presented in chapters 7 and 8, respectively. Daily prayer, as introduced in chapter 6, and weekly participation in the Eucharist form and prepare Catholics to enter Christ's vision and story through their lives. By loose comparison, the Eucharist forms for Christian life the way daily training, film study, and a pregame team meal prepares an athlete for competition. Living the life of an athlete prepares one to be an athlete and actually makes one an athlete. One becomes who one trains to be, whether it is a Christian or an athlete. Athletes know that when fatigue sets in, and things have not gone as planned, their training and preparation take over. This is analogous to how a life of prayer and the Eucharist sustain and support Christian life. By participating in the life of the church, which includes communal worship, prayer, and the Eucharist, one ever more deeply immerses oneself into the Christian life, including the paschal mystery. Practices and habits such as daily prayer and regular Eucharist train Christians to be open to God naturally and unconsciously, and so form Christians into the people they are created to be. This habitual and open stance to God's presence sustains a relationship with God that frees one to love others and embrace one's life, which includes personal and terminal deaths, in a way that results in new, transformed life. Such formation through the Eucharist becomes evident in every facet of life, including sports.

---

37. Himes, *Doing the Truth*, 128–29.
38. *Catechism of the Catholic Church*, 1324.

CONCLUSION

When experiencing suffering and loss, people intuitively reach out to God. It is often phrased as a question, sometimes with an expletive; basically, "Why did this happen?" Michael's and Maya's stories illustrate this clearly. Reaching out to God (or the heavens or one's center of meaning and value) recognizes God's always-present, welcoming invitation. Humans' questions, inherent desire for answers, and even restlessness, when honestly addressed, lead to God. When things are going well, which can go on for years, people get distracted from, or complacent about, their relationship with this mystery. Some may have never really learned about this mystery in life-giving ways. Maya's and Michael's experiences with Catholicism illustrate this; we have seen this lack of understanding many times in those we teach. When people are successful, it is easier to accept the delusions that one is in control, solely responsible for one's achievements, and uniquely deserving of the spoils of success—overlooking the obvious facts that one did not create oneself or the world one inhabits, and that one's personal success reflects the efforts and skills of many people through the years. For example, a Hall of Fame quarterback relies on the skill of his offensive line, the preparation of his receivers, and the ability of his team's defense. Likewise, many coaches, doctors, and mentors helped him develop and maintain his talents, supporting and guiding him every step of the way. He is also flat-out lucky to have never suffered a debilitating injury like Michael did. It is sometimes only in the face of loss and death that questions about meaning, value, and God become urgent, and one accepts the invitation that has been there all along. People think they are reaching out to God, but they are truly responding to God's eternal reaching out to them. In the next chapter, we will see how rituals and prayers can help one respond more fully to God through sport.

CHAPTER 6

Kneeling in the End Zone

Ritual, Superstition, and Prayer in Sports

IN 1977, RUNNING BACK Herb Lusk broke free for a seventy-yard touchdown run. It is what he did next, though, that cemented his legacy in the NFL and North American sports culture more broadly.[1] After crossing the goal line, "The Praying Tailback" paused, took a knee, and gave thanks to God. And so entered the end-zone prayer into the lexicon of modern sports rituals.

Lusk's act should not be a surprise, theologically speaking. If Christians are to follow the rhythms and patterns of Christian life, it seems only natural for them to incorporate Christian practices into sports. From Lusk to Tim Tebow to the local high school basketball game, famous and unknown athletes alike have publicly prayed before, during, and after games, both individually and as a team. But should sporting-event prayer be enabled and endorsed? Is Lusk's quiet sign of prayer a true act of devotion, or is it overly pious? If a coach thumbs through rosary beads in her pocket while on the sidelines, is that sacrilegious? One might further question if using explicit religious rituals in sports causes an unwanted distraction, perhaps harming the purposes of sports.

In this chapter, we offer a theological examination of rituals in sports and religion in order to understand, judge, and support spiritual practices used by individual athletes, coaches, and fans. First, we present some background to this question by showing how sports historically have borrowed

---

1. Goldenbach, "After NFL's First Prayer." Lusk went on to serve as a religious advisor for President George W. Bush.

much from religious rituals. Although few athletes today believe that their act of competition is primarily a religious act, it remains helpful to understand the ritualistic side of sport that opens the door to religious practices. In the chapter's second step, we complete a deep dive into personal rituals that athletes use in sports, whether religious or not. We describe why Christians have traditionally used spiritual practices, posit how religious and nonreligious alike can easily fall prey to superstitious mindsets, and differentiate how prayer and ritual ought to be incorporated into sports.

ANCIENT RELIGIONS AND SPORT RITUALS

Anthropological studies reveal how ancient peoples often created sports from their religious rituals. In his classic work, *From Ritual to Record*, Allen Guttmann explores the abundance of evidence that shows how "primitive societies frequently incorporated running, jumping, throwing, wrestling, and even ball playing in their religious rituals and ceremonies."[2] It is not that all sporting activities by early peoples were necessarily religious, but Guttmann explains that "sports ... may indeed have entered the lives of primitive adults primarily in conjunction with some form of religious significance."[3] He added that modern societies tend to underestimate the cultic aspects of these original sports. For many ancients, "the contest was in itself a religious act."[4]

Consider the most widely known example of the coming together of sport and religion: the ancient Olympics. In a five-day festival in honor of Zeus, the greatest of the gods, the ancient Greeks made games a part of their religious devotion.[5] Spectators and athletes alike made a pilgrimage to Olympia, a holy site, where there was an impressive Temple of Zeus and a statue to the namesake. As the Games opened, the Greeks stood shoulder to shoulder, offering prayers, hymns, incense, and animal sacrifice.[6] In light of the large number of temples found around Olympia, there were many opportunities for athletes to pray and make ritual offerings between competing in events like running, discus, javelin, boxing, and pankration.[7] Other

---

2. Guttmann, *From Ritual to Record*, 16.
3. Guttmann, *From Ritual to Record*, 19.
4. Guttmann, *From Ritual to Record*, 25.
5. Bain-Selbo and Sapp, *Understanding Sport*, 137.
6. Bain-Selbo and Sapp, *Understanding Sport*, 139.
7. Although nationalistic and athletic ambitions appeared to overtake the festival's religious dimensions over time, cultural historian Johan Huizinga maintained that the ancient Olympics remained closely aligned with religion (Bain-Selbo and Sapp,

sports and religious rites came together for Indigenous peoples. Anthropologist Michael Zogry observed a contemporary form of a traditional Cherokee game played in North Carolina.[8] The autumn-season game includes an amalgamation of pre- and postgame rituals, including dancing, fasting, and a water ritual, which bridge the Cherokee religious system and lacrosse. In what is now known as Central America, Aztecs and Mayans competed in a ball game on stone courts adjacent to their religious temples, with religious priests closely observing.[9] The game included a solid rubber ball that was hit with players' hips—not their hands and feet—and put through a wooden or stone hoop turned sideways on the wall.

These three above examples show how the divide between ancient games and religious rites was ambiguous, to say the least, but do they provide historical evidence of sports' religious basis? We argue that the religious rituals of ancient sports provide analogous connections to contemporary sport, where through a sacramental perspective (as described in chapter 3) we see how sport can mediate the divine. Along with Guttmann, we agree that contemporary sport does not publicly endorse religious traditions through its rituals, but disagree that the bond between the secular and the sacred has been fully severed.[10] Historian Johan Huizinga explains that what has happened is that highly organized, scientifically driven sports have "stiffened" the spirit of play with greater seriousness, which in effect has weakened the play-element in sport. Yet Huizinga is also unwilling to deny a transcendent possibility in sport because of its spirit of play, although he rejects the idea of making today's sport an explicit religious practice.[11] In other words, the veil that hangs between the secular and the sacred, between the material and the spiritual worlds, has become more permeable in the sporting world. Further investigation is required.

Ritual time and space

At a human level, rituals can open communities to transcendence. They convey significance through symbolic words and gestures, moving participants beyond the literal meaning. They align values, as people recognize others and themselves in them. They enact values by symbolically representing

---

Understanding Sport, 140–41).

8. Zogry, *Anetso, the Cherokee Ball Game*, 4, 18.

9. Baker, *Playing with God*, 7.

10. Guttmann, *From Ritual to Record*, 26. He notes exceptions, like the sporting involvement of devout Christians and those who see sport as a civic, secular religion.

11. Huizinga, *Homo Ludens*, 199.

them, which forms participants in their mold. Rituals are repeated over time and accompany significant events; they link people, past and present, usually through a community. They are profoundly human and are the glue that holds together social groups.[12] Rituals reflect and mediate meaning; they are a human and created experience. They include honoring former athletes, singing the national anthem, stretching during the seventh inning, or watching the Opening Ceremonies of the Olympics.

For religious persons, rituals provide unique opportunities to encounter God's grace through the created reality. The ritual does not replace God and is not a face-to-face encounter with the divine; yet the ritual mediates God's grace to those who are open to the encounter and experience. The ritual is tethered in reality, tradition, and experience; it does not float around and latch on to random meanings. For Christians, religious rituals often develop over time and are based on belief in the incarnation and a sacramental approach, as outlined in chapters 3 and 4. They are ways that transcendence reaches through the veil between heaven and earth. Just as human beings use time and space to analyze culture and interpret reality, religious persons use these categories to incorporate the divine.

Time

Secular time is generally marked in two ways: 1) calendars based on lunar and solar cycles organize time into categories of days, months, and years, while 2) history marks out significant events that shape the course of time.[13] From these, people speak of time in terms of past, present, and future. For religious persons, sacred time is a category that transcends these temporal standards and introduces the eternal, where the past and future become coterminous with the present.[14] Christian churches mark out this eternal time according to sacred rituals and seasons. As noted in chapter 5, the season of Easter brings together the solar cycle of spring in the northern hemisphere, the significance of Christ's death and resurrection (in connection with the Jewish Passover), and the aspiration for a future of full communion with others and God.

---

12. Jones, "Social Evolution," 470–72. For more about rituals and their connections to rites, see also Zuesse, "Ritual," 7833–43; Chauvet, *Sacraments*, 173–84; Cooke, *Sacrament and Sacramentality*, 39–40; Irwin, *Sacraments*, 29–32.

13. Seasoltz, "Sacred Time," 504.

14. Seasoltz, "Sacred Time," 504.

Ritual sacraments, like Eucharist, enable experiences of what Charles Taylor calls "higher times."[15] "Higher times" are disruptions to our conventional notions of chronological time. Taylor boldly writes: "Good Friday 1998 is closer in a way to the original day of the Crucifixion than midsummer's day 1997. Once events are situated in relation to more than one kind of time, the issue of time-placing becomes transformed."[16] Where linear time ran for three days between Christ's death and resurrection, kairotic time (which is a deeper time, or "the right moment") recognizes the significance of an event in the here and now. Instead of a moment merely being one second within sequential time, kairotic time denotes an important moment of action and has a permanent, in-depth nature. Easter is not a yearly anniversary like a birthday celebration; it stands outside linear time. It defies the limits of chronological time.

Sports have a similar "outside-of-time" dimension. Sports move according to seasons—football and ice hockey are seen as cold-weather sports, while baseball and beach volleyball are summer sports. Significant sporting events mark the course of the year, too: the Super Bowl, the Winter X Games, March Madness, the Run for the Roses, and the Fall Classic. Michael Novak analyzes the concept of time in baseball: "The time of a baseball game is a special time, measured in outs rather than in minutes. The clock time required to play a game is always listed in the box score, as though to assist one in translating one time measure into another. Every baseball game has its own distinctive clock time. Each *is* its own distinctive unit of time."[17] The baserunners even move in a counter-clockwise direction. Sports with game clocks introduce alternative notions of time. The last three minutes of a basketball game, "basketball time," can take fifteen minutes or more in chronological time. Despite these different forms of sports time, baseball fans complain that more strikeouts, pitcher changes, and the like have slowed the pace of play and made games over an hour longer than before. Its kairotic time has weakened, and the demands of fans' chronological time press in upon the game. Finally, the quality of time in North American sports is meant to improve, where a season progresses toward a championship game and the eternal moment of crowning a victor.

If Taylor is right that we moderns live in a flattened world, then it is unsurprising that some view the notion of time "slowing down" as merely a psychological phenomenon. Mihaly Czikszentmihalyi terms this experience "flow," where an athlete is so focused on hitting a ball or outrunning an

---

15. Taylor, *Secular Age*, 55.
16. Taylor, *Secular Age*, 55.
17. Novak, *Joy of Sports*, 126 (italics original).

opponent that she enters into a psychological state of being "in the zone," as noted in chapter 2. Kelly counters that this scientific approach can complement insights from Christian spirituality, along with Taoism and Zen Buddhism.[18] As when archers focus completely on shooting at a target, there is a centering of attention, loss of self, a sensation of effortlessness, and a connection to their surroundings. Kelly believes that when time slows down in a state of flow, it is somewhat comparable to the spiritual experience of consolation: people become more aware of God's presence, have more energy, and desire to help others more.[19] Kelly and others would agree that the spiritual life is about more than simply becoming self-forgetful.[20]

Rituals' repeated patterns break up the movement of chronological time. They are possible moments of lifting the veil between the material and spiritual worlds. They provide a lens through which "real" time is viewed. Kelleher notes how rituals have a heightened sensitivity to receiving the world as it really is.[21] Rituals, such as a baseball game or a baptism, speak to the way things *really are* instead of the way they *appear to be*, enabling the unveiling of hidden and deeper truths. Consider "home" as baseball's central metaphor.[22] It speaks of life's journey: we depart from home (plate), travel around the world (i.e., the bases), and return home. Other sports are built upon their own metaphors. For instance, the archetype of football is war, thus it includes throwing "bombs," running "blitzes," and "pounding" the defensive line.

In the rituals of Christian worship, even more so than sport, there is a pointing to things of ultimate, cosmic concern. In the ritual prayers recited at baptism, attendees are reminded that the universe is created by God despite its broken nature. In the action of washing the candidate, one's past life dies, sin is cleansed, and the person becomes a new creation with new life in Christ. An individual's personal growth is set within a larger church narrative: the neophyte is now part of the progression of creation in time and space, where everything is believed to reach its fulfillment in the person of Jesus Christ.[23] In this eternal moment, by participating in the ritual sacrament, the truths of kairos speak.

---

18. Kelly, "Flow, Sport, and Spiritual Traditions," 50–54.
19. Kelly, "Flow, Sport, and Spiritual Traditions," 55.
20. Ward, "Question of Sport," 60.
21. Kelleher, "Sport as Ritual Performance," 40.
22. Giamatti and Robson, *Great and Glorious Game*, 95.
23. Seasoltz, "Sacred Time," 504.

Space

Space is another important category for understanding religious rituals. Connections to transcendence, awe, or a specific religious memory can take place at religious shrines, like a church or temple, or geographical entities that are spiritually understood, such as a mountain, cave, desert, or river.[24] Because God has intervened or continues to intervene at some unique location, its physical makeup has at the very least something like the residue of the divine presence.[25] This manifestation of God means that this part of the physical world represents how life on earth should look. For instance, early Christians paid tribute to "the morning star," which was symbolic of the Risen Christ, by praying eastward toward the sun.

Sacred places do not limit God's transcendence. Saint Paul proclaimed this teaching at Athens: "The God who made the world and everything in it, being Lord of heaven and earth, does not dwell in shrines that our hands have made" (Acts 17:24). Seasoltz explains that Christian teaching holds that God is not confined to an edifice built by human hands.[26] Christianity has a universal character. As declared in chapter 3, because God is present everywhere, God can be found wherever people search for the divine. Paul's affirmation of God's transcendence was not meant to be understood with a strict literalism, however. While no one church or pilgrimage site can circumscribe God's presence, people are often more aware of God in certain holy sites. Numerous biblical examples speak to this truth. For instance, Moses was asked to remove his sandals when he met God near the burning bush on Mount Sinai: "Come no nearer . . . for the place where you stand is holy ground" (Exod 3:5).[27] Christians reserve special privilege to churches as places of assembly and prayer. Nevertheless, the early church remained focused on understanding the church primarily as those people following Jesus. For example, Peter asks Christians themselves to be like "living stones, built into a spiritual house" (1 Pet 2:4–5).

Likewise, athletes and fans have connections to special, "holy" sites in sports, whether iconic locations such as Daytona Speedway and Notre

---

24. Seasoltz, "Sacred Space," 500.
25. Seasoltz, "Sacred Space," 501.
26. Seasoltz, "Sacred Space," 501.

27. Seasoltz, "Sacred Space," 501–3. Because people needed a visible representation of the invisible God, God's presence was captured in the symbol of the ark, which was housed in a tent. Later God was regarded as present in the temple, which was in Jerusalem, the heavenly city. Yet King Solomon knew that the God of heaven and earth could not be confined to one place (1 Kgs 8:27), and God also condemned the people of Israel for representing God as a golden calf (Exod 32).

Dame Stadium, or more intimate places known locally. Novak explains: "There is a special awe that arises when one enters for the first time—or at any time—one's high school gym, or Madison Square Garden, or Pauley Pavilion, or wherever the symbolic center of achievement may be."[28] More recently, Ellis differentiates "sacred space" from "sacred place." The field, court, or track is no longer neutral *space*, but a *place* of connection that itself communicates meaning relative to one's relationship to the community that honors the place.[29] A *space* becomes a *place* when it is no longer a neutral spot, but a site of special connection among people.[30] The special, even "hallowed," places in which sport is played and celebrated contribute significantly to these experiences for fans, evoking and mediating them in a semi-sacramental way.[31]

For scholar John Sexton, visiting Yankee Stadium brings back connections to past games and championships, along with players who were larger than life like Mickey Mantle and Babe Ruth. In that place, he finds a connection to something deeply meaningful. He does not naively equate a stadium to a place of worship, but nuances that the stadium acts as an *axis mundi*: "a channeling of the intersection between our world and the transcendent world."[32] For example, Pittsburgh Steelers fans are allegedly the most dedicated fans in the NFL. Tens of thousands cram into Heinz Field to become the mythical "twelfth man" who will lift the team to victory. Others participate in pregame tailgating or watch the game with friends at a favorite sports bar.[33] Some in Steeler Nation even host funerals and weddings at the stadium. Weddings as major life events are made exceptional with twirling "Terrible Towels," a photo opportunity on the field, and a tour of the Steelers' locker room for the wedding party. Emotions connected to the team, its symbols, and these special places, bolster the intensity and elation of the wedding day.[34] In this sport setting, fans of the team feel the regenerative, communal, and nurturing elements that peel back the limits of the regular-day world.[35]

---

28. Novak, *Joy of Sports*, 130.

29. Ellis, "Sporting Space, Sacred Space," 50. Ellis builds on the ideas of theologian Oliver Donovan.

30. Ellis, "Sporting Space, Sacred Space," 50.

31. Ellis, "Sporting Space, Sacred Space," 61.

32. Sexton, *Baseball as a Road*, 21.

33. Cottingham, "Interaction Ritual Theory and Sports Fans," 173–76.

34. Cottingham, "Interaction Ritual Theory and Sports Fans," 180.

35. Ellis, *Games People Play*, 179–89.

Hallowed places can return to being flattened spaces when larger connections are lost. The Brooklyn Dodgers' Ebbets Field was torn down and turned into an apartment building, while the Montreal Forum, the heart of "the Mecca of hockey," became a shopping mall. As sports venues, they called attention to this mediating capacity, where what is most real or magical can be touched, like Gil "The Miracle Man" Hodges hitting four home runs in one game at Ebbets Field,[36] or Canadiens fans celebrating one of the twelve Stanley Cup-clinching games at the old Forum. Further, economic pressures and the prominence of broadcast sporting interests can turn sporting events into spectacles, where they are transformed into a commodity for the production and consumption of images and airtime.[37] Philosopher James K. A. Smith adds that these deeper meanings can be replaced by a staunchly militaristic nationalism or an engrossing consumeristic desire to devour as much sporting content as possible[38]—whether on television or via fantasy pools, gambling wagers, or e-sports. If the rhythms and places of sporting rituals are dismissed or embraced half-heartedly, their spell can be broken and potentially overtaken by meanings antithetical to values of community, friendship, and development.[39]

In concluding this section, it is important to note how the special times and places of the sporting world carry the potential to mediate the transcendent in human lives. Sports are common initial symbolic experiences to the extent that they mediate human encounters and communicate values. Anthropologically, sports address a human need for relationships and connection. Sporting seasons and venues act like a flare gun, signaling the breaking-in of the spiritual in our lives. Sports fans demonstrate by their lived example that the transcendent has not been completely severed from sport, despite what Guttmann argued. Huizinga was right to challenge a highly institutionalized and scientifically driven sport that has "stiffened" the spirit of play in modern sports. Maintaining a ritual playfulness is necessary in order to salvage sport. Holding to the rules and ritualistic conventions of sports can reenable the lusory (or playful) reality felt through gatherings at games.

---

36. Sexton, *Baseball as a Road*, 27.

37. Lasch, *Culture of Narcissism*, 121. See also Hoven, "'Sport as a Celebrative,'" 218–19.

38. Smith, *Desiring the Kingdom*, 93–109.

39. Lasch, *Culture of Narcissism*, 101, 108–10.

PERSONAL RITUALS, SUPERSTITIONS, AND PRAYER

It is helpful for a theology of sport to understand sport as a ritual performance. This is not to declare that modern sport is an explicitly religious event, but rather that it carries meanings of time and space that allow a glimpse of the sacred. Ritual enables a richer understanding of sport, where it and ancient sport communicate social values and can affirm human connectedness (e.g., endorsing human attributes such as camaraderie, courage, and creativity). Overall, a broader view of sport as a ritual performance makes it easier to understand why people incorporate their own personal rituals into sporting events, where the veil between the sacred and secular is more easily lifted.

As an extension of this thinking, we spend the rest of this chapter examining personal rituals enacted by sporting participants: rituals and routines, superstitions, and prayer. In these practices, we find ordinary uses of religion within sport that highlight the possibility of encountering God's grace in the sporting world.[40]

Rituals and routines

Competitive sports can be anxiety-inducing for everyone involved. Much is left to chance and out of the control of the athlete and coach, to say nothing of the spectators. Increased awareness about mental health issues over the past decade has led superstar athletes like tennis's Naomi Osaka and ice hockey's Carey Price to take time away from their sport.[41] It is little wonder that athletes use personal routines, rituals, and superstitions to exert some control in high-anxiety environments that are filled with random threats.

Clarification of terminology is important here. Sports rituals differ from routines in that routines neither convey meaning or value nor link people to past and present. Routines serve a function and practical purpose: to maximize athletes' control of the relatively few elements they can control. To use Charles Taylor's terminology, sports routines are part of an immanent frame. This relates to any athlete meticulously making sure all the equipment is ready and their uniform is appropriately worn so nothing is forgotten or deficient. Further, sport psychology helps demonstrate this in its definition of pre-performance routines (PPR), which are undertaken as the immediate preparatory steps before the execution of a sporting

---

40. Hoven and Kuchera, "Beyond Tebowing and Superstitions," 62.
41. Dawson, "'They Are Human Beings."

performance. Positive self-talk, visualization, physical and verbal cues, and relaxation techniques can be part of a healthy PPR.[42] Ultimately, the difference between routines and rituals is analogous to the difference between a blink and a wink. Both involve moving one's eyelid. The former serves a function to clear one's eye, while the latter is intentionally infused with meaning intended to communicate and connect. PPRs are simply a blink.

Athletes can have personal rituals that open them to God's grace in the sporting world. Prayers and actions, such as pointing to the heavens, can be spiritual practices when they are part of a lived awareness of God's relationship to the athlete, the sport, and humankind. Religious rituals can personalize religious doctrines and values within a given context. In this light, religious rituals open one up to those around them, as well as God, and the possibilities inherent in these connections. At their best, religious sports rituals are part of a larger matrix of spiritual practices that reminds, aligns, and opens athletes and fans to recognize and respond to God's grace in sports and life. More specifically, through the paschal mystery, Christians can unite their challenges and suffering with Jesus, and in so doing join in his cross and resurrection (see chapter 5). Through divine grace, their fears and their best efforts can be transformed into new life.

The personal rituals or spiritual practices athletes undertake in their sporting life are not merely a mark of their personality. Instead, the enactment of these rituals forms them. Wearing a cross or a pair of football gloves from a deceased friend is a practice that reminds players of their identity and offers continued support. These spiritual practices can impact sporting performances, too, as highlighted in the research of Broch and Kristiansen. They compared pregame rituals of Norwegian and Polish athletes, where the devoted, Catholic Poles felt a boost in confidence prior to their match because they performed spiritual practices, like prayer.[43] When athletes' seasons or personal worth are on the line in a contest, they often rely on everything possible, which includes their most cherished beliefs. Broch and Kristiansen thus considered the possibility of faith doping—*glaubensdoping*—when elements of faith are linked to athletes' personal identity authentically and meaningfully.[44] Making the sign of the cross before a wrestling match can be an important element of personal integration that builds confidence in athletic endeavors.

One point should be added. Spiritual practices in sport do not typically arise spontaneously from sport itself. Instead, they are more likely

---

42. Podium Psychology, "Coach & Athlete Resource," 5.
43. Broch and Kristiansen, "'Margin for Error,'" 837.
44. Broch and Kristiansen, "'Margin for Error,'" 842.

borrowed from the spiritual storehouses of a religious tradition.[45] One study found that sporting participants primarily borrowed rituals from their religious traditions.[46] Generally, religious persons have the privilege of knowing these practices.

Superstitions

What about rituals known as superstitions? Both sport sociology and theological studies criticize them, yet the vast majority of elite athletes practice them.[47] Sport sociology defines superstitions as "actions, which are repetitive, formal, sequential, distinct from technical performance and which the athletes believe to be powerful in controlling luck or other external factors."[48] Examples abound. Athletes admit to wearing pink goggles from their childhood (swimmer Lydia Jacoby), inscribing a slogan on their underwear (karateka Ariel Torres), watching the movie *Kill Bill* the night before the big event (high jumper Vashti Cunningham), or "flipping off" his dad before a race (swimmer Santo Condorelli).[49] Tennis superstar Serena Williams admitted, "I have too many superstitious rituals and it's annoying. It's like I have to do it and if I don't then I'll lose."[50] She explained, "It's totally ridiculous because I have to use the same shower, I have to use the same sandals, I have to travel with the same bags." As captured by Williams, the problem with superstitious routines is that they follow excessively rigid processes and time schedules. This contrasts with PPR, which are focused on regulating intensity, enhancing concentration, and optimizing physiological and psychological states.[51] Superstitions run the risk of acting as a scapegoat, where poor performance is blamed on not following the superstition properly.[52]

From a theological perspective, it is understandable that athletes desire to amplify their perceived means of control, but their rituals can easily shade into problematic superstitious practices. Watching a movie the night before competing is a relaxing distraction, but it can become twisted into a rigidly performed superstition. Further, these rituals can digress to the

---

45. Ammerman, *Sacred Stories, Spiritual Tribes*, 87.
46. Hoven and Kuchera, "Beyond Tebowing and Superstitions," 61.
47. Bartosova et al., "Rituals in Sport," 6.
48. Bartosova et al., "Rituals in Sport," 6.
49. Dodd, "Olympic Athletes Share," paras. 1, 2, 4, and 12.
50. Dodd, "Olympic Athletes Share," para. 7.
51. Bartosova et al., "Rituals in Sport," 7.
52. Bartosova et al., "Rituals in Sport," 8.

point of athletes trying to control the sporting gods, who affect many sporting intangibles, like the way a football bounces or the stiffness of a breeze. Superstitions imitate an open encounter with God in the world but distort a ritual's potential and meaning. Superstitions open people to manipulation and false security, and they ultimately take away players' freedom, chaining athletes to habits out of fear of the consequences for deviating from the superstitious practice.

The line between a meaningful, liberating ritual and superstitions can be blurred in sport, as is the case with the use of numbers. Numbers are prominent in sport: playing fields are carefully measured and jersey numbers can correlate to a specific player position, as with rugby. Strict numerical order in sport enables scorekeeping (and betting) while advanced analytical statistics find new ways to understand the game and even change game strategies. Certainty that comes with mathematics can produce numerical affections for fans and players alike, who desire a favorite jersey number or believe a number of a deceased player should be retired (like that of Australian cricketer Phillip Hughes' One-Day International shirt).[53] Similarly, peoples in the ancient Near East and the Greco-Roman worlds assigned symbolic power to numbers: for example, "2" noted important pairs (e.g., left and right, heaven and earth, female and male), "4" modeled completeness (e.g., the four seasons and phases of the moon), and "7" were the number of celestial bodies known to Babylonians and used to order the days of the week.[54] For biblical authors, numbers also symbolically expressed reality: for example, "1" is associated with God's uniqueness, "6" marked the efforts of humankind (the six days of creation) but that lacked the final completeness of sabbath rest, and "12" noted the months in each year and the number of apostles.[55]

In sport, many still hold to belief in the symbolic power of numbers. Tim Tebow, a devout Christian who had a brief stint as a NFL quarterback, wrote with a white marker "John 3:16" on his eye black for a Denver Broncos' playoff game in 2012.[56] After throwing the winning touchdown pass in overtime, Tebow learned that he threw for 316 yards, averaged 31.6 per completion, that the opposition time of possession was 31:06, and that the end of the game registered a 31.6 overnight TV ratings.[57] Tebow believed

---

53. Hughes was struck by a ball and died during a match.

54. McGuire, "Numerology," 475–76.

55. Sorensen, "Numerology (In the Bible)," 477–78.

56. John 3:16 reads: "For God so loved the world that he gave his only Son, so that everyone who believes in him might not perish but might have eternal life."

57. Schefter, "Tebow Phenomenon," paras. 4–8.

that the numbers showed that God had bigger plans for him than simply winning a football game; tens of millions of viewers googled the biblical passage. Believing that a lucky number symbolically connects a player to God or others seems reasonable, but sportspeople can take belief in numbers too far and lose perspective, falling into a superstitious mindset of control instead of a theological understanding that God uses the created world as an invitation to grace through human desires, thoughts, and feelings. People need coherence in the world—and numerical connections can signify this—but these can easily give way to misplaced trust in idolatrous sources.

Superstitions are an example of contemporary materialists misinterpreting and then inadequately responding to the human desire to connect with transcendence sensed throughout the world. Many athletes and fans maintain superstitious practices that are flatly unscientific and irrational, yet simultaneously scoff at the possibility of transcendence in an open framework. Several fans explain their superstitious rituals as a means to influencing sports while watching from home: wearing a particular sweatshirt or lucky charm, turning off their screen for important plays, sitting in the right chair, or even avoiding a shower prior to the game so as to feel as dirty as the players.[58] Ironically, at times sport superstitions are seen to be more acceptable than religious rituals, perhaps because their superficial nature is more accommodating to an immanent worldview.

When people use routines to try to manipulate or control their relationship with the mystery of God, they become superstitions. It is not uncommon for religious people to fall prey to superstitions, where they turn spiritual practices into rigid rituals based on fears and obsessions.[59] These seemingly religious acts become something they were unintended to be, namely mere psychosocial interventions performed by athletes. Properly constructed, however, religious behaviors can provide a wide range of psychological benefits, give holistic meaning to sporting experiences, and endorse ethical action and moral growth.[60]

Prayer

To close the chapter, it is important to examine the most common ritual performed by sporting participants: prayer. For instance, despite the fact that coaches in US public schools are legally restricted from prayer or participating in religious activities while performing their role as coach, one

---

58. Eastman and Riggs, "Televised Sports and Ritual," 260, 266–68.
59. Bartosova et al., "Rituals in Sport," 10.
60. Maranise, "Superstition and Religious Ritual," 89.

study found that 40 percent of public high school football coaches reported their team praying before games.[61] This long-standing football tradition has staying power. Some coaches are adamant that team prayer gives confidence and energy to players, heightens team unity, and inspires better on-field performance, while also helping coaches maintain social control of their team.[62] Others add that prayer helps athletes lead a morally sound life, sanctifies their commitment to sport, and puts things in proper perspective.[63]

Prayer is more than simply asking God for things. According to Ward, prayer is an open stance to, and experience of, God. It is an act of faith, where one maintains a fundamental disposition of reception because "God gives continually, without abatement."[64] Instead of being concerned with whether God will give the gift asked for, a more authentic stance focuses on opening oneself to God by asking for assistance. At a fundamental level, humans have been gifted with life from the Creator; in prayer, they willingly receive other gifts as a sign of acceptance of this original gift.[65]

To use a leisure metaphor, prayer is sometimes described as a "walk with God." This demonstrates how Christians cultivate a friendship with Jesus, but it should not be interpreted literally. God is not a friend in the sense another human can be.[66] To be in relationship with God necessitates realizing that human beings are not God's equal. The same can be said of calling God "Father." This title is a sign of God's transcendent authority and parental tenderness; at the same time, the *Catechism of the Catholic Church* clarifies that "God transcends the distinction between the sexes" and is neither man nor woman.[67] The God who is fully other, nonetheless, wishes to walk with human beings.

Prayer is about sharing one's life with Jesus and involves aligning oneself with God's love. God offers love and grace for whatever is best for oneself, others, and creation. This selfless love is inherently creative and life-giving and is the power that began and sustains the universe. Christians seek

---

61. Utrup, "Coach's Fight to Pray," 339.

62. Hochstetler, "Striving towards Maturity," 330. The author adds that perhaps those coaches who require pregame prayers should themselves be required to attend church each week.

63. Coakley, *Sport in Society*, 28.

64. Ward, "Question of Sport," 62.

65. Ward, "Question of Sport," 62.

66. Martin, *Learning to Pray*, 45.

67. *Catechism*, 239. "God's parental tenderness can also be expressed by the image of motherhood," affirms the *Catechism*. Certainly, Jesus taught his disciples to pray the words, "Our Father," as a sign of God's adoption of his children through his only Son, Jesus (*Catechism*, 2779–80).

to align themselves with (or walk alongside) God's love, as it is prayed in the *Our Father*, "Thy will be done." They grow through various forms of prayer, such as blessing and adoration, petition (when they cry out to God for help), intercession (praying for others and the world), and prayers of thanksgiving and praise.[68] Prayer moves people away from their smallness toward a trust in God's ways and promises. In the midst of finding themselves through prayer, Christians should acknowledge that they come to prayer with mixed attitudes: altruistic, selfish, merciful, hateful, loving, and bitter.[69] As reflected in the diversity of the biblical Psalms, prayer often reflects this range of emotions through profound reflections on anger, grief, joy, gratitude, and fear. Managing this emotional energy, people of faith open themselves to growth in virtues like honesty, humility, openness, and trust.

Such an integrated, sporting approach to prayer was reported to researchers by recreational marathon runners.[70] Huffman and Etnier found that runners of varied religious backgrounds wove prayer into their running life. While one marathoner said that prayer is communication with God, another added that "marathon running makes my connection, my prayer connection, stronger and more direct."[71] Prayer helped these runners to change their outlook during a run when they reflected and put their life in proper perspective or more honestly admitted their mistakes and sought to make changes.[72] Running was also a moment to feel thankful, and prayer improved their relations with others.[73] Through personal reflection, these runners enabled prayer to create a spiritually edifying environment both inwardly and outwardly.

The openness of prayer is fundamentally illustrated by forgiveness as expressed in the *Our Father*: "Forgive us our trespasses as we forgive those who trespass against us." Prayer opens people up and reflects an openness to forgive others and be open to accept God's forgiveness, which is sacramentally expressed and experienced in the Sacrament of Reconciliation.[74] Christians cannot accept God's ever-extended offer of forgiveness unless they ask for it. They may need to offer forgiveness to a teammate, opponent, referee, or coach, and it may be the case that they most need to forgive

---

68. *Catechism*, 2623–43.
69. Hochstetler, "Striving towards Maturity," 328.
70. Huffman and Etnier, "Use and Meanings of Prayer," 147. See also Hochstetler, "Running as Liturgy," 85–96.
71. Huffman and Etnier, "Use and Meanings of Prayer," 153–54.
72. Huffman and Etnier, "Use and Meanings of Prayer," 152.
73. Huffman and Etnier, "Use and Meanings of Prayer," 157–58.
74. See *Catechism*, 1424.

themselves. Prayer can help people get over hatred of themselves, especially for driven players and coaches. Maranise outlines prayer practices specific to sport, of which we note two.[75] Talking to oneself as a friend instead of an enemy is his first technique. It requires players to trust in their abilities because God fully trusts in them.[76] Athletes need to be driven toward the love of the game, not toward hating themselves or teammates for mistakes and deficiencies. Second, when dealing with worry or cognitive anxiety, a life of prayer enables players to bring fears and concerns to God. It is an act of faith to admit a lack of control, just as a healthy relationship does not demand control from the other. Sitting with God in the quiet, for instance, helps human bodies: muscles relax, breathing slows, blood pressure declines, perspiration drops, serotonin and dopamine are produced.[77] In prayer, Christians become more likely to sense things around them that are normally blocked out because of the busyness of life.[78] Fears and concerns become smaller when they are taken from minds and bodies and offered to God.[79]

Prayer is not the means of escaping from the material world, but, according to Ward, is an entering into the materiality of the human condition more profoundly. Instead of overspiritualizing prayer, Christians should see it as the total embrace of embodiment, where integration of cognitive, emotional, and physical dimensions is possible.[80] Of course, sometimes competitive athletes overlook or avoid this movement toward integration. In the midst of a competitive sports atmosphere, one study identified athletes who compartmentalized sport and their faith, where, for instance, they pushed aside moral teachings in the heat of the game.[81] The athletes believed that religious beliefs could weaken their resolve to win. They felt the tension between an integrated, spiritual understanding of themselves and an internal performance narrative, overly focused on victory. Praying, believing in developing God's gifts, and circumventing unethical actions helped combat the dominant sport narrative.[82]

---

75. Maranise, "Superstition and Religious Ritual," 88–89.

76. Maranise, "Superstition and Religious Ritual," 88. Maranise highlights the Scripture passage often used by athletes: "I can do all things through Christ who strengthens me" (Phil 4:13).

77. Ward, "Question of Sport," 61.

78. Ward, "Question of Sport," 61.

79. Ward, "Question of Sport," 61.

80. Ward, "Question of Sport," 61.

81. Hoven, "Faith Informing Competitive Youth Athletes," 284–86.

82. Hoven, "Faith Informing Competitive Youth Athletes," 286.

Praying to win?

Does God care about athletic contests? One survey found that about 3-in-10 Catholics believe that God plays a role in the outcome of a sporting event.[83] Some claim that miracles do happen in sport, especially when Catholic imagery is evoked.[84] As a wordplay from the doctrine about Mary's Immaculate Conception, Terry Bradshaw's last-minute pass to Franco Harris became known as "The Immaculate Reception." Decades later, Stefon Diggs's last-play-of-the-game reception led his Vikings to a playoff victory in the "Minneapolis Miracle." Both plays are transcendent moments where a final catch in each game was an eternal, kairotic moment, as if God Almighty had initiated the fantastic endings.

Is it wrong for an athlete who has trained for years to ask for divine assistance before their big event? This may seem like a stretch to some, but often people intuitively offer a prayer of petition when facing a predicament. Ethical problems arise when people start to rationalize why their team should win. Some people have altruistic reasons for victory, where a player's fame can be a witness to faith. Or, when there is a cheater, like cyclist Lance Armstrong, people pray for his demise so that he can face public-shaming.[85] Motives should be examined before making such bold prayers. For philosopher Anthony Kreider, the worst part of praying for victory is the bartering that goes along with it: I'll be a better person, or I'll go to church on Sunday.[86] Surely, seeking outside help toward victory based on religious devotion is problematic, if not sacrilegious.

Theologian Lincoln Harvey raises an interesting critique around God's involvement in sport.[87] He argues that sport is an area of life that is strictly within the human realm. In fact, sport marks out human contingency; that is, future human events cannot be predicted with certainty, and sport celebrates this. Sport is simply something of human culture. Religion, for Harvey, is a celebration of God's presence with humankind. He argues that it would be wrong to commune with God in sport because people should do sport simply for its own sake. The obvious problem with this position is that it contradicts a sacramental perspective. In response, one theologian argues that the problem is not that athletes find God in all things, but that people

---

83. Cox et al., "Nearly 3-in-10 Americans." This number was about the same as the general population.

84. Hochstetler, "Striving towards Maturity," 332.

85. Kreider, "Prayers for Assistance," 21; Meyer, "Redemption of 'Fallen' Hero-Athletes," 1.

86. Krieder, "Prayers for Assistance," 17.

87. Harvey, *Brief Theology of Sport*, 93–94.

should see God so utterly involved in sport that they make God something less than the Creator of everything.[88] The problem is anthropocentrism: one equates God's sovereignty over the world to a person's control over an Xbox game, where someone manipulating controller buttons forces an outcome. Smith adds that it seems rather silly "to imagine a picture of God playing video games in the sky."[89] God's providence over life's many contingencies is surely not like this, where it is nonsense to make claims about a divine perspective determining who won or lost a game. (For Kreider, asking for outside assistance—whether from God, or the trainers deflating air pressure in footballs—is an attempt to gain an unfair advantage and is thus cheating, as we explain in chapter 7.[90])

If sporting participants pray for victory, they misunderstand what salvation is about. People are not saved when victory is forged, despite the slapdash use of redemption metaphors in sports media. Christians are not redeemed through their victories or worldly successes. Ironically, they are united with God and thus saved through loss and death. This is the pattern of the paschal mystery, as discussed in chapter 5. Redemption is not returning from injury, a mistake, or scandal to help the team or win a championship; redemption is recognizing that loss is not the end. This *may* involve a return to the team or championship game, but often does not, though audiences like Hollywood-ready happy endings where redemption is simply about victory.

What should sport enthusiasts pray for? Prayers of petition ask God for assistance. They remind people of their dependence on God and place hope in the God who sustains all things. They also remind people of their weaknesses and hurt, where they fear rejection or wonder why life has not been easier on them. Asking for God's intercession can be a good thing. More specifically, it is good to pray for one's best effort, where one somehow digs deeper than ever before. This type of intercession by God might be comparable to asking a hometown crowd to cheer their racer to a first-place finish.[91] Prayers for avoidance of injury for oneself, one's team, and one's opponents are entirely sporting.[92]

---

88. Smith, "Praying to Win," 335.

89. Smith, "Praying to Win," 335.

90. Kreider, "Prayers for Assistance," 18. It doesn't seem right that a contest would be determined by an outside force. If praying for victory worked, would that not fundamentally change the nature of sporting competition?

91. Kreider, "Prayers for Assistance," 22.

92. These prayers may lead to an ethical question: If you're so concerned about injury in your sport, should you perhaps play a less violent one?

Prayers of petition are a first step toward a mature faith. God wants people to use their gifts to find solutions to problems.[93] Their development and greater independence do not compete with God's power because the Maker of the universe is unafraid of creatures' powers or abilities.[94] God wants human flourishing. For Hochstetler, it is important to grow past seeing prayer as a good luck charm and embody it as an act of faithful devotion.[95] This is captured by one marathoner: "I'm not asking for any magic shoes that are going to make me faster . . . it's just really asking to let me bring out that potential that I know I have inside of myself . . . to bring out the best in yourself."[96] God wasn't micromanaging the race. Instead, working through this person's openness, God's grace can enable an athlete's fullest potential. As Patrick Kelly has pointed out, there is more to prayer than mere psychology.[97] Grace perfects our nature, theologically speaking, and thus it develops what people already are—it does not make them into something they are not. God's grace, therefore, does not transform people without their permission or by ravishing their humanity. Rituals and prayers open athletes up to this grace within a lived relationship with God and the recognition that they are not ultimately in control. This in turn can be an important lesson for prayer in life when people face more serious questions of suffering, such as the premature death of a friend or family member.

CONCLUSION

Rituals embody what is most important to human communities. As in the ancient world, today's athletes can understand how sport triggers their spiritual awareness through its connections to play, spatial and temporal dimensions, commonalities to ritual, and the modeling of spiritual acts like prayer incorporated by fellow competitors, coaches, and fans. These rituals can reveal how things really are and what really matters, even to a larger, cosmic purpose for living. Yet modern sport is not worship, and long-distance running is not a substitute for Sunday Mass. Liturgical, communal worship has a privileged place in the Christian faith; Christianity is not an individualistic endeavor or a set of practices for elites (as is often the case in athletics). Engaging the spiritual life in sport is not wrong or superficial, however.

93. Hochstetler, "Striving towards Maturity," 331.
94. Smith, "Praying to Win," 332.
95. Hochstetler, "Striving towards Maturity," 332.
96. Huffman and Etnier, "Use and Meanings of Prayer," 156.
97. Kelly, "Youth Sport and Spirituality," 151.

Combining sport and Christian spirituality requires careful reflection and commitment. The mix can help people realize their dependent, creaturely nature. Finding the root of their identity in spiritual beliefs rather than in sporting performances can facilitate a deepening of one's sense of self. Thoughtful and embodied engagement in spiritual practices in sport is not a distraction from the spiritual life. It can enable greater sensitivity to human bodies and better awareness of a person's psychological and emotional condition.[98] Ward explains that entering into the spiritual life is a corporeal event, where a stony heart becomes a heart of flesh (Ezek 36:26–27). Sportspeople who slowly uncover their bodily and spiritual realities are on a path to their sanctification. People misunderstand self-sacrifice and asceticism when their objective is not set within deeper, ritualistic meanings of love, community, and maturity of faith.

Openness to sport as a ritual performance requires the balancing of values. The self-sacrifice enabled in the notion of "Christ the Athlete," as outlined in chapter 1, needs to find harmony with the give-and-take of Christian life. A model of athleticism for Christian discipleship balances the ardor of self-sacrifice with a welcoming spirit to others. Sports can be a form of training in giving of oneself, but along with virtues there are vices that can harden the hearts of sport performers. In the next chapter, we examine morals and ethics in sport, seeking to determine if modern sport remains a place of training for virtue.

---

98. Ward, "Question of Sport," 64.

CHAPTER 7

The Virtuous Life

Morality and Human Flourishing in Sports

AT THE 1988 SUMMER Olympics in Seoul, South Korea, Jamaican-born Canadian Ben Johnson defeated American Carl Lewis in the 100-meter sprint in world-record time.[1] Canadians celebrated his gold medal with great satisfaction, particularly because a humble patriot had defeated the former Olympic champion. When Johnson's postrace drug test revealed an illegal, performance-enhancing substance, joy turned into shame which led to a national inquiry of the Canadian sport system. A race that took less than ten seconds to win was transformed into a multiyear drama of finger pointing, confessions, and banning of additional athletes and some coaches. Why did Johnson lack the moral character to refuse steroids? More importantly, how could the sporting system unwittingly endorse banned substances?

Sport ethics philosopher Mike McNamee explains that sports today act like moral plays of medieval times. In an age before widespread literacy or the internet, moral plays told stories about good and evil for regular folks. McNamee argues that today when many commentators question the possibility of a shared, societal morality, sports present "neither complex cognitive nor moral vocabularies" but nonetheless offers opportunities "to understand cheating and courage, . . . fair and foul play."[2] Sports distill life for today's society like medieval morality plays did for that time period. While those morality plays were clear in their didactic intent, today's sports

1. Montague, "Hero or Villain?"
2. McNamee, "Youth Sport and the Virtues," 74.

spectacles are more ambiguous and ambivalent. As in the case of Johnson, the personal character of the individual was at fault, but it would be shortsighted to think that sporting institutions and organizations had no culpability for creating the system Johnson competed in. For a Catholic theology of sport, sport's social dimension creates human stories about individuals and groups, where anybody can discuss the unfolding of a moral play on social media, sports talk radio, or in the locker room.

Contemporary sports affect sporting participants for both good and ill. Whereas chapter 8 will address larger structural justice issues through Catholicism's deeply social vision of sports, this chapter focuses on sports as a place of human stories that reveal personal character and the possibility of the virtuous life. First, we begin by asserting that sport is a moral activity that should primarily build up human persons. Because of this aspiration, secondly, we present an ethical model based upon character, where concern is focused on virtue as a means of personal growth and fulfillment in sports. The chapter concludes by examining a darker side of sports: dehumanizing factors, like a comparison culture and athletic enhancements, that challenge the cultivation of personal character.

SPORT AS A STAGE OF MORAL ACTIVITY

There is a longstanding tradition of character development in sport. As explained in chapter 1, the origins of modern sports drew upon the ideals of muscular Christians who, following in the tradition of Saint Paul and his comparison between discipleship and athletics,[3] sought to make sporting fields places where boys became virtuous and physically strong.[4] Highly structured sports like rowing, football, and wrestling were incorporated into college curricula as a means to build student character at the end of the nineteenth century. For instance, an early-twentieth-century priest-teacher exclaimed, "No other force can do so much for the [moral] happiness and contentment of the boy."[5] It is easy to see why historically some people assume the best about sports, especially when its modern ideal is rooted in character development.

It is dangerous to assume, however, that sports naturally cultivate good character. Some research, for instance, points out that sports participation might actually undermine character and moral development.[6] Something as

---

3. Friedrichsen, "Disciple as Athlete," 13–14.
4. Bundgaard, *Muscle and Manliness*, 29–33.
5. St Michael's College, *Yearbook* (Toronto, 1911), 41.
6. Power, "Playing Like a Champion Today," 91.

good as giving one's best for team victory can easily get twisted and result in different forms of cheating or letting anger and resentment fuel play. Even parents, who should have the best interests of their child in mind, can obsess about their child's sporting success with a win-at-all-costs mentality. The documentary *Trophy Kids* tells one story about a tennis mother who ceaselessly trained her children.[7] She declares that she made a covenant with God that her two pre-teen sons would become World No. 1-ranked players in doubles tennis. This mother's drive for world domination in tennis seems to supplant her children's dreams for their own personal development.

Sports participants are not only formed by the rules and strategies of a particular sport, but also its particular play-ethos. Philosopher Randolph Feezell explains that alongside the rules, each sport contains a "prescriptive atmosphere" or "ethos" that "sanctions . . . behavior and generates expectations" for participants' strategies within the game.[8] This unwritten code specifies what is allowed and disallowed in each sport. For instance, the game of baseball has a long history of stealing opponents' signs and pitchers marking up or adding something onto the ball to create more dramatic movement when thrown. In golf, on the other hand, it is most dishonorable for a player to place Vaseline on the front of her club to increase ball control or mismark a ball on the green by a few inches. Because there are many opportunities to cheat in golf, the ethos of golf has a strict code to follow compared to baseball's more lenient approach to bending the rules.[9] Each has its own playing-ethos, which can be influenced over time by internal and external forces. Golf's strict playing code meant dressing in formal attire on the PGA tour and at local golf courses. Over time, however, these unwritten codes have loosened as the sport tries to increase participation and become more inclusive of different sociocultural groups. In baseball, too, technological advancements pushed the boundaries for sign-stealing when the 2017 and 2018 Houston Astros used video cameras and special dugout audio cues, like banging a trash can, to signal the next pitch to their batters.[10] MLB eventually handed out substantial fines and suspensions to the team's leadership because the creation of a technologically driven system went too far even for baseball. Playing codes may change over time, but it is clear that a play-ethos informs and shapes participants—perhaps more than the formal rules of the game do.

---

7. Bell, *Trophy Kids*.
8. Feezell, *Sport, Play, and Ethical Reflection*, 103.
9. Feezell, *Sport, Play, and Ethical Reflection*, 103.
10. Verducci, "Why MLB Issued Historic Punishment."

Because each sport has its own playing code, following the rules closely does not necessarily create good, moral persons. Thus, determining what is right and wrong in sport is more complicated than it might seem at first glance. For instance, even something as simple as cheating is complicated. Feezell explains that "cheating involves the attempt to gain an unfair advantage over your opponent by violating the agreements underlying the game."[11] If someone cheats—for example, by bribing a referee—they should be disqualified from competing. However, if someone steals baseball signs with the human eye, this act of *stealing* is acceptable within the ethos of the game although it may not display angelic obedience.[12] This act might seem borderline in goodness, but it is "part of the game" and accepted in the unwritten code of the sport.

In sum, rules in every sport must be kept for the integrity of each game, but simply following the rulebook does not translate into being a moral person. Obeying the rules means that athletes accept the formal logic or operating principles of their sport, where, for instance, they dribble a basketball if they wish to move with the ball in their possession.[13] This is an inefficient way to travel, but that is part of the challenge of playing basketball. Forms of play demand obedience to rules (as described in chapter 2), thus athletes relinquish their freedom to the rules of the game, making a highly organized, competitive contest possible. However, keeping the written code within sport does not mean that athletes and coaches act with moral integrity. Blindly following the hidden codes within a game, for instance, might lead players to brutally haze a rookie teammate, or a coach to explode in a temper tantrum in reaction to poor officiating. Human persons play and coach sports; their performances are often public displays of moral activity.

As a moral stage, sporting environments can reveal the best and worst of human persons. Because sports evoke moral discussions, a theology of sport can assist with insight into human nature and how best to enable human flourishing.

THE CATHOLIC MORAL TRADITION AND VIRTUE-ETHICS

The Catholic moral tradition engages a virtue-ethics approach that focuses on dispositions that benefit human individuals, freeing them from destructive or distorted habits. Other moral approaches have different

---

11. Feezell, *Sport, Play, and Ethical Reflection*, 109.
12. Feezell, *Sport, Play, and Ethical Reflection*, 109.
13. Kretchmar, "Why Do We Care So Much?," 185–86.

priorities. For instance, some moral systems emphasize duties and rules (i.e., deontological), while others weigh the consequences of actions (i.e., consequentialism). Faced with an issue of benching a weaker player in a championship game, coaches who want to do the right thing in principle would ensure that everyone plays at least some of the time. On the other hand, consequentialist coaches would weigh the outcomes of their decision (e.g., how might benching a player affect his self-esteem or the team camaraderie, or hurt the team's chances for victory?). In both mindsets, coaches' free will is limited by either an externalized law (perhaps learned from a mentor coach) or the possibility of choosing an action that produces poor consequences. From a virtue-ethics perspective, these are "freedom of indifference" positions, where freedom is simply the ability to choose between different possibilities. Every choice is seen as a free act independent of the last choice made.

Virtue-ethics are different in that the moral quality of freedom is not simply a matter of the freedom to make a choice but is something that grows and develops over time. Moral theologian and Dominican priest Servais Pinckaers calls this "freedom for excellence."[14] In this approach, what is right is neither an obligation nor a utilitarian weighing of the maximum pleasure for the most people. In the latter instance especially, people can become overwhelmed by the finer details of each particular ethical situation. However, a "freedom for excellence" position focuses upon both knowing and acting well, where individuals are motivated by principles endowed by the Creator and seek the flourishing of persons and communities. By thinking reasonably, persevering, and longing for truth, goodness, and happiness, moral freedom matures, and people can live more wisely and happily. Doing what is right is not so much a duty, but an act of freedom that ultimately results in joy. Happiness, which is not the same as external pleasure or comfort, is the end point of this traditional thought. Happiness is an interior joy and moral good: "Nature warns us by a clear sign that our destination is attained. That sign is joy. . . . Joy always announces that life has succeeded, gained ground, conquered."[15] As people become moral persons and seek wisdom, they find joy in doing what is good. Thus, people actually become freer: "The more one does what is good, the freer one becomes. There is no true freedom except in the service of what is good and just," as declared in the *Catechism of the Catholic Church*.[16] Simply doing

---

14. Pinckaers, *Morality*, 65–81.

15. Pinckaers, *Morality*, 79. Pinckaers quotes the words of philosopher Henri Bergson here.

16. *Catechism of the Catholic Church*, 1733.

whatever one wants, like an athlete who cuts corners in training, limits the human potential of oneself.

Following a "freedom for excellence" mindset rests on the ancient ideal that humans are inherently moral beings and that moral laws are not merely external pressures from social life. Instead of externalizing morality, this tradition holds that there is a natural law within each person, where there are universal attributes of human beings that transcend social mores and personal tastes. These are called transcendentals;[17] we highlight three of them here. Most well-known is the "human yearning for the good," where people are attracted to the fulfillment of others and things around them. Children often display this on the school playground when they hotly debate an unfair play in a game. They are repulsed by the wrongness of the action and demand justice. This attribute is the root of the human rights tradition. Of course, people can be attracted to what is wrong because moral judgment and tastes can become distorted.[18]

Two other transcendentals are importantly related to sport. The natural inclination to "preserve one's being" includes conserving one's life and promoting good health. More than that, it is also a dynamic that pushes one toward flourishing: taking care of one's body, developing one's mind, and progressing in sport skills. Another universal attribute of the natural law tradition is the inclination to "know the truth." When the public learned of Johnson's positive drug test, they wanted to know what exactly had happened. This transcendental creates trust and communion among reasonable people.[19] People yearn for truth, where religious faith is not blindly obedient but loves truth gained through knowledge and understanding.[20] These three transcendentals—yearning for good, preserving one's life, and seeking the truth—reveal the nature of human beings as made in the image and likeness of God,[21] where human happiness and flourishing are enabled within a loving communion with the Creator.

Living a moral life does not happen automatically, as if these universal attributes magically lead people in all moral choices. To mature these innate truths within, human beings need stable dispositions that can incline themselves to act toward these attributes. These dispositions are called virtues. Virtues are good habits. And because people become what they do, people's

---

17. Pinckaers, *Morality*, 98.
18. Pinckaers, *Morality*, 99.
19. Pinckaers, *Morality*, 105.
20. Pinckaers, *Morality*, 106.
21. *Catechism*, 1702.

actions shape their fundamental character in decisive ways. Forming good habits are vital to living a moral life.

Excellence in virtue bears strong similarities to sporting proficiency, which can explain the importance of good habits in the moral life. Moral theologian William Mattison asks readers to imagine two tennis players, as was noted in chapter 2.[22] One is accomplished and the other unskilled. The good player still makes mistakes but can more reliably hit good shots than the poor player. Just as the habits of a tennis player reveal the quality of his skills, people's habits reflect more clearly the sort of person they are. Being a good player is more important than simply making a good shot for two reasons. First, the good player "does good actions more frequently and consistently" because his "goodness abides in the self in the form of a habit, rather than in the acts." Thus, the good player is such even when he is not playing tennis: "he is in shape, has certain muscle memory, a well-trained eye, a sense of tennis strategy, and so on." Having a virtue changes a person. This change leads to greater frequency of good acts. Second, a habit indicates past action and helps anticipate future acts. Just as a tennis player arrives on the court with skills and strategies, a virtuous person has a dynamic disposition that provides an inclination to do what is good. The good player's habits make him more likely to make shots consistently. In a nutshell, the Catholic moral tradition endorses the principle that humans become what they habitually do.

This connection between the moral life and sport has led Catholics to traditionally understand sport as an education, where people learn virtues and moral principles in athletic programs offered in schools, parishes, and colleges. Ideally, character development should not be reduced to forming youth according to societal expectations that foster only social and achievement virtues.[23] Sporting opportunities in these faith-based settings have been meant to engage moral situations and develop a sense of right and wrong. Coaches, for instance, can embolden moral freedom in their athletes by promoting discussions about fair play and addressing personal responses to moral situations that arise.[24] In this way, hard-nosed Catholic coaches like basketball's John Thompson and football's Vince Lombardi sought to forge better people through sport. Thompson, who provided an educational environment for Black players at Georgetown, kept a deflated basketball in his office to remind players that everyone's athletic career comes to an end sooner or later:

22. Mattison, *Introducing Moral Theology*, 62.
23. Power, "Playing Like a Champion Today," 94.
24. Power, "Playing Like a Champion Today," 106.

> I started thinking about the thousands and thousands of kids across the country chasing the basketball, focused on the basketball, treating the basketball like the most important thing in the world. This leather object seemed to represent the sum total of their life experiences. But once the air came out of the ball, it felt like the player had no value. I thought, You never want the sum total of your value to be eight or nine pounds of air inside a basketball.[25]

Thompson believed that the educational component of his coaching ultimately outweighed other considerations.

THE VIRTUOUS LIFE

Early Christians found great value in Greek thinking about the virtues. The ancient Greek concept of *aretē* has the general meaning of "excellence," which can refer to striving for excellence in sport and is also translated as "virtue" in moral discourse.[26] For instance, Saint Paul's Letter to the Philippians (4:8) commends readers to think about "whatever is true, whatever is noble, whatever is right, . . .—if anything is excellent [*aretē*] or praiseworthy . . ." Virtues are good habits and are within the reach of anyone. They incline people to act one way or another, as explained in the tennis example above, and they form and develop over time as people consider the needed proportion of each virtue in each circumstance. For example, courage in a wrestling match is virtuous. However, an excess of courage (foolhardiness) will lead a wrestler to make high-risk moves that could backfire, whereas a deficiency (cowardice) could make her timid and allow her opponent to pin her quickly. Thus, an excess or deficiency in virtue causes it to become vice. Over time, this difference becomes better known to a virtuous person as she improves at finding this learned mid-point between these extremes. This notion is what Aristotle called the golden mean, which is not a mathematical point, but a balance learned over time.[27] Proper actions may vary given the circumstances and the persons involved (e.g., depending upon their temperament and skill), where a wrestler will get a feel for courageously wrestling as she grows in experience. Moreover, trusting in the power of virtue can be revelatory.

---

25. Thompson, *I Came as a Shadow*, 92.
26. Holowchak and Reid, *Aretism*, 162.
27. Holowchak and Reid, *Aretism*, 162.

Among the many virtues, seven stand out in the Catholic tradition.[28] The first four—justice, temperance, fortitude, and prudence—are traditionally called the cardinal virtues, from which minor virtues hinge or pivot around. The other three are the theological virtues of faith, hope, and love, which for Christians are believed to perfect the cardinal virtues.

The first of the four cardinal virtues is justice. Classically, and particularly as reflected in the teachings of Aristotle, this virtue grows through giving each person their due. Because humans live interdependently, the road to happiness requires fairness in relationships. Temperance is the habit of well-ordered desires toward pleasures. For instance, it is good to moderate one's desires for fame, as obsession for attention can ruin integrity and open a door to many vices. Fortitude is synonymous with courage, where one faces difficulty well whether on the field or when she stands up to a racist teammate. Prudence is the ability to make wise decisions. It requires moderation and perspective.

Consider how cardinal virtues shape a virtuous approach to victory in sport. To begin, an athlete should naturally want a fair competition where everyone can excel and thus be recognized for their skills and tenacity. This means appreciating the gifts of opponents and realizing that their excellence makes everyone strive for greater excellence. This justice perspective requires courage, where athletes are not afraid of losing (or becoming a champion) and thus can persevere in developing their gifts. Temperance allows them to appropriate proper value to winning: victory is commendable and worth achieving, but should not overshadow a sense of fairness, friendship, or basic human goodness. A moderate competitive spirit of agonism (i.e., *agon* is an ancient Greek term for "struggle" or "contest") is better than a pan-agonistic attitude that is driven excessively to victory with a winner-take-all attitude.[29] Finally, this mindset becomes a disposition over time as virtuous people prudently weigh the importance of victory. On the court, players should give their full effort, but this drive should not become a fixation that blinds them to justice issues within human communities.

The three theological virtues are different because they connect directly to God. Good actions arise from integrating them with cardinal virtues. Similar to how Catholic belief holds that grace builds on nature, the three theological virtues offer direction and even a reshaping of how to practice the cardinal virtues. Love is the primary virtue of the Christian life (1 Cor 13:13), as Jesus commanded his listeners to love God and their neighbor as they love

---

28. This paragraph and the two below rely on Mattison, *Introducing Moral Theology*, 66–68.

29. Holowchak and Reid, *Aretism*, 165.

themselves (Matt 22:35–40). To love another is to give of oneself and receive from others, where a person wants others' happiness and fulfillment and acts accordingly.[30] Love, or charity, is the virtue that gives form to all the virtues. When American Abbey D'Agostino and New Zealand's Nikki Hamblin accidentally tripped each other in a 5,000-meter heat at the 2016 Rio Summer Olympic Games, D'Agostino helped up the New Zealander and encouraged her to finish, while Hamblin later assisted D'Agostino who, it turned out, had torn a knee ligament. D'Agostino recalled why she helped and encouraged her competitor: "I don't think that was me, I think that it was literally the spirit of God in me, like, 'let's go.'"[31] One could argue that the virtue of charity directed her other-centered actions during that race; the acts were habitually shaped and made her more open to God's voice within.

The virtue of hope envisions future communion with God despite recognizing that full communion will not be realized on earth. Hopeful people trust that their inner restlessness—that human drive that wants more, is not satisfied, and feels insignificant—can find satisfaction through a loving God who made the universe.[32] Two positions in particular threaten the moral virtue of hope. First, instead of finding completion in divine communion, people can seek satisfaction in passing things like power or social status, where they want control over others through dominance or by looking impressive. Second, they rightfully become disillusioned by chasing these things, but then settle for less in life. If they cannot have everything they want, nothing has worth. For example, many newly retired athletes struggle to find something equivalent to the excitement of playing in front of thousands of fans. Many go off the rails and end up in bankruptcy or in detox, often faced with mental health issues. Making the necessary changes in their postperformance lives seems impossible. When Simone Biles failed to win a gold medal at the Tokyo 2020 Olympics, the sporting world felt tremors. Weeks later Biles recognized that "I should have quit way before Tokyo."[33] Performing became a way to rebuild her confidence after sexual abuse by a team doctor, but later she could see that it was time to move on from the sport. While Biles can only explain her gymnastics success as "a God-given talent," she will need to continue to hope that God has other gifts waiting for her.[34] Mattison summarizes that hope sustains religious persons on their

---

30. Mattison, *Introducing Moral Theology*, 300.
31. Dawn, "US Runner Who Helped Rival," para. 3.
32. Mattison, *Introducing Moral Theology*, 259.
33. Felix, "Simone Biles Chose Herself," para. 15.
34. Felix, "Simone Biles Chose Herself," para. 8.

journey: it enables them to see the goods of this life more truthfully and trust the paschal mystery acting in their lives, as explained in chapter 5.[35]

The remaining theological virtue is faith. Faith is a natural human activity.[36] People have faith in what they believe to be true, especially when it comes to questions about the universe's origins and purpose. Science cannot speak conclusively on such topics, as poets and theologians try to help understand humanity's reason for living.[37] Mattison thus describes faith as follows: "To believe is to cling to something as surely true, much in the way you do when you see clearly the truth of the matter at hand."[38] Those things which might not be scientifically verifiable, like a close friendship or an encounter with God, may feel more certain than a scientific law studied in a classroom. One's gut convictions are invaluable, and also require introspection from a clear mind that weighs external evidence and challenges lies and misinformation.

It is easy to find sports media examples of faith in related terms like *belief* and *trust*. Players on Cinderella teams, like the 1980 "Miracle on Ice" US hockey team, or the 2021 Arizona Wildcats women's basketball team (who upset powerhouse UConn in the Final Four), often speak about their belief in each other despite those outside the team doubting their chances for victory. Talking about faith in other areas of modern life usually implies doubt, where believing goes against conventional thinking. To the contrary, medieval thought understood "to believe" as "to hold dear."[39] Faith was not a fleeting feeling or whim but required dedication and putting one's heart into things. No wonder sporting Cinderella stories resonate with sport spectators. Faith is palpably felt by a group of players who deeply trust teammates and try to win for each other. It is also common to hear players speaking about *confidence*, which literally means *with faith* or *full trust*. For instance, golfer Jordan Spieth explains that confidence "is the most important thing in the game of golf," where mastering body mechanics, visualizing the perfect shot, and dedicating oneself to the game can stabilize and develop confidence.[40] Here faith requires careful attention to many truths in sport, leading to subsequent success.[41] Confidence is not certitude but an act of trust in one's abilities and purpose.

35. Mattison, *Introducing Moral Theology*, 259.
36. Mattison, *Introducing Moral Theology*, 214–30.
37. Mattison, *Introducing Moral Theology*, 217.
38. Mattison, *Introducing Moral Theology*, 216.
39. Marthaler, *Creed*, 23.
40. Dick's Pro Tips, "Jordan Spieth on the Importance of Confidence," para. 3.
41. Hoven, "Re-Characterizing Confidence," 298.

Faith is the glue that holds people together on and off the pitch. Sport psychologist Mark Nesti, who has worked professionally with soccer teams in the English Premier League, notes how questions of identity and meaning also impact the confidence of athletes.[42] Nesti questions understandings of confidence that are limited to measurable qualities like past success or visualization techniques. If faith is connected to that which people hold dear, it makes sense that Nesti argues for a broader understanding of confidence that includes athletes' self-identity, social networks, and even their religious beliefs. In his experience, moral dilemmas, family disputes, and grief over the loss of a loved one can dramatically affect player confidence. When those people or things players trust in fall apart, a dip in player confidence often follows.

The virtuous life requires reflection on choices and habits. This is difficult, but as choices become habits, they are made permanent. Virtues are like muscles: when exercised, they become stronger. With the support of worthy mentors, doing what is morally good increasingly becomes second nature. At the same time, people can act "out of character" or inconsistently with their previous decisions, like an athlete having an "off" game. If those decisions are repeatedly made, they become the character of the person or quality of the player. According to educator Thomas Likona, to grow in good habits requires cultivation of our moral knowing,[43] where people become more sensitive to the morality of actions, learn about moral virtues,[44] and give time to self-reflection and conversations about their actions. (We will talk more about the related "see-judge-act" method in Catholic social teaching in chapter 8). In addition to moral knowing, Likona adds that a virtue-based response also requires feeling compelled to do what is right. When people love doing what is good, they become joyful when doing the right thing. A moral feeling stance requires a healthy self-esteem, an ability to empathize and have self-control, and the humility to appreciate people's strengths and weaknesses. For a Christian approach to sport, the moral stage of sport demands developing character instead of overlooking the depth of the moral dimension of human living.

---

42. Nesti, *Psychology in Football*, 137–53.

43. Likona, *Educating for Character*, 49–63.

44. For Christians, moral virtue is inspired by multiple sources, including biblical sources, like Jesus' Sermon on the Mount (Matt 5–7), Saint Paul's Letters, and the Ten Commandments, and tradition sources like the writings and examples of saints and the *Catechism's* third part on the moral life (1691–2557).

SIN AND DEHUMANIZED SPORT

Just as athletes face great obstacles on their path to sporting success, the virtuous life faces deeply rooted impediments within the human heart and human communities. Historian Sheldon Rothblatt captures well how sport unearths the shadows within the human heart that people instinctively cover up. A careful exploration of competitive sport, he writes, "reveals something disturbing about human character, an urge to violence, even sadism, struggling to the mat with other urges to control them."[45] Christians try to comprehend this dark element within human beings through the theological notion of sin (as described in chapter 4). At one level, sin is personal, where individuals "miss the mark" and are responsible for their own actions.[46] For example, a coach who belittles players through public scorn is dehumanizing and alienating them from their teammates. Of course, coaches, like anyone else, can avoid reflecting on their lack of care for others and themselves.[47] Obvious moral failings, like physically abusing a player, are more likely to command repentance than owning up to an anger issue, especially when the team wins games.

Sin is doubly complicated because of its social nature. Sprinter Ben Johnson not only sinned personally by taking steroids, but there were structures within the sport that supported his choices (e.g., top athletes were able to avoid being caught, and coaches often supported athletes' cheating). Theologically speaking, all human persons have the propensity to sin because of humankind's sinful nature or original sin.[48] Today, each person is born into a world marred by individual sins that over generations have sedimented into sinful structures and dynamics that dehumanize and alienate people from themselves, others, God, and creation. A theology of sin is too often misunderstood. The point is not to shame people, but instead is an attempt to unpack the complex nature of moral living and, in sport, to give athletes a framework to understand dehumanizing trends in competition.

Human selfishness is a default behavior that virtuous living and divine grace help humans overcome. Despite sport's capacity to reveal the worst of human nature, it also represents, as noted by Rothblatt, "an awakening of the moral sense, a glimpse of a frightening existential moment when it is realized that clubbing one's neighbour senseless is not always . . . easily

---

45. Rothblatt, "James Anthony Mangan," 3.

46. *Catechism of the Catholic Church*, 1868.

47. Concupiscence is the propensity for human desires to unreflectively lead towards sin (*Catechism of the Catholic Church*, 405).

48. *Catechism of the Catholic Church*, 388–90, 1869.

rationalized."⁴⁹ When a person of faith is awakened and feels the far-reaching effects of sin in his life and the world, there is also a sense of hope that another way to live is possible. But to do so, sporting persons must acknowledge the dehumanizing effects of sin that limit the cultivation of virtue in sport. We provide two instructive examples below: comparison culture and athletic performance enhancements.

Comparison culture

The nature of sport appears to promote a competitive, comparison culture, which can quickly become destructive. Athletic contests pit opponents against one another to determine a sole victor. Even within a team, players vie for starting positions or a coach's approval. Philosophers Brian Bolt and Chad Carlson summarize: "athletes compare talents, advantages, genetic traits, practice habits, and opportunities against those of competitors. Indeed, if not instinctive, they are encouraged to do so from many directions" in their sporting lives and beyond.⁵⁰ Sports' ugly comparison culture can bring out the worst in people.

The source of this comparison culture is greater than merely wanting what others have. As cultural anthropologist René Girard argued, a comparison culture is heightened through the fact that people often learn mimetically or through imitation, where they desire the things that are desired by the people they imitate.⁵¹ The act of imitation enables learning and binds people to others as they form mutual connections. Trust and friendship are built through imitating others. However, at the same time, human capacity for imitation can also become destructive. It can pull people apart through the occurrence of rivalry, which often leads to violence.

Take one of the greatest tennis rivalries of all-time: top-ranked Chris Evert and Martina Navratilova competed against each other for most of the 1970s and 1980s and nearly split the eighty matches played against each other, including sixty in tournament finals.⁵² The media portrayed them as stereotypical opposites: Evert was seen as the classic "American girl," whereas Navratilova was viewed as a masculine eastern European woman. Their different playing styles clashed as they learned each other's playing tendencies over time and pushed one another to the absolute limit. Early on they actually played doubles tennis together, but Evert broke the partnership

---

49. Rothblatt, "James Anthony Mangan," 3.
50. Bolt and Carlson, "Sport, Envy, and the Conundrum," 137.
51. Pisk, "Mimetic Desire," 12–13.
52. Cambers, "'We Are Still Fighting.'"

because she noticed that Navratilova was learning her weaknesses from playing and practicing together. Evert recalls Navratilova's coach further separating them, where she was told not to invite Evert for dinner because Navratilova needed to end their relationship and learn to hate Evert.[53] Their friendship turned into an embittered on-court rivalry. Near the end of their careers, however, they began to wonder if they could separate tennis from an off-court friendship. Evert summarized the possibility of a new relationship: "[Together] you go out there and try to beat your brains out, but I can also care for you, be your friend."[54] The two athletes' desire for singles championship trophies resulted in a decade-long rivalry that only broke near the end of their playing careers.

According to Girard's research, ancient peoples knew how imitation often ignited the human capacity for violence and rivalry. Rituals, like human and animal sacrifices, and taboos, like avoidance of a woman during menstruation, could limit retaliatory and aggressive actions stemming from mimetic desire.[55] Making things off-limits or finding a scapegoat to relieve tensions between rival parties helped determine a peaceful resolution.[56] This thinking is still present today, most obviously with scapegoating. It was perfectly captured when a Chicago Cubs baseball fan, wearing a bright green turtleneck sweater, reached out to catch a foul ball and interfered with a Cubs outfielder during a playoff game in 2003.[57] The team was just five outs away from reaching the World Series for the first time since World War II, but the interference set off a number of mistakes, and the lovable loser Cubs went down to defeat. While there were several errors made by the team, many cast sole blame on the fan, who had to flee the stadium fearing for his life. He went into hiding and declined any interviews about the incident. Making him the scapegoat of a fanbase's disappointment quenched their anger, but at what cost?[58]

The rivalry between Evert and Navratilova and the scapegoating of a baseball fan enable reflection on the workings and consequences of mimetic desire and assist in understanding its larger significance. For Girard, seeking resolution to the rivalry and violence stemming from mimetic desire is the hidden reason that initiated religions centuries ago. In his research, he was struck by the Judeo-Christian Scriptures' unique response. Instead of

---

53. Cambers, "'We Are Still Fighting,'" para. 20.
54. Cambers, "'We Are Still Fighting,'" para. 22.
55. Kaplan, *René Girard*, 28.
56. Girard, *Girard Reader*, 11–12.
57. Kaplan, *René Girard*, 32.
58. Kaplan, *René Girard*, 26.

accepting human and animal sacrifice, biblical authors challenged the logic of mimetic violence. Theologian Kaplan explains: "Girard discovered [biblical] tales that revealed this violence . . . that God has nothing to do with violence and that God sides with the victim. In the New Testament, God not only sides with the victim, but God is the victim."[59] Instead of finding a human scapegoat who can quell the violence between competing groups, biblical authors showed another way. For instance, God stops Abraham from sacrificing his own son Isaac in Gen 22, and Jesus freely offers himself as the victim in his crucifixion. For Girard, biblical authors pull back the veil on rivalry and violence stemming from mimetic desire. In Jesus' passion and death, religious leaders plotted murder against the Messiah to bring stability during a societal crisis. For Christians, however, Jesus's death breaks the cycle of rivalry and violence.[60] His death reconciles the world to God because he humbled himself and became "obedient to death—even death on a cross!" (Phil 2:8). Because God "exalted him" and raised him from the dead, Christians need not seek out a scapegoat or fall for rivalry violence. Instead, they share in this new life and are told by Saint Paul to "have the same mindset as Christ Jesus" (Phil 2:9, 5).

Sports bring the human drama explained by Girard to center stage, if in a lower-stakes fashion. Rather than repressing the worst of humanity, sport lays it on the table and shows how it powerfully plays on human psyches. A response is needed. Being aware of desires, naming them, and learning how to reconfigure them are vital. Envy should not be taken lightly, as the biblical tradition repeatedly prohibits it. The story of the first murder, where Cain kills his brother Abel out of envy (Gen 4:1–16), or the Ten Commandments' ban on coveting others' belongings, are prominent examples. Rigid prohibitions may seem inflexible, but the dramatic consequences of comparison culture are stark, especially in today's social media-soaked age. Bolt and Carlson explain that once human desires become restless and fan the flames of envy and rivalry, people obsess about what they want and can easily gravitate toward "unethical, envy-perpetuating behavior."[61] In response, athletes can carefully reflect and pray about their actions and consider the example of Jesus Christ. As Paul declares in 1 Cor 11:1, "Be imitators of me, as I am of Christ." By imitating both Christ and his saints, people can repattern desires and form new habits. Instead of obsessing over

---

59. Kaplan, *René Girard*, 40.

60. For a fuller explanation of Girard's thinking on this, see Girard, *Girard Reader*, 177–88.

61. Bolt and Carlson, "Sport, Envy, and the Conundrum," 140.

victory, comparing themselves with Christ places his mercy and love within their striving for excellence.

Athletic performance enhancements

Mimetic desire and its subsequent violence forge a pattern that challenges the moral life. As expressed in the example of sprinter Ben Johnson, sportspeople feel the need to keep with the competition even if that means gaining an unfair advantage. These are direct threats to the virtuous life in sport. Athletic performance enhancements are a prime example of how vices like envy and comparison can radically change sport and impact those playing the games.

Athletes use performance enhancements to improve their chances of winning and reduce uncertainties in sport. Some athletic enhancements are accepted by sport governing bodies, and others are not. Following a healthy diet and sleep schedule are widely accepted practices that heighten athletic performance. Improvements in sporting equipment are advantageous, but not always fair. The international swimming federation, FINA, banned long polyurethane super-swimsuits because they made racing too easy (for those who could afford them).[62] Genetic anomalies are usually accepted as a fair advantage. Being a seven-foot, six-inch-tall basketball player like Yao Ming, or having exceptional body proportions like swimmer Michael Phelps, is a tremendous advantage. However, more artificial enhancements, like injecting bodies with human growth hormones, are considered unfair augmentations because these are unhealthy, undermine basic beliefs about fairness and equity, and twist the purpose of sport, where gaining a pharmaceutical advantage overshadows the actual sporting performances. The prevalence of performance enhancements requires institutions and officials to debate and enforce rules that protect athletes and the purpose of sports.

How does one determine which athletic enhancements are allowed in sport? From a virtue-ethics perspective, sport must build up communities and lead to the flourishing of individuals. If athletes become obsessed with drugs and genetic fixes, according to philosopher Michael Sandel, their sporting achievement is minimized because it diminishes their human freedom instead of increasing it.[63] Sandel envisions a bionic baseball player whose implanted computer chips enable him to hit the ball at the perfect angle and with perfect timing, such that he hits every quality pitch for a homerun. While this bionic player's heavy reliance on enhancement

62. Trothen, *Spirituality, Sport, and Doping*, 41–43.
63. Sandel, "Bionic Athletes," 208.

would diminish his human freedom, Sandel claims that the larger issue is that the bionic ballplayer represents a remaking of human nature to serve individuals' purposes and desires. He argues that the deeper problem lies in the human drive for mastery or perfectionism, which can lead to the destruction of people's "appreciation of the gifted character of human powers and achievements."[64] Instead of believing that talents are fundamentally gifts from God that ought to be developed because that is what they were created for, perfectionism can make sporting actions become pharmaceutically and genetically enhanced, individualistically charged, and take away from achievement on the diamond. Sandel explains:

> To acknowledge the giftedness of life is to recognize that our talents and powers are not wholly our own doing, nor even fully ours, despite the efforts we expend to develop and to exercise them. It is also to recognize that not everything in the world is open to any use we may desire or devise. An appreciation of the giftedness of life . . . [produces] a certain humility. It is, in part, a religious sensibility.[65]

An assertion about the giftedness of life, which reflects Christian belief in the intimate relationship possible between each person and God, humbly affirms the limits of human beings and how they fall short of perfection. Father Athol Murray, who established a twentieth-century ice hockey program at the Notre Dame Collegiate on the Canadian prairies, was fond of paraphrasing Saint Augustine: "He who does what in him lies, God will not deny his grace."[66] Murray preached how players should cultivate their God-given gifts and trust that God's grace would help fulfill their nature—whether in life or sport. Trying to live a virtuous life is a way that a personal God can work through human actions and enable flourishing. It is an act of faith despite human failings, and shifts people away from following a narrow perfectionism.

Enhancements can enable human flourishing, but sports shouldn't become only about winning or perfectionism. Limitations are a part of human living, and sporting excellence is about confronting athletic limitations as best as one can. Sandel explains:

> Excellence consists at least partly in the display of natural talents and gifts that are no doing of the athlete who possesses them. This is an uncomfortable fact for democratic societies. We want

---

64. Sandel, "Bionic Athletes," 208.
65. Sandel, "Bionic Athletes," 209.
66. Gorman, *Père Murray and the Hounds*, 111.

to believe that success, in sports and in life, is something we earn, not something we inherit. Natural gifts, and the admiration they inspire, embarrass the meritocractic faith; they cast doubt on the conviction that praise and rewards flow from effort alone.[67]

The problem with the bionic baseball player is that he would corrupt athletic contests instead of honoring natural talents cultivated and on display.[68] When enhancements are pushed to their absolute limit, they see creating super intelligent, physically dominant, and immortal human beings as their ultimate purpose. No longer *homo sapiens*, people become cyborgs that are part human, part machine.[69] Sporting enhancements need limitations. Improved sporting equipment, training methods, sport psychology practices, and the like can improve performances, but ought not make human perfectionism or empirical efficiency the sole aim of sport.

Sport should remain a stage for the drama of human living, where moral questions are paraded before spectators and the limits of the human condition (e.g., injuries, disease, aging, and sex) are confronted. This is perhaps most beautifully displayed in the Paralympics and Special Olympics, where physical or mental challenges are incorporated into the fabric of sport, and spectators can see individuals overcoming human expectations while revealing the frailty of life. At the same time, it should be remembered that the limits of the human condition can lead to questions about the very structures of sport. For instance, sport has often reflected and perpetuated the sexist standards of society, where females had far fewer opportunities in sport. Today, with the recognition of transgender athletes and better understanding of those whose chromosomal sexual identity is ambiguous, simple male-female categories can seem exclusivist. When transgender collegiate swimmer Lia Thomas transitioned from competing as a male to a female, however, she beat her female counterparts easily at a 2021 swim meet—she had competed as a male for most of her life.[70] Advocating for transgendered athletes' participation in sport is unquestioned, but undue competitive advantage can also be problematic. There is no clear solution: some suggest that all nonfemale competitors should compete in an "open" category inclusive of all males and transgendered persons, while others think athletes should be classified according to various categories (e.g., age, weight, impairment)

---

67. Sandel, "Bionic Athletes," 209.
68. Sandel, "Bionic Athletes," 209.
69. McNamee, "Whose Prometheus?," 217–18.
70. Kay, "Case for an 'Open' Category."

instead of merely by gender.[71] What is obvious is that limitations are necessary in competition, and this corresponds to a theological sporting response. Placing restrictions on human sporting performances highlights the limits of human reality, embraces the giftedness of human life, and seeks a balance in the mutual relationship between male and female.

CONCLUSION

Viewing sport as today's morality play highlights sport's power, especially in a globalized, high-speed media world. As analyzed through Girard's work on rivalry, violence, and scapegoating, the spectra of human wretchedness and grace are brought into full view in stadiums and living rooms. Whereas some Christians might walk away from sport because of the seeming prevalence of vice, this is also true in nearly every other facet of human life, whether politics, music, art, or education. Sport is not free of vice, but sport participation can still be a place where a virtuous life is fostered in light of the Catholic moral tradition, encouraging both athletic and moral excellence. The moral life does require owning up to one's vices and the need for forgiveness. Sin is prevalent, as dramatically displayed in many athletes' "fall from grace," and one can offend truth and one's fulfillment while transgressing against God and breaking Jesus' commandment to love one another.[72] For Christians, the virtuous life is an adventure where God-given gifts are developed in a broken world. Life is about more than winning and personal success.

It is important that Christians help shape sporting organizations so that sport institutionally prioritizes the flourishing of human persons and the celebration of God-given gifts. Whereas this chapter focused on developing personal character in sport, the next chapter presents Catholicism's deeply social vision and related theological principles that can help accentuate contemporary sport's potential to build a civilization of love and culture of encounter.

---

71. Pike et al., "Fair Game," 8.
72. *Catechism of the Catholic Church*, 1849–50.

CHAPTER 8

Building a Culture of Encounter

Sport and Catholic Social Teaching

In November 2020, Pope Francis met at the Vatican with a delegation of five NBA players to discuss social justice, economic inequality, and racism. Francis himself had initiated the meeting. During the conversation, he spoke of his concern and interest in ongoing racial justice protests in the United States that followed the police killing of George Floyd earlier that year. Describing sports as a vehicle for Christian discipleship and building social unity, he encouraged the players to live out their vocations as role models and activists for social change.[1]

This meeting exemplifies an important if not always recognized dimension of a Catholic theology of sport. Namely, in the Christian tradition sport is linked with social justice, an essential element in building what Pope Francis calls a culture of encounter and what his predecessor Pope Saint John Paul II named a civilization of love. This chapter will first explore the theological roots of this deeply social vision of sport, including the rise of the modern tradition of Catholic social teaching (CST). Second, we will analyze John Paul's and Francis's understanding of the social role of sport, especially regarding questions of justice, human dignity, and building a culture of mutual respect. Third, we will show how this Catholic social vision has been exemplified on the ground in two case studies from twentieth-century America and twenty-first-century Uganda. At the end of the chapter, we will apply CST principles and social analysis to two contested questions

1. Abrams, "N.B.A. Players Meet."

in contemporary North America: the role of money in youth and college sports, and gender and racial discrimination in sports leadership.

THE SOCIAL ROOTS OF THE CHRISTIAN AND CATHOLIC THEOLOGICAL TRADITIONS

Contrary to the spirit of modern individualism, the biblical narrative has deeply social and political ramifications. The Jewish people's primary salvation narrative was the story of Exodus, where God liberates the people of Israel from the tyranny and slavery of Pharaoh's Egypt. This deeply historical understanding of salvation recurs throughout the Old Testament, whether in the brief triumph of the Davidic monarchy, or the restoration of Israel to the promised land after the Babylonian exile. In turn, prophets such as Amos, Hosea, Micah, and Isaiah continually lambasted their leaders and their people for their unjust treatment of the poor, often described by the Hebrew term *anawim* ("the little ones"), and embodied in the categories of resident aliens, widows, and orphans. In the words of the prophet Micah, God does not desire ritual sacrifice, but rather the conversion of heart exemplified in socially just relations: "He has told you, O mortal, what is good; and what does the Lord require of you but to do justice, and to love kindness, and to walk humbly with your God" (Mic 6:8). For the Old Testament prophets, being created in God's image entails mirroring God's own care for the *anawim*.

This integral connection between discipleship, social concern, and justice is carried forward in the New Testament. While eschewing traditional Davidic understandings of the Messiah as a kingly warrior, Jesus by no means limits discipleship to an exclusively individualistic, "me and Jesus" spirituality. If anything, one of the genuine signs (and scandals) of Jesus' kingdom-of-God ministry was the way in which he shared table fellowship with the socially outcast and suspect of his day (Matt 9:10–13), whether tax collectors serving the Roman Empire, Jewish Zealots fighting to overthrow Rome, prostitutes, poor Galilean fishermen, or ostracized lepers.[2] Whether in Matthew's Beatitudes or Luke's Sermon on the Plain, Jesus announces God's blessing on the poor, symbolizing a striking social reversal that echoed the Old Testament prophetic tradition. In Luke's words, "Blessed are you who are poor, for yours is the kingdom of God. Blessed are you who are hungry now, for you will be satisfied. . . . But woe to you who are rich, for

---

2. As Catholic theologian Elizabeth Johnson notes, such concrete actions show how Jesus moved beyond "abstract ideals" to "powerfully enact the values of the reign of God" (*Consider Jesus*, 75).

you have received your consolation. Woe to you who are full now, for you will be hungry" (Luke 6:20–21, 24–25). The social radicality of the Christian gospel was further embodied in the early Acts community, which held "everything in common" (Acts 4:32), as well as Saint Paul's exhortations to early Christians in Rome to go so far as to share food and drink with their *enemies* in need (Rom 12:20). In summary, the heart of Jesus' teaching in the gospels—"to love God with all your heart, all your soul, and all your strength, and to love your neighbor as yourself" (Mark 12:30–31)—has an inherent social dimension, and a particular concern for the poor and marginalized. Inspired by this gospel witness, Christian churches over their long history developed an unmatched network of charitable works, schools, and medical facilities.

This Christian social apostolate grew, deepened, and changed in the late-nineteenth and early-twentieth centuries in response to the rise of modernity, industrialization, and capitalism. At the same time that Protestant social reformers were developing muscular Christianity on the playground and pitch (see chapter 1), Protestant ministers such as the Baptist Walter Rauschenbusch were propagating the social gospel.[3] Reacting to trends of economic dehumanization in the modern world, these reformers argued that the proclamation of the good news of Jesus Christ entailed more than getting souls to heaven, and Christians needed to commit themselves to the structural reform of society in the spirit of the impending kingdom of God.

During the same era, Catholic popes initiated the modern tradition of Catholic social teaching (CST). Inaugurated in Pope Leo XIII's 1891 encyclical, *Rerum Novarum*, on the labor question in modern Europe, the CST tradition originated through a series of papal and other magisterial statements. It has been incarnated in social movements and organizations such as Catholic Action, Caritas, Pax Christi, Catholic Relief Services, and the pro-life movement. CST draws on the theological riches of the Christian tradition to serve the common good, defined at Vatican II as "the sum total of social conditions which allow people, either as groups or as individuals, to reach their fulfillment more fully and more easily."[4] It is based on the conviction that human beings are relational, social, and creative by nature. In the words of the *Compendium of the Social Doctrine of the Church*, "Man, in fact, is not a solitary being, but a 'social being,' and unless he relates himself to others he can neither live nor develop his potential."[5] The Catholic Church

---

3. Rauschenbusch and Fahey, *Walter Rauschenbusch*.

4. Vatican II, *Gaudium et Spes*, §26.

5. Pontifical Council for Justice and Peace, *Compendium of the Social Doctrine*, §110.

thus encourages the broadest possible community participation, balancing personal rights with social responsibilities. Finally, the CST tradition shifts the traditional Catholic focus on "charity"—defined here as relieving the symptoms of poverty and oppression—to a lens of "justice." By nature, a justice approach entails discerning, engaging, and transforming the structural, economic, and sociopolitical causes of a particular social problem.

There is no dogmatic list of the essential teachings of CST. However, most commentators agree that the foundational principle is the *dignity and sanctity of human life created in the image of God*. The biblical foundation of this teaching is Gen 1:27: "So God created humankind in his image, in the image of God he created them." Defending human dignity entails protecting life from conception to natural death and publicly safeguarding a variety of other human rights, including "food, housing, work, education and access to culture, transportation, basic health care, the freedom of communication and expression, and the protection of religious freedom."[6] Second, the CST tradition sees *the family as the foundation of society*. This stands in sharp contrast to the individualistic, consumerist vision of liberal capitalism, or Marxism's prioritization of class or social identity. Going back to *Rerum Novarum*, CST supports legal protection of *private property rights*, yet the tradition also relativizes this right within the broader principle of *the universal destination of goods*—namely that "all created things should be shared fairly by all [humankind] under the guidance of justice tempered by charity."[7] Fourth, CST respects the *dignity of labor*, including workers' rights to a living wage, free association, and the formation of unions. Under the influence of Latin American liberation theology, CST in the latter half of the twentieth century developed what is often described as a *preferential option for the poor*. Rather than merely encourage charitable relief toward the symptoms of poverty, this approach aims to transform the structural causes of poverty and support integral human development.[8] Sixth, in response to the rise of nuclear weapons during the Cold War, CST developed a new focus on *peacebuilding*, shifting from a predominantly just-war posture to encouraging nonviolent alternatives to war and addressing the root causes of conflict and violence.[9] In the twenty-first century, *care for creation and*

---

6. Pontifical Council for Justice and Peace, *Compendium of the Social Doctrine*, §166.

7. Pontifical Council for Justice and Peace, *Compendium of the Social Doctrine*, §171, quoting *Gaudium et Spes*, §69. See also Pope Francis, *Fratelli Tutti*, §§119–20.

8. Important encyclicals here would include Pope Paul VI's *Populorum Progressio* (1967) and Pope John Paul II's *Sollicitudo Rei Socialis* (1987).

9. For example, see Pope John XXIII's *Pacem en Terris* (1963) or the National Conference of Catholic Bishops' 1983 encyclical, *Challenge of Peace*.

ecological concern have risen to the fore. In the face of widespread environmental degradation and the unprecedented global threat of climate change, Pope Francis released the 2015 encyclical, *Laudato Si': On Care for Our Common Home*, the first papal social teaching to focus predominantly on the environmental crisis. In recent decades, there has been growing reflection on what it means to live out these principles in the world through what ethicist Bernard Brady calls "Catholic social living."[10]

A final Catholic social teaching worth highlighting is *solidarity*. In his social encyclical, *Sollicitudo Rei Socialis*, John Paul II defined solidarity as a "firm and persevering determination to commit oneself to the common good; that is to say to the good of all and of each individual, because we are really responsible for all."[11] Solidarity recognizes that we are all members of the same human family, created in God's image, and called to see each other as brothers, sisters, and neighbors sharing communion, rather than as rivals or enemies struggling over scarce resources. It also can inspire a deeper concern and engagement with the social ills afflicting our neighbors near and far, whether related to economics, politics, health, gender, race, or sexuality. In calling people from a variety of backgrounds into deeper mutual relationship, solidarity humanizes and dignifies the other. To borrow one of Francis's own sporting metaphors, solidarity reminds people that when it comes to human flourishing, they are "saved as a team," not as individuals.[12]

Catholic popes have seen sport as a crucial dimension of the modern church's social apostolate, and a primary means by which Catholics, Christians, and other people of good will live out these social virtues in their daily lives. While recognizing the dangers and excesses of modern sport culture, the popes have consistently argued that sport can help construct a more just society that respects human dignity and fosters reconciliation across lines of social division. Sport can also be a crucial dimension of the human journey toward holiness as people grow more fully into the image of God by enacting these social values in all aspects of life. It is to this papal application of Catholic social thought to sport that we now turn.

SPORT, THE CIVILIZATION OF LOVE, AND THE CULTURE OF ENCOUNTER

Both Pope John Paul II and Pope Francis were avid sports *aficionados* in their day. Even into his early years as pope, John Paul loved to hike, ski, and

---

10. Brady, "From Catholic Social Thought," 352.
11. John Paul II, *Sollicitudo Rei Socialis*, §38.
12. Nanko-Fernández, "Pope Francis," para. 12; Francis, *Fratelli Tutti*, §137.

climb, carrying forward the twentieth-century tradition of "papal alpinists" going back to Pope Pius XI. For his part, Pope Francis shares his native Argentina's passion for soccer, and he has recalled fond childhood memories cheering for the Buenos Aires football club San Lorenzo.[13] Their mutual love of sport may explain why these two pontiffs both embraced sport as a key pillar of their respective social visions, namely John Paul's civilization of love and Francis's culture of encounter.

Let us begin with John Paul's vision. As a bishop at Vatican II, John Paul was well-aware of the council's call for the church to constructively engage the signs of the times in the modern world.[14] More than his predecessors, though, John Paul saw sport as one of the crucial signs of the times, a "cultural mediator" uniquely "capable of interpreting contemporary man's hopes and needs."[15] In addition, sport's global popularity gave it a special potential to help build a civilization of love and an "integral humanism," or what John Paul described as "anything that contributes constructively to the harmonious and complete development of man, body and soul."[16] As John Paul further shared in his 2000 "Jubilee of Sports" speech:

> Because of the global dimensions this activity has assumed, those involved in sports throughout the world have a great responsibility. They are called to make sports an opportunity for meeting and dialogue, over and above every barrier of language, race or culture. Sports, in fact, can make an effective contribution to peaceful understanding between peoples and to establishing the new civilization of love.[17]

More specifically, John Paul commended sport for transcending barriers of race, religion, politics, and ethnicity, a trajectory that we will discuss in more depth later in this chapter.[18]

Pope Francis built on John Paul's civilization of love with his own vision of the culture of encounter. Beginning with his first major papal teaching, *Evangelii Gaudium* (2013), Francis has argued that the Christian faith does not grow primarily through cultural or even family inheritance, but

---

13. Bergonzi, "Papa Francesco," para. 2.

14. Vatican II, *Gaudium et Spes*, §4.

15. John Paul II, quoted in Mazza, "Sport in the Magisterium," 127–28.

16. Mazza, "Sport in the Magisterium," 128–29; John Paul II, "Sport as Training Ground," in Feeney, *Catholic Perspective*, 60.

17. John Paul II, "Jubilee of Sports People," §2.

18. John Paul II, "Address of the Holy Father John Paul II to the Executive Committee," para. 4; John Paul II, "Jubilee of Sports People."

rather through a personal encounter with God's mercy in Jesus Christ.[19] One experiences God's mercy not only in church but also in the streets, namely by getting "involved by word and deed in people's daily lives" and "touching the suffering flesh of Christ in others."[20] A culture of encounter thus becomes a culture of contact rather than isolation, a culture of dialogue rather than monologue, and a culture of respecting difference and listening, even in the face of firmly held commitments. In Francis's words, "To speak of a 'culture of encounter' means we, as a people, should be passionate about meeting others, seeking points of contact, building bridges, planning a project that includes everyone."[21]

Francis holds that sport can play a critical role in fostering a culture of encounter, as well as the church's overall evangelizing mission. Crossing lines of "race, sex, religion, and ideology," the sporting field can be a place of "unity and encounter among people."[22] For Francis, sport's role is especially important for the furthering of peacebuilding and international harmony, especially through fostering coexistence and the types of personal encounters that can break down ingrained national and cultural stereotypes. As he said in the run-up to the 2016 Rio Olympics, "Sports make it possible to build a culture of encounter among everyone for a world of peace.... I dream of sports as the practice of human dignity turned into a vehicle of fraternity."[23] Building on Francis's thinking, the 2018 Vatican document on sport, "Giving the Best of Yourself," made a direct connection between sport's inclusive spirit and the catholicity, or universality, that is one of four creedal markers of the church: "In this sense, the very idea of being 'Catholic' goes hand in hand with what is best in the spirit of sports."[24]

This is not to say, however, that the recent papal magisterium has been wholly uncritical of some of the darker social dimensions of sport. In one of his final speeches on sport in 2004, John Paul noted that "in our time, organized sport sometimes seems conditioned by the logic of profit, of the spectacular, of doping, exasperated rivalry and episodes of violence."[25] On several occasions, Francis has castigated the problem of doping in sport,

---

19. Ivereigh, *Wounded Shepherd*, 155.
20. Francis, *Evangelii Gaudium*, §24.
21. Francis, *Fratelli Tutti*, §216.
22. Francis, "Message of the Holy Father," para. 2.
23. Francis, "Sports, a Culture of Encounter," 0:24–0:30, 0:48–0:56. Francis has echoed this theme of sport as a means of "building a culture of encounter and a world of peace" before many other major sporting events, including the 2014 World Cup in Brazil and the 2017 Super Bowl in Houston.
24. Holy See Dicastery for Laity, Family, and Life, "Giving the Best," §5.2.
25. John Paul II, "Address of John Paul II," para. 8.

especially cycling.²⁶ In general, though, these Catholic leaders have emphasized the positive social potential of sport over negative trends.

To summarize, sport has the potential to build solidarity across boundaries of class, race, ethnicity, and poverty, and it *can* be a critical element in the construction of both a civilization of love and a culture of encounter. Nothing is inevitable about this, however, and history is replete with examples of sport exacerbating ethnic, religious, and political tensions, as Franklin Foer so thoroughly demonstrates in his study of sports-based violence in Serbia and Scotland.²⁷ So it is important to examine how sport in the real world can contribute to a culture of encounter and simultaneously address the root causes of poverty, inequality, and injustice. To achieve this goal, we will now examine two modern examples of Catholic sports apostolates that offer tangible examples of both Catholic social teaching and the culture of encounter in action.

CASE STUDIES IN CATHOLIC SPORTS, CST, & THE CULTURE OF ENCOUNTER

Bishop Bernard Sheil and the Chicago CYO

The American Catholic Youth Organization (CYO) arose as a Catholic alternative to the Protestant Young Men's Christian Association (YMCA). The Vatican and the American Catholic hierarchy had discouraged Catholics from participating in the YMCA, yet also saw the value in using sports to connect with youth in the post–World War I setting.²⁸ The CYO was organized explicitly under the authority of the Catholic hierarchy, in part to prevent the violent and racist excesses associated with lay Catholic athletic clubs like the "Irish Catholic Ragen's Colts," which instigated race riots in Chicago in 1919.²⁹ In 1930, Chicago Archbishop George Mundelein asked his auxiliary bishop, Bernard J. Sheil, to start a CYO program that would respond to the multifaceted recreational needs of Chicago's burgeoning, panethnic Catholic youth population.

In Bishop Sheil, the Chicago CYO was getting more than just an administrator. Born in 1886, Sheil studied at a Catholic secondary school

---

26. Bergonzi, "Papa Francesco," §2.

27. Foer, *How Soccer Explains the World*, 7–64.

28. Neary, "Bishop Sheil," 49. Such negative Catholic views toward Protestants gave way to much more positive, ecumenical attitudes after the Second Vatican Council in the 1960s.

29. Neary, "Bishop Sheil," 50.

that strongly emphasized Pope Leo XIII's charter social encyclical, *Rerum Novarum*, and its concomitant commitment to workers' rights in industrial society.[30] Sheil was also an outstanding baseball player who pitched a no-hitter in college and nearly pursued a career in the sport before deciding to enter the priesthood.[31] As a young priest, Sheil served as a chaplain at Chicago's Cook County jail. Accompanying young men to their executions imparted on him an urgent commitment to use recreation and sport to forestall juvenile delinquency. In the spirit of Catholic Action, an international movement founded in the 1920s to encourage Catholic laity to engage and transform their social contexts, Sheil also saw his sports apostolate as a way to reinforce democratic and American civic principles without losing a deeply Christian moral and spiritual foundation.[32] The holistic nature of the CYO's mission is exemplified in its 1932 Charter: "The Catholic Youth Organization was established to promote among youth a recreational, educational, and religious program that would adequately meet the physical, mental, and spiritual needs of boys and girls without regard to race, creed, or color . . . while instilling in their minds and hearts a true love for God and country."[33] Beginning as a downtown boxing program for young men, the CYO developed a wide array of programs for both boys and girls across Chicago, including basketball, track and field, baseball, softball, tennis, golf, bowling, swimming, water polo, and even chess and checkers. It also influenced Catholic dioceses to start similar programs across North America.[34]

The language of the CYO charter exemplifies one of the most prophetic dimensions of the Chicago CYO: its bedrock commitment to racial integration. In one of the most racially and religiously segregated cities in America, the Chicago CYO welcomed African Americans as well as Protestants.[35] CYO's boxing program pitted black and white athletes in competitive yet friendly competitions, and championship bouts drew as many as 20,000 spectators.[36] Black athletes also found significant success in CYO

30. Neary, *Crossing Parish Boundaries*, 75.
31. Neary, "Bishop Sheil," 48; Neary, *Crossing Parish Boundaries*, 76.
32. Neary, "Bishop Sheil," 49.
33. Neary, "Bishop Sheil," 45–46. Showing the direct influence of CST, one of the CYO "creeds" of the 1930s went so far as to call participants to "promote social justice by rigid application of the principles expressed in the Encyclicals of Leo XIII and Pius XI" (Neary, *Crossing Parish Boundaries*, 85).
34. Neary, *Crossing Parish Boundaries*, 72, 81.
35. To quote the Chicago CYO, "Whether they are Catholics, Protestants, Jews, or Colored, they are welcome to the free education and supervision which the Catholic Youth Organization provides" (quoted in Baker, *Playing with God*, 177).
36. Neary, "Bishop Sheil," 51; Baker, *Playing with God*, 178; Neary, *Crossing Parish*

competition. Between 1931 and 1949, 46 percent of team champions in CYO's most popular sports—basketball, boxing, and track and field—were African American or represented Black parishes.[37] Coming during the Jim Crow era and at the height of the "great migration" of southern Blacks to northern cities, this interracial Catholic sports apostolate was decades ahead of its time.

The Chicago CYO's interracial character and commitment to serve all urban youth also involved the organization in a striking variety of civic programs. Reflecting his pragmatic philosophy that the CYO should respond to the social needs of the community, Bishop Sheil's CYO grew to encompass summer camps, a Juvenile Delinquency Prevention Service, the Sheil Guidance Clinic to provide psychological counseling for youth, and even a tuition-free "workingman's college" in downtown Chicago. This latter initiative included the Sheil School of Social Studies that integrated Catholic social thought with American principles of democratic self-government. The Sheil School initially enrolled a 75 percent majority of female students, and it employed Black faculty who taught courses on labor relations and African American history.[38] Without losing the CYO's primary focus on sports, Bishop Sheil managed to integrate critical elements of social analysis and social ethics into the formation of young people.

The collapse of Sheil's CYO in the 1950s is also illustrative. As white families fled to the suburbs, CYO programs became more Black-dominated, leading racist skeptics to mockingly call it the "Colored Youth Organization."[39] In 1954, Bishop Sheil came out against Senator Joseph McCarthy's virulent anti-communist campaign, precipitating a conservative backlash that led him to resign his leadership position. At the parish level, CYO programs became much more decentralized and simultaneously "de-socialized," losing the energy and vision of Catholic social teaching that had infused them during their first two decades.[40] The ultimate decline of Sheil's project reminds us that in practice, the civilization of love and culture of encounter are always fragile and contested, and therefore must be constantly nourished and sustained.

Bishop Sheil's Chicago CYO offers a powerful historical example of the potential breadth and depth of a genuinely Catholic social understanding of sport. It modeled and tutored young people in how to be whole persons,

---

Boundaries, 72.

37. Neary, *Crossing Parish Boundaries*, 126.
38. Neary, "Bishop Sheil," 47, 57; Neary, *Crossing Parish Boundaries*, 140–42, 160–61.
39. Neary, *Crossing Parish Boundaries*, 128.
40. Neary, "Bishop Sheil," 58–59.

impressing upon them that bodily well-being matters to God. The CYO literally embodied solidarity by putting different colored bodies in the same teams, gyms, and pools to engage in friendly and collaborative competition. In this sense, Sheil's CYO exemplified later papal teaching on solidarity and demonstrated how sport could serve as an entrée into a much wider social apostolate that engages the root causes of urban poverty and juvenile delinquency, or what Pope Francis has described as sport's mission to "promot[e] human development through an education of the whole person."[41] It also demonstrates the church's potential to facilitate a culture of encounter that "crosses parish and neighborhood boundaries," bridging seemingly immutable lines of race, geography, religion, and gender.[42] For another more recent example of this type of boundary-crossing sports apostolate, we need to travel halfway around the world to the refugee camps of Northern Uganda.

"That they may be one": Father Robert Ayiko and Uganda's refugee camp sports programs

In the late 2010s, Bidi-Bidi camp in northwestern Uganda was the largest refugee camp in East Africa. It hosted over 230,000 residents, most of them fleeing a brutal civil war across the border in South Sudan. At the peak of the refugee influx in 2016, upwards of 2,000–3,000 refugees were arriving in Uganda's West Nile region every day. Two-thirds of the refugees were under the age of thirty-five, 90 percent were Christian, and a majority were Roman Catholic. For all of its deprivations, Bidi-Bidi was also a center for international development. The fifty-three NGOs working in the camps included the prominent international Catholic groups Caritas and Catholic Relief Services, known for their work in agricultural development, vocational training, and initiating income-generating activities among the refugees. Yet even as these NGOs brought much-needed development opportunities, they also drew local teachers away from their home communities to seek better-paying jobs in camp schools. The population influx also exacerbated land and water conflicts. In turn, the refugee population included Dinka, Nuer, and other ethnic communities embroiled in South Sudan's civil war, which created significant political tensions within the camp itself.[43]

---

41. Pope Francis, quoted in Barbieri, "Sport is a School for Peace," 557.

42. Neary, *Crossing Parish Boundaries*, 12.

43. Carney, field notes, Yumbe, Uganda, May 10, 2019; Robert Ayiko, interview with J. J. Carney, Yumbe, Uganda, May 10, 2019. On the origins of South Sudan's civil war, see D. Johnson, *Root Causes*.

Into this volatile mix stepped Father Robert Ayiko, a Catholic diocesan priest based at Mary Queen of Heaven Catholic Parish in Yumbe, a 95 percent Muslim town adjacent to Bidi-Bidi camp. Previously diocesan director of Caritas, Ayiko was known locally as the "football priest." A former player and coach, Ayiko briefly managed a top-division professional club in northwestern Uganda and served as chair of the local district's football association. Ayiko recognized that whatever the religious, political, economic, and ethnic divisions within and around the camp, refugees and local residents both shared a common love of sport. So in 2017 he started a new refugee camp sports program for both young men and women. By 2019, the programs had taken off, with 665 men participating on soccer teams, and 380 women playing volleyball and netball (a derivative of basketball).[44]

Key themes in Catholic social teaching, such as dialogue, peacebuilding, and solidarity, course through the Bidi-Bidi camp sports program. The motto of the program, "That they may be one," was inspired by John 17:11.[45] This reinforced Ayiko's vision that "we are all human persons created by the same God," called to foster "harmonious coexistence" and "unity in diversity."[46] Club names reflected this theme, such as the girls' volleyball teams with monikers like "Peace Club," "United Stars," and "Hope Club."[47] In a nod to the interreligious context of Uganda's West Nile region, program organizers also cited Surah 49:13 of the Qur'an, a verse that emphasizes the common humanity of all people.[48] In this spirit, players were asked to lead prayers and share peace messages before games that explicitly focused on applying themes of love, harmony, and unity to healing conflicts within the camps.[49] To emphasize unity, team jerseys included program mottoes, such as "harmonious coexistence," rather than individual names. Critically, teams

---

44. Ayiko, interview.

45. The scriptural text reads as follows: "And now I will no longer be in the world, but they are in the world, while I am coming to you. Holy Father, keep them in your name that you have given me, so that they may be one just as we are" (John 17:11).

46. Ayiko, interview.

47. Kiden, interview.

48. Ayiko, interview. In English, Surah 49:13 is translated as follows: "O mankind, indeed We have created you from male and female and made you peoples and tribes that you may know one another. Indeed, the most noble of you in the sight of Allah is the most righteous of you" (https://corpus.quran.com/translation.jsp?chapter=49&verse=13). Or in the looser translation of a local Muslim program coordinator in Yumbe, "God says that we are all human beings and we are all together. No one in this world can do the judgment unless it is God himself who judges" (Ratib Alahai, interview with J. J. Carney, Arua, Uganda, May 13, 2019).

49. David Andama, interview with J. J. Carney, Yumbe, Uganda, May 11, 2019; Moses Aloro, interview with J. J. Carney, Yumbe, Uganda, May 11, 2019.

were intentionally mixed to include Muslims, Christians, locals, refugees, and members of various ethnic communities.[50] The relationships that developed from this "mixing up" helped to break down ethnic and religious stereotypes as players got to know each other "by name" rather than simply by ethnic affiliation.[51] The effects rippled out as players went home to their families, with youth encouraging their parents and grandparents to be more open to the ethnic and religious other. In Ayiko's words, "When a child goes home and says 'This man is good,' the parents will take this as the gospel truth."[52]

These positive influences also extended into the broader community. In interviews, several Christians spoke of significant improvement in Muslim-Christian relations in Yumbe since the introduction of Ayiko's sports apostolate. As one Catholic school teacher put it, "You can now put on a rosary without receiving abuse. Christians can organize a Way of the Cross through town in peace."[53] Bidi-Bidi's sports programs also reinforced interreligious social apostolates in the surrounding community, such as Muslim, Anglican, and Catholic leaders' joint work to combat gender-based violence, teen pregnancy, and alcohol and drug abuse. In turn, Father Ayiko and other leaders ran a regular Saturday sports program on local radio that provided a forum for speaking about the social challenges in the camps.

The Bidi-Bidi refugee sports apostolate embodies many key dimensions of Pope Francis's culture of encounter, as well as CST. Significantly, Ayiko noted how he conceived the program during Francis's 2016 jubilee "year of mercy," seeing this as a way for the church to embody compassion for refugees who had suffered tremendous trauma and stigmatization. The program also exemplifies the CST theme of solidarity and reinforces the fundamental human dignity of the religious or ethnic "other." In turn, the Bidi-Bidi sports refugee program exemplifies a key dimension of CST's notion of integral development: one should work *with* and not just *for* the poor, strengthening their local agency so that they can pursue development and human flourishing on their own terms, rather than terms dictated by outsiders. Finally, one sees in a tangible way how sport can serve the CST commitment to peacebuilding, nonviolence, and reconciliation. In the words of local Ugandan Catholic and sports radio announcer Vicente di Costa, sports are never just an end in themselves, but rather a way to

50. Ayiko, interview.

51. Alex Hakim Thomas, interview with J. J. Carney, Bidi-Bidi Refugee Camp, May 11, 2019.

52. Ayiko, interview.

53. James Vigas Ayimani, interview with J. J. Carney, Yumbe, Uganda, May 11, 2019.

contribute to social harmony and reduce conflict.[54] Or as Muslim tournament coordinator Ratib Alahai put it, "We [Muslims and Christians] just want to build peace and stay together as we are all brothers and sisters!"[55]

Bidi-Bidi's model of using soccer to facilitate interreligious harmony and build social peace is not unique to Uganda. In Northern Ireland, PeacePlayers International has encouraged basketball as a form of "peaceful integration," while also facilitating storytelling among Protestant and Catholic youth.[56] In Nicaragua, the Jesuit parish of Santo Domingo requires its 300 soccer players to participate in social workshops on themes of spirituality, social leadership, machismo culture, and drug and alcohol addiction.[57] In Nigeria, the Kaduna City Interfaith Football Club was founded in 2000 in the aftermath of Muslim-Christian riots and grew to include ten Muslim players and twenty Christian players. In the words of its Christian founder, Thomas Jimiko, "If Jesus were alive today in Nigeria he would be using football to break down barriers and build peace. . . . Jesus is all about reconciliation and that is what we hoped the club could achieve by using football to mediate the process."[58] In this sense, sport—and perhaps soccer in particular, given its near-universal popularity around the world—has unique potential to contribute to the type of culture of encounter that Pope Francis envisions.

CRITICALLY ENGAGING SPORT THROUGH THE LENS OF CATHOLIC SOCIAL TEACHING

Pope Francis's culture of encounter and Pope John Paul II's civilization of love emphasize sport's potential to positively reinforce human dignity and strengthen human relationships. In turn, the two case studies from Chicago and Uganda exemplify sport's ability to bring people together across lines of race, citizenship, and ethnicity, exemplifying Catholic social principles of solidarity, shared respect for human dignity, and peacebuilding.

But the world of sport is not always as upbuilding as the popes or even these two cases imply. Sports are a profoundly human endeavor marked by moral ambiguity; they reflect the personal and structural sins that deeply mark the human condition as well as the church. Soccer has the social popularity to contribute to communal harmony in a Ugandan

54. Vicente Di Costa, interview with J. J. Carney. Arua, Uganda, May 13, 2019.
55. Alahai, interview.
56. Jarvie, *Sport, Culture, and Society*, 195.
57. Meléndez, "Football *Plus* Human," 67.
58. Williams, "Religion and Sport," 120.

refugee camp, but it also has the income-generating power to embroil FIFA, soccer's governing body, in a far-reaching corruption scandal. Likewise, the Chicago CYO offers an inspiring example of how sports programs can serve the integral development of the human person. Yet youth sport programs, Catholic or otherwise, can also become hypercompetitive money pits where upper-middle-class American parents and their children pursue their sports dreams at any price.

In response, we would like to propose the principles of Catholic social teaching as a grid for evaluating if and how sport is actually "at the service of humanity," as the Catholic Church calls for. In particular, CST offers a welcome justice perspective that can be occluded in the paeans offered to sport by popes and sports fans alike. Our goal here is not to provide the definitive response to contested questions of social ethics and sport. Rather, we hope to raise "CST-inspired questions" that could facilitate a more substantive Christian dialogue around these difficult issues.

Money in youth and college sports

The rising costs of youth sport are posing dual challenges in modern North America. On one side, wealthier suburban parents are paying record sums of money to place their kids in select and travel sports leagues, most of which play year-round. In 2014, for example, American families spent an average of $2,300 per year on youth sports.[59] On the other hand, sports participation is declining among minority communities and the poor, especially in urban cities and rural areas. The two phenomena are linked, as the increasing cost and expanded travel logistics of youth sport combine to drive lower-income families out of the game. In 2018, one-third of American children with a household income under $25,000, and one-quarter of children with a family income under $50,000, engaged in *no* sport activity during the entire year. In contrast, only 10 percent of youth in families earning over $100,000 did not play a sport.[60]

The issue of money in sport is sparking a different debate at the college level, where a major dispute revolves around the question of college athlete compensation. "Amateurism" is the classic ideal of collegiate sport going back to its founding in the nineteenth century. This tradition holds that athletes should compete in sport purely for the love of the game rather than for financial incentive. The origins of this amateur ideal reflected the independent wealth of nineteenth- and early-twentieth-century collegians

59. Tracy, "Closed Door," para. 7.
60. Tracy, "Closed Door," para. 1.

who were drawn almost exclusively from the upper classes. It also reflected classist and often racist notions of "keeping sport pure" by excluding Americans from working-class and ethnic minority backgrounds.[61] And as Ronald Smith points out, the amateur ideal might better be described as the "amateur myth"; college boosters found ways to pay athletes going back to the first intercollegiate rowing regatta between Harvard and Yale in 1852.[62] In the 1950s, the NCAA started awarding athletic scholarships to student athletes, even as governing bodies resisted the idea that athletes were employees and therefore entitled to workers' compensation. The question has taken on renewed urgency in a twenty-first-century context where unpaid black athletes, often from poor backgrounds, dominate the rosters of men's basketball and football teams while their predominantly white coaches and universities rake in millions of dollars.

What could the CST tradition contribute in the face of these challenges? On the issue of youth sport costs, it should be noted that CST prioritizes "participation." In the words of ethicist Thomas Massaro, the Catholic Church teaches that humans have a "right and duty to participate in the full range of activities and institutions of social life."[63] Sport is clearly one of the central social activities and institutions of modern life, and it is therefore unjust to deny participation to large numbers of people simply because they are not wealthy. Second, the CST tradition prioritizes the family as both the "domestic church" where children first learn the faith, as well as the bedrock social institution in society itself. This raises the question of whether some families' financial and time commitments to youth sport exceed what might be considered balanced, fair, and proportional. Sport can and should be a key dimension of a child's life. But it should not monopolize or dominate life, producing burnout, imbalance, unhealthy attachments, a disregard for Sunday worship, or unnecessary delays in starting kindergarten to maximize future sports success. Third, CST emphasizes a preferential option for the poor as well as subsidiarity. The first teaching posits that the church and community are called to give particular concern and attention to the poor and marginalized in our society. Subsidiarity teaches that this is done by "rely[ing] as much as possible on those solutions that are closest to the people affected."[64] In this regard, subsidiarity professes that solutions to the problem of youth sport access will not be resolved solely at the state or national level. Rather, Catholic parishes, CYOs, and sports leagues need to

---

61. Grundy and Rader, *American Sports*, 69, 109–10.
62. Smith, *Myth of the Amateur*, 12, 235.
63. Massaro, *Living Justice*, 90.
64. Massaro, *Living Justice*, 93.

find creative ways to expand access, keep costs down, and strike a balance that takes sport seriously without letting it become the new golden calf of Christian family life.

In terms of the question of college athlete compensation, a CST lens would again highlight several key questions for consideration. First, the social background of today's money-sport athletes is radically different from that of their predecessors in the late nineteenth century. Doak Walker and Walter Camp's wealthy, white Yale football players have been replaced by a far more diverse group, both racially and socioeconomically.[65] Reflecting its prioritization of both family and the preferential option for the poor, the CST tradition would challenge the NCAA to ask how poorer players can best support themselves and their families. For example, in 2010, the average American college football player had an annual shortfall of $3,222 in living expenses not covered by his scholarship, which led a consortium of Division 1 universities to introduce "cost of living stipends" in 2015.[66] In turn, going back to its charter document *Rerum Novarum*, a core commitment of the CST tradition has been the "dignity of workers," as exemplified in the tradition's support for unions, safety and health regulations, a limited-hour workweek and, most importantly, just and fair wages for workers.

At the same time, the tradition has been skeptical of hyperconsumerism and super-abundance, where power and profit are king, which could be applied to the entire landscape of modern televised sport. To keep our lens on college sports, over half of Power Five football schools made over fifty million dollars in revenue in recent years, enabling them to pay their coaches millions of dollars, while 85 percent of players lived under the federal poverty line as recently as 2010.[67] The opportunities associated with the 2021 introduction of Name, Image, and Likeness (NIL) for student-athletes will alleviate some of this inequality. But NIL will not lift all student athletes in light of the major disparities in conference size, college revenue, sport popularity, and social media savvy. And given the extensively documented risks of depression, dementia, violent behavior, and suicide associated with

---

65. In 2019, 48 percent of college football players and 56 percent of men's basketball players were Black. Overall, 70 percent of women's athletes were white, which is roughly the same percentage for all college athletes (Axson, "College Football Means Big Money," para. 13; Gough, "Share of Female Student Athletes"; Burns, "Racial Divides Persist").

66. Huma and Staurowsky, "Price of Poverty," 4; Jones, "Can NCAA Policy Effect Student Costs?," 2. "Cost of living" expenses would include travel, bills, laundry, and other living expenses beyond tuition, books, and room and board. In 2015, 65 NCAA Division 1 universities adjusted their athletic scholarship policies to include higher cost-of-attendance stipends.

67. Mount Shoop, *Touchdowns for Jesus*, 43.

CTE (Chronic Traumatic Encephalopathy), one could ask whether college football has become a modern version of the Roman gladiatorial games, exploiting and discarding the poor for the entertainment of the rich.[68] In light of these health risks, as well as the huge amount of money flowing through college sports, much more could be done to support all student-athletes. In addition to boosting the overall cost-of-living stipends for scholarship athletes, another intriguing idea is to place a portion of athletic revenue in an "educational lockbox" that could be used to pursue postgraduate degrees after the expiration of athletic eligibility.[69]

Gender and racial inequities in sports leadership

A second pressing social case concerns how to address the gendered and racial disparities in sports coaching, management, and ownership. To be fair, women's participation in sport has grown markedly over the past several decades. One sees this at the Olympic level, where the percentage of female athletes has been on a steady upward trend from 1 percent of competitors in 1904, to 14 percent in 1972, 29 percent in 1992, 44 percent in 2012, and, most recently, 49 percent in the 2020 Tokyo Olympics.[70] Women's recreational participation has also grown, although rates fall off at lower socioeconomic levels.[71] In large part due to the 1972 Title IX legislation, American women's college athletics leads the world, and female athletes now comprise 44 percent of NCAA athletes.[72] However, women continue to face a glass ceiling for sport leadership positions. In 2020, only one-third of the International Olympic Committee's executive board were women,[73] and among American colleges only four of the sixty-five Power Five university

---

68. CTE is not limited to football and has also been found in soccer and hockey players, among others.

69. Huma and Staurowsky, "Price of Poverty," 5. Signs of progress are also evident. Undergraduate graduate success rates (which include transfers) rose to 90 percent in 2020. For men's basketball, the graduation rate was 87 percent, and 81 percent for men's football. Graduate rates for Black men's football and basketball players improved by 24 percent and 39 percent, respectively, between 2010 and 2020. Federal graduation rates, which are limited to the original school of enrollment, remain only 56 percent for Black male student-athletes, and 66 percent for Black female athletes. (NCAA Research Staff, "Trends in Graduation Success Rates," 6, 10).

70. Ellis, *Games People Play*, 63; Minsberg, "When Gender Equality."

71. Ellis, *Games People Play*, 68.

72. Jenkins, "NCAA's Message," para. 4.

73. Minsberg, "When Gender Equality," para. 4.

athletic directors were women.[74] And not only are women almost universally denied coaching opportunities over men's teams, but they have even struggled to gain opportunities to coach female teams.[75] This exclusion of female coaches has been accompanied by a growing scandal of male sexual, verbal, and physical abuse against female athletes, such as the systemic sexual abuse of female gymnasts by a USA Gymnastics team doctor, or the verbal, physical, and sexual abuse of players perpetrated by multiple male coaches in the National Women's Soccer League.[76]

The situation of racial minorities is also stark. In 2020, 83 percent of NBA players were people of color, yet only 30 percent of head coaches and 28 percent of general managers were nonwhite. The discrepancy was even worse in the NFL, where 75 percent of players, 13 percent of head coaches, and 7 percent of general managers were nonwhite.[77] This link between race and team ownership is even more glaring. Nearly twenty years after Robert Johnson became the first African American owner of a major professional sports franchise in North America, there remains only one Black principal owner—Michael Jordan, who succeeded Johnson as owner of the NBA's Charlotte Bobcats.[78]

Catholic social teaching can again contribute insights to this question of gender and racial inequity in sports leadership. First and foremost, the core CST tenet of human dignity, namely that all humans share a common origin, nature, and destiny that stems from their creation in the image of God, provides a powerful transcendent justification for challenging the status quo. Shared human dignity also underscores the imperative of equal opportunities for education, professional advancement, and social mobility,[79] including coaching, management, and other sports leadership positions.

Second, the CST principles of participation and the common good call for the widest engagement and empowerment of the most people in a society, to support the flourishing of all. In sport, full participation entails

74. Jenkins, "NCAA's Message," para. 4.

75. For example, the percentage of women coaching women's college teams actually *declined* between 1977 and 2002 (Ellis, *Games People Play*, 67).

76. Hensley-Clancy, "NWSL Commissioner"; Crawford and Haneline, "Follow IndyStar's Investigation."

77. Whitaker-Moore, "Strong Barriers," para. 1. Similar inequities exist outside of America. In 2014, only one manager in the English Premier League was black (Kuper and Szymanski, *Soccernomics*, 112).

78. See Rhoden, *Forty Million Dollar Slaves*, 247–61, and Shea, "5 North American Major Leagues." Even when one expands this lens beyond Black Americans, only five of the 150 major professional teams in 2020 had Asian-American or Latino owners (Hinton, "You Know Michael Jordan").

79. Massaro, *Living Justice*, 85.

leadership, responsibility, and decision-making, whether through coaching, managing, investing, owning, or hiring and firing personnel. Such opportunities in turn contribute to greater economic opportunities within the booming sports industry unfolding around the game. As legendary Georgetown men's basketball coach John Thompson used to say, "far more money is made sitting down than standing up."[80]

Third, the CST tradition grows out of a tradition of social analysis in which one "sees, judges, and acts" in response to what Vatican II calls the signs of the times. This requires becoming aware of, analyzing, and discerning the root causes of the major inequities in society (*seeing*); discerning where the social, political, and economic dynamics holding them in place are sinful and unjust in light of the Christian gospel (*judging*); and then working for systemic change in policy and society (*acting*). Let us apply this to the NFL's "Rooney Rule," introduced in 2003 to require teams to interview at least one minority candidate for an open head coaching or senior leadership position.[81] One could say that the NFL has helpfully seen a key "sign of the times," that is, the massive discrepancy in minority hiring in coaching. It has judged that this is a problem in a league where 75 percent of players are ethnic and racial minorities, predominantly African American. And it has acted to require at least one minority candidate interview. And yet at the beginning of the 2021 season, only five NFL coaches were minorities, including three Black coaches, and five of the league's thirty-two general managers were Black.[82] The lingering question remains as to why this rule has not resulted in more systemic improvements in minority hiring nearly two decades after it was first implemented. It seems that the NFL can require a team to interview a Black candidate, but that does not alter implicit biases that see a white coach as a more natural fit for the job. One can see why Pope Francis is so insistent on the necessity of broader cultural evangelization, for there are deeply embedded, structural biases occluding genuine racial and gender equity in sports.

---

80. Thompson, *I Came as a Shadow*, 301. A Catholic with a deep Marian devotion, Thompson was the first Black coach to win the NCAA men's basketball championship in 1984.

81. Feinstein, *Raise a Fist*, 130.

82. Feinstein, *Raise a Fist*, 134. Speaking in early 2021, former NFL coach Tony Dungy noted that only "two of the last twenty head coaching hires in the NFL have been African American" (Feinstein, *Raise a Fist*, 116).

CONCLUSION

In this chapter, we examined sport in the context of the Catholic social tradition. The Christian gospel has deeply social ramifications, and any theological analysis of sport must entail a close consideration of sport's social context and social impact. To their credit, Pope John Paul II and Pope Francis have proclaimed sport's centrality to their understandings of the civilization of love and the culture of encounter. In turn, notable past and current Catholic sports apostolates in Chicago and Uganda reveal sport's potential to contribute to social justice and reconciliation across lines of ethnic and racial division. Finally, we have argued that the principles of Catholic social teaching provide important ethical resources for engaging intractable social challenges in contemporary North American sport such as the cost of youth sport, compensation for NCAA athletes, and stark racial and gendered inequities in sports coaching, management, and ownership. If nothing else, one can see that Pope Francis's meeting with NBA players to discuss sport and racial injustice was not an exception, but rather an exemplification of a longstanding Catholic commitment to orient sport toward the service of humanity and society writ large. This meeting also demonstrates that while popes, bishops, and priests can exhort and encourage, it is ultimately up to regular laypeople to bring sports into line with the values of the kingdom of God. Clearly, much has yet to be achieved, pointing to the need for sustained action toward a more hopeful future. It is with this theme of eschatology that we now conclude this book.

Conclusion

Sport and Eschatology on the Eighth Day

BEFORE TENNESSEE, UCONN, BAYLOR, and Notre Dame, there were the Immaculata College Mighty Macs. The first Catholic women's college in Philadelphia, Immaculata emerged as a city and mid-Atlantic basketball power in the decades following World War II. Under the leadership of Coach Cathy Rush, Immaculata's success culminated with a remarkable stretch in the 1970s when the team won the first three women's collegiate national championships and made it to six Final Fours in a row.[1] Run by the Congregation of the Sisters, Servants of The Immaculate Heart of Mary, a Catholic religious order of women, Immaculata was known for its religious devotion. Before every game, the team would recite the same prayer: "O God of Players, hear our prayer/To play this game and play it fair/To conquer, win, but if to lose/Not to revile nor to abuse/But with understanding start again/Give us the strength, O Lord. Amen."[2] The Mighty Macs' petition was a prayer of hope—hope for victory, yes, but also hope for fair play, good sportsmanship, perseverance through loss, and, most of all, God's grace and strength.

If theology is "faith seeking understanding, love and hope,"[3] then in this conclusion we take up the final horizon of hope. The title of our book, *On the Eighth Day*, references an imagined day that follows God's six days of creation and a seventh day of rest. In this sense, the language of "eighth day" moves into the area of theological inquiry most closely associated with hope. This is eschatology, or what Christians anticipate as the final unfolding of the

---

1. These championships were organized under the umbrella of the Association for Intercollegiate Athletics for Women (AIAW), founded in 1971 to govern women's college athletics in the USA. It was ultimately supplanted by the NCAA in the early 1980s.
2. Byrne, *O God of Players*, 121.
3. Orobator, *Theology Brewed*, 3.

divine plan or *eschaton*. In this conclusion, we will first describe the general Catholic theological approach to eschatology. Second, we will consider how these eschatological themes are reflected in sports. Finally, we will provide our own threefold vision for salvation and redemption in sport on an ecological, communal, and personal level. In summary, if eschatology "points us toward the future,"[4] what is hoped for in sport on the eighth day?

CATHOLIC ESCHATOLOGY

Eschatology is literally defined as the "science of the last things."[5] This includes contemplation of the "eschata," or the ultimate mystery of humanity's and creation's final destiny in God. Traditional eschata include death, particular judgment, purgatory, heaven, hell, the end of the world, the parousia (or second coming of Christ), and the resurrection of the dead at the general judgment of humanity. Eschatology also refers to the inauguration of the "*eschaton* in Christ," or the initiation of a new time or final age through the life, death, and resurrection of Jesus Christ. In this sense, eschatology describes not only what is anticipated in the distant future, but how the future age is already unfolding in human history. Christ's resurrection anticipates future hope—enjoying the beatific vision of God—yet also offers a horizon for interpreting the present moment.

As in sport, so in life: future hope determines how one lives in the present. Every competitor enters a game anticipating victory and has an implicit sense of what type of effort and achievement is necessary to make the win possible. At the same time, no athlete can fully control the outcome of a contest. The final result remains unknown, yet the end goal of an activity determines its purpose, where a person knows what she is only by saying what she wants and what she can become.[6] This corollary has had a profound impact on Catholic notions of holiness. The monastic "athletes for Christ" discussed in chapter 1 lived an ascetic life out of anticipation that heaven would be a place of leisure, contemplation, prayer, and removal from the cares of the world.[7]

In the classic eschatological phrase, the kingdom of God is both "already" and "not yet." Signs of the kingdom abound wherever justice, unity, reconciliation, freedom, peace, love, and truth are found, and Christians believe they are already incorporated into the body of Christ through Christ's

---

4. Williams and Lane, "Eschatology," 347.
5. Williams and Lane, "Eschatology," 342; Lane, "Stirrings," 577.
6. K. Rahner, *Foundations*, 431.
7. Williams and Lane, "Eschatology," 343.

sacrifice and their baptism, which unites humans with Jesus' paschal mystery. Yet people are simultaneously always becoming as they grow more deeply into the image of Christ, just as they continue to await the fullness of Christ's reign in the world, when God will be all in all (1 Cor 15:28).[8] In Augustine's classic phrase, human hearts are "restless until they rest in you [God],"[9] and this restless desire for fulfillment marks both human life and, as we will discuss later, the life of sport.

For the Christian, then, the proper eschatological attitude is one of hope rather than certainty.[10] Human beings do not know the details of what awaits them after death, but it will surely be quite different from life as now known. The gospel resurrection accounts demonstrate that while there is continuity between the crucified and risen Jesus—he shows his disciples his wounds, after all—there is also radical discontinuity, mystery, and uncertainty as the disciples fail to recognize the Risen Christ.[11] Saint Paul likewise describes the perishable physical body as a seed, incomparable to the imperishable "spiritual body" that God will raise up on the last day (1 Cor 15:35–57). But all of this lies in the realm of faith, rather than knowledge. As Swiss theologian Hans Urs von Balthasar claims, seekers are "permitted to hope that God's redemptive work for his creation might succeed. Certainty cannot be obtained, but hope can be justified."[12] This Catholic perspective of uncertain hope contrasts with the salvific certitude that can emanate from some (if by no means all) Protestant and Pentecostal circles, as reflected in the title of the classic Evangelical hymn, "Blessed Assurance, Jesus Is Mine."

This contrast between hope and certainty reflects the Catholic conviction that people are *free*, not compelled, to love God and their neighbor. A life of freedom is found in the service of what is good and just, as explained in chapter 7, where humans voluntarily care for their brothers and sisters in need and imitate the life of Jesus and the saints. However, freedom can also be twisted toward violence, indifference, dehumanization, alienation, pride, and egoistic selfishness. And such actions can be ossified in deeply held patterns and structures of sin that permanently break relationships with God

---

8. Williams and Lane, "Eschatology," 350; Lane, "Stirrings," 578.

9. Augustine, *Confessions*, 1.

10. L. Johnson, *Creed*, 295.

11. See, for example, Luke's Emmaus story when Cleopas and his companion do not recognize Jesus on the road, only to have their eyes opened "in the breaking of the bread" (24:13). In the Gospel of John, Mary Magdalene confuses the risen Christ for a gardener (20:15). In Matthew, the disciples doubt even as they worship the risen Lord on the mountain (28:17). And in Mark, the women run in fear and terror from the tomb, unable to make sense of the angel's news of Christ's resurrection (16:8).

12. Balthasar, *Dare We Hope*, 187.

and neighbor. In other words, freedom can lead to heaven, but it can also lead to hell; humans have the freedom to "decide against God forever."[13] The possibility of cutting oneself off from God is not meant to stir fear as a motivation for faith, but shows that human actions have moral weight and consequences. How lives are lived today matters now and forever.

Catholic and classic creedal eschatology envisions final life with God in corporeal terms, namely through the "resurrection of the body." As already mentioned, this "spiritual body" should not be confused with the historical, biological body. At the same time, this Christian vision of eternal life does not just transpose a Platonic notion of immortal souls flitting about in the ether (captured in pop culture by the Pixar film *Soul*, in which recently deceased souls simply disappear into God's light). Rather, the Catholic vision of eternal life is deeply incarnational and holistic, recognizing that human beings are not just disembodied immortal souls, but soul-body unities.

This emphasis on the unity of the resurrected person also extends to the social and ecclesial plane. Rather than focus only on the afterlife, twentieth-century Catholic theology emphasized the historical and social dimensions of eschatology in response to the existential, apocalyptic threats of genocide, nuclear war, and ecological collapse. In a century that saw more people die in war than all previous centuries combined, Catholic theology recognized the urgency of eschatological hope, a hope that discerns and responds to the call of God in the midst of the darkness, suffering, and death that mark culture, politics, and life itself. In this context, Vatican II described the Catholic Church as a "pilgrim Church" pointing to the inaugurated yet unrealized kingdom of God.[14] Likewise, Catholic eschatology moved back toward the early church's understanding of "social salvation,"[15] seeing redemption not just as an individual matter, but also as a unity between people and the cosmos.[16]

In summary, then, Catholic eschatology considers both the last things of eternal life, as well as what historical life should mean in light of the new age inaugurated by Christ's life, death, and resurrection. Human beings are

13. K. Rahner, *Foundations*, 435.

14. Vatican II, *Lumen Gentium*, ch. VII. See in particular the deeply eschatological language of §48: "Already the final age of the world is with us (cf. 1 Cor 10:11) and the renewal of the world is irrevocably under way; it is even now anticipated in a certain real way ... until there be realized new heavens and a new earth in which justice dwells (cf. 2 Pet. 3:13), the pilgrim Church, in its sacraments and institutions, which belong to this present age, carries the mark of this world which will pass, and she herself takes her place among the creatures which groan and travail yet and await the revelation of the sons of God (cf. Rom 8:19–22)."

15. De Lubac, *Catholicism*, 120.

16. Lane, "Stirrings," 584.

people of hope, and hope for the future has a determinative impact on how one lives in the present. Reflecting its deeply incarnational and social ethos, Catholic eschatology follows the Nicene Creed in anticipating the resurrection of the body after death, yet also calls for discernment and action in the face of the existential opportunities and threats of this age. Whether on a personal or global level, history is contingent rather than preordained; it is up to human beings to respond in freedom to God's promises of fulfillment and redemption. Part of this human response unfolds in the world of sport, as we will now explore.

ESCHATOLOGY AND SPORT

To be clear, we do not wish to exaggerate the connections between sport and Christian eschatology. As Lincoln Harvey argues, part of the giftedness of sport is its finitude and status as a "radically contingent activity,"[17] rather than the ultimate arena for humans to work out their salvation before God. And as we have noted at several points in this book, there is a danger in our sports-obsessed society of asking sport to do too much, to bear more theological weight than it should. With Robert Ellis, one should recall the paradox of sport as both "terribly important yet utterly unimportant."[18] On a very important level, sport is *not* life, and in a healthy way can even serve as an escape from the realities of life.

We must also name a second danger that connects to themes of eschatology and soteriology (or the study of salvation). Namely, sport can easily become a modern version of the ancient heresy of Pelagianism that taught that humans control their destiny and earn their salvation through individual force of will and perseverance in good works. Such heresies find fertile ground in the world of sport. If an athlete works hard enough and does the right things, so the story goes, she will experience "salvation" in making the team, earning a starting role, perhaps starring and even winning championships. This meritocratic myth—one could even call it a kind of sports "prosperity gospel"[19]—fails to take into account all of the graced factors beyond one's effort, such as the arbitrary nature of birth dates in determining who moves ahead in Canada's youth hockey system.[20] In turn, the

---

17. Harvey, *Brief Theology of Sport*, 93.
18. Ellis, *Games People Play*, 215.
19. Associated especially with modern Pentecostalism, the prosperity gospel directly connects faith and financial tithing to future personal prosperity, arguing that God will materially reward those who trust in God.
20. Gladwell, *Outliers*, 16–30.

church is ultimately a place of grace, not an arena of achievement. To invoke Augustine's imagery, the church should be a hospital for sinners that welcomes and loves all wherever they may be in life's journey. One should not have to "earn" a place in church like you earn a spot in the starting lineup, much less "buy" grace in the way that elite athletes' families connect them to private coaches, travel teams, or expensive training facilities. In sum, the Christian account of salvation by grace is a counternarrative to the Pelagian pseudomeritocracy that dominates so much of the world of sports.

With these caveats in mind, the human experience of sport can still foreshadow eschatological hopes for the eighth day. First, sports trade in the language of hope. Athletes continue to train and compete in hopes of a better performance, a long-sought victory, or a personal breakthrough. Baseball teams enter spring training with dreams of October grandeur. In an American college football town, there is no greater month of expectation than August. This is not to equate a high school state championship with heaven, but if heaven is the "ultimate end and fulfillment of the deepest human longings, the state of supreme, definitive happiness,"[21] then perhaps sports can offer the types of *metaphors* for heavenly hope that resonate with the modern mind. Just as the prophet Isaiah's audience of pastoralist shepherds could envision God's reign through symbols of the "mountain of the Lord of hosts" and its "feast of rich food and well-aged wines" (Isa 25:6), so many modern Christians can envision beatific hope through their images and experiences of hope in sport.

This is due in large part to sport's ability to deliver fleeting yet unforgettable tastes of glory. One could name here the deep sense of fulfillment and joy that a soccer player feels in scoring a game-winning goal, or that the runner experiences through achieving a personal record in a marathon. On a communal level, one can point to the "day of salvation" that fans experience when their team wins a long-awaited championship. See for example this sampling of Twitter responses to the 2016 Chicago Cubs' World Series championship, bringing an end to the north-siders 108-year title drought:[22]

- "All of our Grandparents that aren't here today to witness what they waited for and never got to witness!"
- "All about getting a title for those who never got to see it. This man passed on to me a lifelong love of the Cubs. That's what means the most." (Posted with a picture of a Cubs hat and jersey on his grandfather's grave).

---

21. Ellis, *Games People Play*, 263.
22. All are taken from SI Wire, "Cubs Fans," paras. 7, 6, 9, and 4.

- "It means I will leave this earth and see a Cubs title. It means my family of life-long Cubs fans suffers no more."
- "Been waitin on this since I was 5. . .BEST DAY OF MY LIFE."

One can see here the potential for sports to elicit language that gestures at our finite experience of the infinite.

In sport, as in life, however, winning is not everything, nor is it the only thing. Often, athletes and coaches are simply seeking personal excellence or team improvement. In this sense, the athlete's task is not just one of *agon*—competing with others to win the perishable crown—but also one of *arête*—seeking excellence or the game well-played. In this way, athletes are Augustinians: just as humans for Augustine are created with an inbuilt, restless desire to seek God, so athletes are always pushing beyond their limits to touch the transcendent. This desire for perfection, if not always competitive victory, is exemplified in the closing scene from the 1996 movie *Tin Cup*, when the golf club pro Roy McAvoy refuses to lay up, preferring to reach the eighteenth green with a near-impossible long-iron shot. As he deposits shot after shot in the water, McAvoy forfeits a chance to get into a playoff and win the US Open. Yet he simultaneously captures the imagination of the crowd, who rejoice when he hits his twelfth shot into the hole.[23]

Yet Roy's reaction to his feat of *arête* is also revealing. Walking off the eighteenth green, he mutters to his girlfriend, "I just gave away the US Open!"[24] In this sense, Roy's triumph is also marked by suffering, loss, and his own self-inflicted wounds, which is one of the dominant themes in the film. In truth, there is no experience of sport shorn of suffering, pain, loss, defeat, or finitude. Likewise, in Christian eschatology there is no resurrection without the cross. The Risen Christ is still the Crucified Messiah, calling Thomas to put his fingers in his wounds (John 20:27). As Robert Ellis writes, "the final victory of God will contain within it some element of what may look to us like tragedy or defeat."[25] The Cubs' World Series triumph did not erase a century of disappointment, pain, and loss, but simply offered a surprising new horizon within which to interpret the long-suffering story of Wrigley's lovable losers.

Christian eschatology also emphasizes the high stakes involved in human life, which is reflected in the world of sport. One only has one life to live, one lifetime to respond definitively to God's self-giving *agapic* love. Humans are free creatures, and in this freedom lies both great hope and

23. For further reflection on *Tin Cup* as a model of *arête*, see Gaillardetz, "For the Love," 166.

24. Shelton, *Tin Cup*, 2:06:34–2:06:35.

25. Ellis, *Games People Play*, 227.

great risk. Death and judgment loom just beyond the horizon, lending a salutary urgency to spiritual and moral decision-making. As the *Catechism of the Catholic Church* claims, "Remembering our mortality helps us realize that we only have a limited time in which to bring our lives to fulfillment."[26] Sports time is also "kairotic" (see chapter 6). The game will end; the race will be over; the season will come to a close. This lends deeper purpose, meaning, and promise to sport, which partially explains its popularity in an immanent world that can seem flat and devoid of teleological energy (see chapter 3).[27]

In addition, sport is all about freedom. An athlete freely chooses to enter into the lusory experience of a particular sport, or tries out for a team, or practices and plays under the doctrines of a particular coach.[28] And with this freedom comes great risk. There are the obvious risks of losing or suffering a career-ending injury. But there are also moral risks: the dangers of insulting each other, quitting on the team, and/or betraying a teammate's trust. If the doctrine of hell is in part about the "possibility of eternal loss for every individual,"[29] then sport in its own small way can exemplify this risk. Many athletes play on clubs that "die" due to a toxic team environment; often there is no resurrection. The gift of freedom comes with great responsibility, and a keen awareness of how quickly things can go awry.

Finally, Christian eschatology strongly emphasizes the resurrection of the body, and the nature of the human person as a spirit-body unity. Knowing that not just his soul but also his body will one day be redeemed, the Christian is called to "treat with respect his own body, but also the body of every other person, especially the suffering."[30] As we have argued throughout this book, sports offer one of the primary ways that modern people engage their bodies, as well as the bodies of their fellow human sojourners. Far from being trivial, exercise, play, and sport are central aspects of human life as embodied, incarnate creatures destined to share body and soul in God's eternal kingdom. In this regard, the monastic "athletes of Christ" were half-right—we will pray in heaven, but we will also surely play.

---

26. *Catechism of the Catholic Church*, 1007.

27. Coming from the Greek term *telos*, meaning "end" or "purpose," teleological refers to the idea that the world has an inbuilt design or purpose.

28. Bain-Selbo and Sapp, *Understanding Sport*, 12–15.

29. K. Rahner, *Foundations*, 444.

30. *Catechism of the Catholic Church*, 1004.

THREEFOLD REDEMPTION ON THE EIGHTH DAY

Eschatology is ultimately about hope for salvation and redemption. In addition to echoing a sports fan's love of "The Great One," our title points to a future horizon for sport, an anticipated redemption or salvation on the eighth day. In this vein, then, we will conclude by considering what the eighth day might look like in the world of sport. In keeping with the holistic vision of Catholic theology, this understanding of sports salvation will entail ecological, communal, and interpersonal dimensions.

Let us begin with the ecological. In a twenty-first century facing the global existential threats of climate change and ecosystem collapse, Christians and all people of good will are experiencing an unprecedented call to environmental awareness. Especially in urban and suburban milieus, sport, play, and recreation provide the primary opportunities for modern people to "live in full harmony with creation" and to rediscover "capacity for wonder" at the beauty of the natural world, to quote Pope Francis's *Laudato Si'*.[31] Sport thus offers the opportunity to enter more fully into the mystery of the created world, whether one is a "papal alpinist" like John Paul II or an agnostic spiritual seeker embracing "extra-theistic" practices of the sacred.[32] Yet the redemption of a rapidly warming world will not happen simply through awareness; collective action is also necessary. A Catholic perspective, then, calls on teams, organizations, leagues, and families to open themselves to what Pope Francis calls an "ecological conversion,"[33] living in solidarity with the local environment rather than with an attitude of self-centered exploitation. Baseball's Nationals Park in Washington DC might offer a helpful model in this regard. The first major professional stadium to become LEED Silver Certified by the US Green Building Council, Nationals Park was built in the mid-2000s as part of a broader effort to revitalize the polluted Anacostia River and southeast Washington. Most fans use the metro rather than cars to reach the stadium; planners established water conservation plumbing techniques that save upwards of 3.6 million gallons of water annually; and the stadium includes extensive energy-saving light fixtures, reflective roof materials, and a state-of-the-art water filtration system.[34] We hope for the expansion of this "green movement" across the sports world as the world moves further into a twenty-first-century climate crisis.

---

31. Francis, *Laudato Si*, §§57, 225.
32. Hoven, "Lived Religion in Sport," 77–79.
33. Francis, *Laudato Si'*, §217.
34. Washington Nationals, "Green Ballpark."

CONCLUSION

Second, "the eighth day" calls for communal redemption. Just as Catholic salvation is premised on the notion of God's justice triumphing over injustice,[35] so a Catholic understanding of eschatological redemption entails a social horizon. As the Lord's Prayer teaches—"thy kingdom come, thy will be done, on earth as it is in heaven"—Christian hope for God's kingdom should lead people to further God's transformative work in the world. In their own unique ways, sports are called to contribute to the building of the civilization of love and the culture of encounter, and to support human dignity and the common good. In doing so, sport can participate in the reunification rather than the further division of the world. Whether through the CYO, refugee sports apostolates, or PeacePlayers International, sport has contributed in tangible ways to a new day in human relations, calling people into the unity for which Jesus prayed (John 17:11). But the challenge here extends to all leagues, teams, coaches, athletes, and parents; all are called to advocate for practices and policies that unite people and communities as opposed to divide. As Pope Francis said, we are "saved as a team," not as individuals.

Finally, "the eighth day" envisions a deeply personal hope for salvation and redemption for each individual athlete, coach, referee, and chaplain. Many of the core themes of this book could be included in this vision. The Catholic imagination celebrates the sensory, aesthetic dimension of life, such as art, music, recreation, play, and feasts. The athlete is likewise called to a spirit of joyful celebration in her sport, recapturing the elusive dimension of play threatened by the escalating costs and professionalization of youth sport. Athletes should seek God in all things, knowing that they can commune with God as much on a volleyball court as in the church. Yet the language of redemption teaches that sin and suffering are ever-present in sport; here too we encounter injury, failure, corruption, betrayal, jealousy, envy, team dysfunction, and even death itself. Redemption comes not through avoiding or escaping these painful realities, but rather through allowing God's grace to enter into and transform them through the paschal mystery. Especially important here is the work of coaches and sport chaplains. Beyond the Xs and Os of sport, coaches must tend to each player and build a communal team spirit, bringing out the unique gifts in each athlete, building a winning culture on and off the court, and serving as some of the most important mentors in young people's lives. Sport chaplains, like the now-famous Sister Jean Schmidt of the Loyola Chicago men's basketball team, provide space and time to pray and reflect with athletes. Such soul work provides a safe place for players to share from their hearts, where

---

35. *Catechism of the Catholic Church*, 1040.

their athletic careers are put into perspective and they can foster a personal identity outside of sport, one which is rooted in spiritual practices. Finally, a Catholic vision of sports redemption points athletes to the virtuous life. It is through the cultivation of virtue—the habitual inculcation of faith, hope, love, justice, prudence, temperance, and courage—that the human person can truly and genuinely flourish.

In a 2014 talk to the Italian Sports Center, Pope Francis encouraged his listeners, and encourages us today, to give the very best of ourselves, not only in sport, but in the rest of our lives as well:

> As sportsmen, I invite you not only to play, like you already do, but there is something more: challenge yourself in the game of life like you are in the game of sports. Challenge yourself in the quest for good, in both Church and society, without fear, with courage and enthusiasm. Get involved with others and with God; Don't settle for a mediocre "tie," give it your best, spend your life on what really matters and lasts forever. Don't settle for lukewarm lives, "mediocre even-scored" lives: no, no! Go forward, seek victory, always![36]

Inspired by Pope/Coach Francis's words of hope, challenge, and promise, and carried by the grace of Immaculata's God of Players, may we all set out with Saint Paul to "run the race in such a way that you may win it" (1 Cor 9:24).

---

36. Francis, "Address of Pope Francis to Members of the Sports Associations," para. 3.

Bibliography

Abrams, Jonathan. "N.B.A. Players Meet with Pope Francis on Social Justice Efforts." *New York Times*, November 23, 2020. https://www.nytimes.com/2020/11/23/sports/basketball/nba-pope-francis-protests.html.

Adogame, Afe, et al., eds. *Global Perspectives on Sports and Christianity*. New York: Routledge, 2018.

Alleyne, Richard. "The Secret Heartbreak Behind Clint Dempsey's Goal Celebration: Team USA's World Cup Hero Dedicates His Career to Sister and Friend Who Each Died Tragically." *Daily Mail*, June 18, 2014. https://www.dailymail.co.uk/news/article-2661342/With-fingers-sky-scoring-Team-USAs-World-Cup-hero-pays-tribute-sister-friend-died-tragically-Clint-Dempseys-secret-heartbreak-revealed.html.

Alpert, Rebecca, and Arthur Remillard. *Gods, Games, and Globalization: New Perspectives on Religion and Sport*. Macon, GA: Mercer University Press, 2019.

Ammerman, Nancy. *Sacred Stories, Spiritual Tribes*. New York: Oxford University, 2014.

Aquinas, Thomas. *Summa Theologiae*. https://www.newadvent.org/summa/.

Armour, Nancy. "Simone Biles Says Mental Health Concerns 'Deeper-Rooted' than Stress of Tokyo Olympics." *USA Today*, August 30, 2021. https://www.usatoday.com/story/sports/olympics/2021/08/30/simone-biles-says-athleta-video-stress-began-before-tokyo-olympics/5654874001/.

Augustine. *The Confessions*. Translated by R. S. Pine-Coffin. London: Penguin, 1961.

Axson, Scooby. "College Football Means Big Money. Black Athletes Stand at the Intersection of Risk and Profit." *NBC News*, August 27, 2020. https://www.nbcnews.com/news/nbcblk/college-sports-mean-big-money-black-athletes-stand-intersection-risk-n1238450.

Bader, Jennifer. "Engaging the Struggle: John Paul II on Personhood and Sexuality." In *Human Sexuality in the Catholic Tradition*, edited by Harold Horell and Kieran Scott, 91–110. Lanham, MD: Rowman & Littlefield, 2007.

Bain-Selbo, Eric, and D. Gregory Sapp. *Understanding Sport as a Religious Phenomenon: An Introduction*. London: Bloomsbury, 2016.

Baker, William J. *Playing with God: Religion and Modern Sport*. Cambridge: Harvard University Press, 2007.

———. *Sports in the Western World*. Urbana: University of Illinois Press, 1982.
Balthasar, Hans Urs von. *Dare We Hope "That All Men Be Saved?"* Translated by David Kipp and Lothar Krauth. San Francisco: Ignatius, 1988.
Barbieri, William A., Jr. "'Sport Is a School for Peace': Sport for Development, the Francis Effect, and New Directions in Catholic Peacebuilding." *Peace and Change* 42.4 (2017) 557–81. https://onlinelibrary.wiley.com/doi/epdf/10.1111/pech.12258.
Bartosova, Katerina, et al. "Rituals in Sport." *Kinesiologia Slovenica* 23.1 (2017) 5–13.
Bauer, David. "Olympic Speech." O'Malley Collection. Regina, SK.
———. "Philosophy of Sport." Basilian Archives. Toronto. Bauer Box 1, File 6.
Bell, Chris, dir. *Trophy Kids*. New York: HBO, 2013.
Bergonzi, Pier. "Papa Franceso: 'Il mio sport è una palla de stracci. Fare il portiere è stata una scuola di vita." *SportWeek*, January 2, 2021. https://www.gazzetta.it/Altri-Mondi/02-01-2021/papa-francesco-esclusivo-gazzetta-il-mio-sport-palla-stracci-3902144306393.shtml.
———. "Papa Francesco in esclusiva con SportWeek: i 7 punti nell'enciclica sullo sport." *SportWeek*, January 2, 2021. https://www.gazzetta.it/Altri-Mondi/02-01-2021/papa-francesco-7-puntiu-encliclica-sport-sportweek-3902138265796.shtml.
Bleacher Report. "The NBA's Top 10 All-Time Worst Free-Throw Shooters." October 11, 2011. https://bleacherreport.com/articles/886876-the-nbas-top-ten-all-time-worst-free-throw-shooters.
Bolt, Brian R., and Chad Carlson. "Sport, Envy, and the Conundrum of Comparison." In *Sport and Christianity: Practices for the Twenty-First Century*, edited by Matt Hoven et al., 133–44. New York: T. & T. Clark, 2019.
Bosschaert, Dries. "Discerning Sports as a Sign of the Times: The Vatican II Fathers' Changing Mentality on Leisure Activities (1959–1965)." *Cristianesimo nella storia* 40.3 (2019) 109–32.
Brady, Bernard V. "From Catholic Social Thought to Catholic Social Living: A Narrative of the Tradition." *Journal of Catholic Social Thought* 15.2 (2018) 317–52.
Broch, Trygve, and Elsa Kristiansen. "'The Margin for Error': Ritual Coping with Cultural Pressures." *Scandinavian Journal of Medicine and Science in Sports* 24.5 (2014) 837–45.
Brown, Daniel James. *The Boys in the Boat: Nine Americans and Their Epic Quest for God at the 1936 Berlin Olympics*. New York: Viking, 2013.
Bundgaard, Axel. *Muscle and Manliness: The Rise of Sport in American Boarding Schools*. Syracuse, NY: Syracuse University Press, 2005.
Burns, Mark J. "Racial Divides Persist on Compensation for Student-Athletes." *Morning Consult*, March 20, 2019. https://morningconsult.com/2019/03/20/racial-divides-persist-on-compensation-for-student-athletes/.
Bushnell, Horace. *Play and Work*. New York: Scribner, 1864.
Byrne, Julie. *O God of Players: The Story of the Immaculata Mighty Macs*. New York: Columbia University Press, 2003.
Cambers, Simon. "'We Are Still Fighting for Recognition'—Evert Explains Why Her Rivalry with Navratilova Is the Biggest in Tennis." *Tennis Majors*, December 19, 2020. https://www.tennismajors.com/our-features/interviews-our-features/we-are-still-fighting-for-recognition-evert-details-why-her-rivalry-with-navratilova-is-really-the-biggest-in-tennis-312867.html.

Carr, Anne E. "Starting with the Human." In *A World of Grace: An Introduction to the Themes and Foundations of Karl Rahner's Theology*, edited by Leo J. O'Donovan, 17–30. Washington, DC: Georgetown University Press, 1995.

Carter, John Marshall. *Medieval Games: Sports and Recreation in Feudal Society*. Westport, CT: Greenwood, 1992.

Cassian, John. *The Institutes*. Edited and translated by Boniface Ramsey. Ancient Christian Writers Series 58. Mahwah, NJ: Newman, 2000.

Catechism of the Catholic Church, Second Edition. Libreria Editrice Vaticana. Washington, DC: United States Conference of Catholic Bishops, 2016.

Center for Action and Contemplation. "My Story of the Cosmic Egg." *Another Name for Every Thing with Richard Rohr* (podcast), February 13, 2021. https://cac.org/podcasts/my-story-of-the-cosmic-egg/.

Chauvet, Louis-Marie. *The Sacraments: The Word of God at the Mercy of the Body*. Collegeville, MN: Liturgical, 2001.

Chrysostom, John. "Address on Vainglory and the Right Way for Parents to Bring up Their Children." In *Christianity and Pagan Culture in the Later Roman Empire*, edited by Max L. W. Laistner, 85–122. Ithaca, NY: Cornell University Press, 1951.

Clemens, Josef. "Sport in the Magisterium of Benedict XVI." In *Sport and Christianity*, edited by Kevin Lixey, 139–55. Washington, DC: Catholic University of America Press, 2012.

Coakley, Jay. *Sport in Society*. 8th ed. Boston: Irwin McGraw-Hill, 2003.

Conroy, Pat. *My Losing Season: A Memoir*. New York: Bantam, 2002.

Cooke, Bernard. *Sacrament and Sacramentality*. Mystic, CT: Twenty-Third, 1994.

Cottingham, Marci. "Interaction Ritual Theory and Sports Fans: Emotion, Symbols, and Solidarity." *Sociology of Sport Journal* 29 (2012) 168–85.

Cox, Daniel, et al. "Nearly 3-in-10 Americans Say God Plays a Role in Outcomes of Sports Events." *Public Religion Research Institute*, January 29, 2013. https://www.prri.org/research/january-2013-tracking-poll-2/.

Crawford, Dakota, and Amy Haneline. "Follow IndyStar's Investigation of USA Gymnastics and Larry Nassar from Start to Finish." *IndyStar*, January 24, 2018. https://www.indystar.com/story/sports/2018/01/24/indystar-larry-nassar-usa-gymnastics-investigation/1062120001/.

Crowther, Nigel B. *Sport in Ancient Times*. Westport, CT: Praeger, 2007.

Cunningham, Lawrence. "Perspectives in Catholic Theology." In *Teaching the Tradition*, edited by John Piderit and Melanie Morey, 47–64. New York: Oxford University Press, 2012.

Czikszentmihalyi, Mihaly. *Flow: The Psychology of Optimal Experience*. New York: Harper Perennial, 1990.

Davis, Charles. *Religion and the Making of Society: Essays in Social Theology*. Cambridge: Cambridge University Press, 1993.

Davis, Zac. "The Spiritual Strength of Simone Biles." *America Magazine*, July 28, 2021. https://www.americamagazine.org/faith/2021/07/28/simone-biles-2020-tokyo-olympics-withdrawal-discernment-241137.

Dawn, Randee. "US Runner Who Helped Rival: This Is What Olympics Are About." *Today*, August 18, 2016. https://www.today.com/news/us-runner-who-helped-rival-what-olympics-are-about-t101980.

Dawson, Tyler. "'They Are Human Beings': Carey Price the Latest Struggling Superstar Athlete to Take a Break in Recent Months." *National Post*, October 7, 2021. https://

nationalpost.com/news/canada/they-are-human-beings-carey-price-is-the-latest-struggling-superstar-athlete-to-take-a-break-from-the-game?r.

De Lubac, Henri. *Catholicism: Christ and the Common Destiny of Man.* Translated by Lancelot C. Sheppard and Elizabeth Englund. San Francisco: Ignatius, 2005.

Dick's Pro Tips. "Jordan Spieth on the Importance of Confidence." https://protips.dickssportinggoods.com/sports-and-activities/golf/jordan-spieth-on-the-importance-of-confidence-and-building-your-game.

Dodd, Sophie. "Olympic Athletes Share Their Pre-Competition Rituals and Superstitions." *People*, July 27, 2021. https://people.com/sports/olympic-athletes-pre-competition-rituals-and-superstitions/?slide=f883268a-f789-4166-a7c2-e8302fb14c00#f883268a-f789-4166-a7c2-e8302fb14c00.

Dych, William V. "Theology in a New Key." In *A World of Grace: An Introduction to the Themes and Foundations of Karl Rahner's Theology*, edited by Leo J. O'Donovan, 1–16. Washington, DC: Georgetown University Press, 1995.

Eastman, Susan, and Karen Riggs. "Televised Sports and Ritual: Fan Experiences." *Sociology of Sport Journal* 11 (1994) 249–74.

Edmonds, Ed. "The Vatican View on Sport at the Service of Humanity." *Notre Dame Journal of International & Comparative Law* 20.8 (2018) 20–34.

Ellis, Robert. "Creation, Salvation, Competition: Elements in a Christian Doctrine of Sport." In *Sport and Christianity: Practices for the Twenty-First Century*, edited by Matt Hoven et al., 35–46. London: T. & T. Clark, 2019.

———. *The Games People Play: Theology, Religion and Sport.* Eugene, OR: Wipf & Stock, 2014.

———. "Sporting Space, Sacred Space: A Theology of Sporting Place." In *Sport, Spirituality, and Religion: New Intersections*, edited by Tracy Trothen, 49–64. Basel: MDPI, 2019.

Epic Work. "Chemistry Counts: 4 Things NBA Champion Steve Kerr Can Teach CEOs About Team Chemistry." https://epicworkepiclife.com/inside-the-mind-of-steve-kerr/.

Farrow, Mary. "These Two Game-Changing Olympians Are Serious Catholics." *Catholic News Agency*, August 9, 2016. https://www.catholicnewsagency.com/news/34330/these-two-game-changing-olympians-are-serious-catholics.

Feeney, Robert. *A Catholic Perspective: Physical Exercise and Sport.* Marysville, WA: Aquinas, 1995.

Feezell, Randoph. *Sport, Play, and Ethical Reflection.* Urbana: University of Illinois Press, 2006.

Feinstein, John. *Raise a Fist, Take a Knee: Race and the Illusion of Progress in Modern Sports.* New York: Little, Brown, 2021.

Felix, Camonghne. "Simone Biles Chose Herself: 'I Should Have Quit Way Before Tokyo.'" *New York*, September 27, 2021. https://www.thecut.com/article/simone-biles-olympics-2021.html.

Foer, Franklin. *How Soccer Explains the World: An Unlikely Theory of Globalization.* New York: HarperCollins, 2010.

Francis, Pope. "Address of Pope Francis to Members of the European Olympic Committee." *Vatican.va*, November 23, 2013. http://www.vatican.va/content/francesco/en/speeches/2013/november/documents/papa-francesco_20131123_delegati-comitati-olimpici-europei.html.

———. "Address of Pope Francis to Members of the Sports Associations for the 70th Anniversary of the Foundation of the CSI (Italian Sports Center)." *Vatican.va*, June 7, 2014. https://www.vatican.va/content/francesco/en/speeches/2014/june/documents/papa-francesco_20140607_societa-sportive.html.

———. *Evangelii Gaudium*. *Vatican.va*, November 24, 2013. https://www.vatican.va/content/francesco/en/apost_exhortations/documents/papa-francesco_esortazione-ap_20131124_evangelii-gaudium.html.

———. *Fratelli Tutti: On Fraternity and Social Friendship*. *Vatican.va*, October 3, 2020. https://www.vatican.va/content/francesco/en/encyclicals/documents/papa-francesco_20201003_enciclica-fratelli-tutti.html.

———. *Laudato Si'*. *Vatican.va*, May 24, 2015. https://www.vatican.va/content/francesco/en/encyclicals/documents/papa-francesco_20150524_enciclica-laudato-si.html.

———. "Message of the Holy Father to the Prefect of the Dicastery for Laity, Family, and Life." *Vatican.va*, June 1, 2018. https://press.vatican.va/content/salastampa/en/bollettino/pubblico/2018/06/01/180601a.html.

Freiberg, Kevin, and Jackie Freiberg. "4 Things NBA Champion Steve Kerr Can Teach CEOs about Team Chemistry." *Forbes*, June 21, 2018. https://www.forbes.com/sites/kevinandjackiefreiberg/2018/06/21/4-things-nba-champion-steve-kerr-can-teach-ceos-about-team-chemistry/?sh=66fa3ee57d11.

Friedrichsen, Timothy. "Disciple as Athlete." *The Living Light* 39.2 (2002) 13–20.

Gaillardetz, Richard. "For the Love of the Game: Toward a Theology of Sports." In *Youth Sports and Spirituality: Catholic Perspectives*, edited by Patrick Kelly, 155–79. Notre Dame, IN: University of Notre Dame Press, 2015.

Ganter, Mike. "Raptors' Pascal Siakam Says He Has 'Joy' for Game Again." *Saltwire*, December 3, 2020. https://www.journalpioneer.com/sports/basketball/raptors-pascal-siakam-says-he-has-joy-for-game-again-527307/.

Gasaway, John. *Miracles on the Hardwood: The Hope-and-a-Prayer Story of a Winning Tradition in Catholic College Basketball*. New York: Twelve, 2021.

Giamatti, A. Bartlett, and Kenneth S. Robson. *A Great and Glorious Game: Baseball Writings of A. Bartlett Giamatti*. Chapel Hill, NC: Algonquin, 1998.

Gilkey, Landon. *Catholicism Confronts Modernity: A Protestant View*. New York: Seabury, 1975.

Girard, René. *The Girard Reader*. Edited by James G. Williams. New York: Crossroad, 1996.

Gladwell, Malcolm. *Outliers: The Story of Success*. New York: Back Bay, 2011.

Goldenbach, Alan. "After NFL's First Prayer, Religion Touched Down." *The Washington Post*, September 28, 2007. https://www.washingtonpost.com/wp-dyn/content/article/2007/09/27/AR2007092702077.html.

Gorman, Jack. *Père Murray and the Hounds*. 3rd ed. Winnipeg, MB: Hignell, 1990.

Gough, Christina. "Share of Female Student Athletes in the United States in 2020, by Ethnicity." *Statista*, March 16, 2021. https://www.statista.com/statistics/1168383/female-student-athletes-ethnicity/.

Greeley, Andrew. *The Catholic Imagination*. Los Angeles: University of California Press, 2000.

Gretzky, Wayne, with Kristie McLennan Day. *99: Stories of the Game*. Toronto: Penguin Canada, 2016.

Grundy, Pamela C., and Benjamin G. Rader. *American Sports: From the Age of Folk Games to the Age of the Internet*. 8th ed. New York: Routledge, 2019.

Guardini, Romano. *The Church and the Catholic and the Spirit of the Liturgy.* Translated by Ada Lane. New York: Seed & Ward, 1935.

Guttmann, Allen. *From Ritual to Record: The Nature of Modern Sports.* New York: Columbia University Press, 1978.

———. *Sports: The First Five Millennia.* Amherst: University of Massachusetts Press, 2004.

Haeg, Larry. *Saint Benedict's Rule for Fair Play in Sports.* Minneapolis: Little, 2007.

Hahnenberg, Edward P. "The Mystical Body of Christ and Communion Ecclesiology: Historical Parallels." *Irish Theological Quarterly* 70.1 (2005) 3–30. https://doi.org/10.1177/002114000507000101.

Harvey, Lincoln. *A Brief Theology of Sport.* Eugene, OR: Cascade, 2014.

Hensley-Clancy, Molly. "NWSL Commissioner, Under Pressure from Players, Resigns after Abuse Claims." *The Washington Post*, October 1, 2021. https://www.washingtonpost.com/sports/2021/10/01/nwsl-abuse-allegations-call-off-games/.

HERO Sports. "Do You Know All 16 Memorial Stadiums in College Football?" May 8, 2019. https://herosports.com/memorial-stadiums-usc-texas-cal-navy-kansas-aiai/.

Hertz, Noreena. *The Lonely Century.* London: Hodder & Stoughton, 2020.

Hill, Brennan R., et al. *Faith, Religion, & Theology: A Contemporary Introduction.* Mystic, CT: Twenty-Third, 1990.

Himes, Michael J. "Boston College 150th Anniversary Mass Fr. Michael Himes' Homily." *YouTube*, September 28, 2012. https://www.youtube.com/watch?v=jzcn6Ay5kbM&t=498s.

———. *Doing the Truth in Love: Conversations about God, Relationships, and Service.* Mahwah, NJ: Paulist, 1995.

———. "Finding God in All Things: A Sacramental Worldview and Its Effects." In *Becoming Beholders: Cultivating Sacramental Imagination and Actions in College Classrooms*, edited by Karen E. Eifler and Thomas M. Landy, 3–17. Collegeville, MN: Glazier, 2014.

———. "Living Conversation: Higher Education in a Catholic Context." In *An Ignatian Spirituality Reader: Contemporary Writings on St. Ignatius of Loyola, the Spiritual Exercises, Discernment, and More*, edited by George W. Traub, 225–44. Chicago: Loyola, 2008.

———. *The Mystery of Faith: An Introduction to Catholicism.* Cincinnati: St. Anthony Messenger, 2004.

Hinton, Eric. "You Know Michael Jordan . . . But Who Are the Other People of Color with Majority Ownership in Pro Sports?" *NBCLx*, October 11, 2021. https://www.lx.com/social-justice/you-know-michael-jordan-but-who-are-the-other-people-of-color-with-majority-ownership-in-pro-sports/20208/.

Hochstetler, Douglas. "Running as Liturgy." In *Sport and Christianity: Practices for the Twenty-First Century*, edited by Matt Hoven et al., 85–96. New York: T. & T. Clark, 2019.

———. "Striving towards Maturity: On the Relationship between Prayer and Sport." *Christian Education Journal* 6.2 (2009) 325–36.

Hoffman, Shirl James. *Good Game: Christianity and the Culture of Sports.* Waco, TX: Baylor University Press, 2010.

———. "Whatever Happened to Play?" *Christianity Today*, February 2010.

Holowchak, Andrew, and Heather Reid. *Aretism: An Ancient Sports Philosophy for the Modern Sports World*. New York: Lexington, 2011.
Holy See Dicastery for Laity, Family, and Life. "Giving the Best of Yourself: A Document on the Christian Perspective on Sport and the Human Person." *Vatican.va*, June 1, 2018. https://press.vatican.va/content/salastampa/en/bollettino/pubblico/2018/06/01/180601b.pdf.
Hoven, Matt. "Faith Informing Competitive Youth Athletes in Christian Schooling." *Journal of Research on Christian Education* 25.3 (2016) 273–89.
———. "Lived Religion in Sport." In *Sport and Christianity: Practices for the Twenty-First Century*, edited by Matt Hoven et al., 73–84. London: T. & T. Clark, 2020.
———. "'A Powerful Sporting Tradition among Canadian Basilians': Early Twentieth-Century Catholic Priest-Coaches at St Michael's College." *International Journal of Sport History* 39.4 (2022). DOI: 10.1080/09523367.2022.2066079.
———. "Re-Characterizing Confidence Because of Religious and Personal Rituals in Sport: Findings from a Qualitative Study of 15-Year-Old Student-Athletes." *Sport in Society* 22.2 (2019) 296–310.
———. "Recovering Spiritual Centers of Gravity through Sport." *McMaster Journal of Theology and Ministry* 15 (2013–14) 51–78.
———. "'f Johnston and Worshipful Act': Taking Back Sport Through Theological Reflection." *Practical Theology* 9.3 (2016) 213–25.
Hoven, Matt, and Samantha Kuchera. "Beyond Tebowing and Superstitions: Religious Practices of 15-year-old Competitive Athletes." *International Journal of Children's Spirituality* 21.1 (2016) 52–65.
Hoven, Matt, et al., eds. *Sport and Christianity: Practices for the Twenty-First Century*. New York: T. & T. Clark, 2019.
Huffman, Mary, and Jennifer Etnier. "The Use and Meanings of Prayer by Recreational Marathon Runners." *Journal of Leisure Research* 51.2 (2020) 147–64.
Huizinga, Johan. *Homo Ludens: A Study of the Play-Element in Culture*. Boston: Beacon, 1955.
Huma, Ramogi, and Ellen J. Staurowsky. "The Price of Poverty in Big Time College Sport." *National College Players Association*, 2011. http://assets.usw.org/ncpa/The-Price-of-Poverty-in-Big-Time-College-Sport.pdf.
Ignatius of Antioch. "Letter to Polycarp." In *The Epistles of St. Clement of Rome and St. Ignatius of Antioch*, edited by James A. Kleist, 96–101. Ancient Christian Writers Series 1. Westminster, MD: Newman, 1952.
Irwin, Kevin W. *Models of the Eucharist*. Mahwah, NJ: Paulist, 2005.
———. *The Sacraments: Historical Foundations and Liturgical Theology*. Mahwah, NJ: Paulist, 2015.
Ivereigh, Austen. *Wounded Shepherd: Pope Francis and His Struggle to Convert the Catholic Church*. New York: Holt, 2019.
Jackson, Kevin. "Should Colleges Pay Their Athletes? What Catholic Social Teaching Has to Say." *America Magazine*, March 20, 2020. https://www.americamagazine.org/politics-society/2020/03/20/church-meets-world-college-athletes-237111.
Janssens, Louis. "Artificial Insemination: Ethical Considerations." *Louvain Studies* 8 (1980) 3–29.
Jarvie, Grant. *Sport, Culture, and Society: An Introduction*. 3rd ed. New York: Routledge, 2018.

Jenkins, Sally. "NCAA's Message to Women's Basketball Players: You're Worth Less," *The Washington Post*, March 19, 2021. https://www.washingtonpost.com/sports/2021/03/19/ncaa-womens-basketball-unequal/.

John Paul II. "Address of John Paul II to the Members of the Italian Sports Centre." *Vatican.va*, June 26, 2004. http://www.vatican.va/content/john-paul-ii/en/speeches/2004/june/documents/hf_jp-ii_spe_20040626_csi.html.

———. "Address of the Holy Father John Paul II to the Executive Committee Meeting of the Fédération Internationale de Football Association (FIFA)." *Vatican.va*, December 11, 2000. http://w2.vatican.va/content/john-paul-ii/en/speeches/2000/oct-dec/documents/hf_jp-ii_spe_20001211_fifa.html.

———. "Address of the Holy Father John Paul II to the International Convention on the Theme: 'During the Time of Jubilee: The Face and Soul of Sport.'" *Vatican.va*, October 28, 2000. http://w2.vatican.va/content/john-paul-ii/en/speeches/2000/oct-dec/documents/hf_jp-ii_spe_20001028_jubilsport.html.

———. "Jubilee of Sports People: Homily of John Paul II." *Vatican.va*, October 29, 2000. https://www.vatican.va/content/john-paul-ii/en/homilies/2000/documents/hf_jp-ii_hom_20001029_jubilee-sport.html.

———. *Sollicitudo Rei Socialis*. *Vatican.va*, December 30, 1987. https://www.vatican.va/content/john-paul-ii/en/encyclicals/documents/hf_jp-ii_enc_30121987_sollicitudo-rei-socialis.html.

———. *Theology of the Body: Human Love in the Divine Plan*. New York: Pauline and Media, 1997.

Johnson, Douglas. *The Root Causes of Sudan's Civil Wars: Old Wars and New Wars*. 3rd ed. Oxford: James Currey, 2016.

Johnson, Elizabeth. *Consider Jesus: Waves of Renewal in Christology*. New York: Crossroad, 1990.

Johnson, Luke Timothy. *The Creed: What Christians Believe and Why It Matters*. New York: Doubleday, 2003.

———. *The Revelatory Body: Theology as Inductive Art*. Grand Rapids: Eerdmans, 2015.

Johnston, Robert. *The Christian at Play*. Eugene, OR: Wipf & Stock, 1997.

———. "How Might Theology of Play Inform Theology of Sport?" In *Sport and Christianity: Practices for the Twenty-First Century*, edited by Matt Hoven et al., 9–21. New York: T. & T. Clark, 2019.

John XXIII, Pope. *Pacem in Terris*. *Vatican.va*, April 11, 1963. https://www.vatican.va/content/john-xxiii/en/encyclicals/documents/hf_j-xxiii_enc_11041963_pacem.html.

Jones, Dan. "Social Evolution: The Ritual Animal." *Nature* 493 (2013) 470–72.

Jones, Willis A. "Can NCAA Policy Effect Student Costs? Evidence from the 2015 Adoption of Student-Athlete Cost of Attendance Stipends." *Journal of Higher Education* (2021) 1–24.

Kaplan, Grant. *René Girard, Unlikely Apologist: Mimetic Theory and Fundamental Theology*. Notre Dame: University of Notre Dame Press, 2016.

Kauffman, Gary. "Babe Ruth Would Now Be Listed as a Contact Hitter." *How They Play*, April 10, 2020. https://howtheyplay.com/team-sports/strikeouts-have-skyrocketed-since-Babe-Ruth.

Kay, Barbara. "The Case for an 'Open' Category to Welcome Trans Athletes in Sport." *The National Post*, December 20, 2021. https://nationalpost.com/opinion/barbara-kay-the-case-for-an-open-category-to-welcome-trans-athletes-in-sports.

Keenan, James. *Moral Wisdom: Lessons and Texts from the Catholic Tradition.* 3rd ed. Lanham, MD: Rowman & Littlefield, 2016.
Kelleher, Margaret. "Sport as Ritual Performance." *The Living Light* 39.2 (2002) 28–35.
Keller, Helen. *Story of My Life.* Garden City, NY: Doubleday, Page, 1927.
Kelly, Patrick. *Catholic Perspectives on Sports: From Medieval to Modern Times.* New York: Paulist, 2012.
———, ed. "Catholics and Sport in a Global Context." *Journal of Religion & Society* Supplement Series 20 (2019) 1–134. http://moses.creighton.edu/JRS/toc/SS20.html.
———. "Christians and Sport: An Historical and Theological Overview." In *Youth Sport & Spirituality: Catholic Perspectives,* edited by Patrick Kelly, 33–61. Notre Dame: University of Notre Dame Press, 2015.
———. "Flow, Sport, and Spiritual Traditions." In *Sport and Christianity: Practices for the Twenty-First Century,* edited by Matt Hoven et al., 47–58. New York: T. & T. Clark, 2019.
———, ed. *Youth Sport and Spirituality: Catholic Perspectives.* Notre Dame: University of Notre Dame Press, 2015.
———. "Youth Sport and Spirituality." In *Youth Sport & Spirituality: Catholic Perspectives,* edited by Patrick Kelly, 133-54. Notre Dame: University of Notre Dame Press, 2015.
Kimball, Roger. *Experiments against Reality: The Fate of Culture in the Postmodern Age.* Chicago: Dee, 2000.
Koch, Alois. "Biblical and Patristic Foundations for Sport." In *Sport and Christianity,* edited by Kevin Lixey, 81–103. Washington, DC: Catholic University of America Press, 2012.
Koehlinger, Amy. *Rosaries and Rope Burns: Boxing and Manhood in American Catholicism, 1890–1970.* Princeton, NJ: Princeton University Press, forthcoming, 2022.
Kohn, Alfie. *No Contest: The Case against Competition.* Rev. ed. Boston: Houghton Mifflin, 1992.
Kreider, Anthony. "Prayers for Assistance as Unsporting Behavior." *Journal of the Philosophy of Sport* 30.1 (2003) 17–25.
Kretchmar, Scott. "Why Do We Care So Much About Mere Games? (And Is This Ethically Defensible?)" *Quest* 57.2 (2005) 181–92.
Kretchmar, Scott, and Nick J. Watson. "The Paradoxical Athlete." In *Sport and Christianity: Practices for the Twenty-First Century,* edited by Matt Hoven et al., 21–34. New York: T. & T. Clark, 2019.
Kuper, Simon, and Stefan Szymanski. *Soccernomics.* New York: Nation, 2014.
Ladd, Tony, and James A. Mathisen. *Muscular Christianity: Evangelical Protestants and the Development of American Sport.* Grand Rapids: BridgePoint, 1999.
Lane, Dermot. "Christian Feminism." *The Furrow* 36.11 (1985) 663–75.
———. "The Equality of All in Christ." *Doctrine and Life* 44.2 (1994) 75–86.
———. *The Experience of God: An Invitation to Do Theology.* Rev. ed. Dublin: Veritas, 2003.
———. *Foundations for a Social Theology.* New York: Paulist, 1984.
———. *Keeping Hope Alive: Stirrings in Christian Theology.* Eugene, OR: Wipf & Stock, 2005.
———. "Reconstructing Faith for a New Century." In *New Century, New Society: Christian Perspectives,* edited by Dermot Lane, 159–73. Dublin: Columba, 1999.

———. "Stirrings in Eschatology." *The Furrow* 40.10 (1989) 577–85.

Lasch, Christopher. *The Culture of Narcissism: American Life in an Age of Diminishing Expectations*. New York: Warner, 1979.

Lawler, Michael G. *Symbol & Sacrament: A Contemporary Sacramental Theology*. Omaha, NE: Creighton University Press, 1995.

Leithart, Peter. "The Mystical Game." *First Things*, July 23, 2021. https://www.firstthings.com/web-exclusives/2021/07/the-mystical-game.

Lewis, Genevieve. "Sport after Death: The Importance of Fan Memorials." *Stadium Business News*, August 19, 2021. https://www.thestadiumbusiness.com/2021/08/19/football-after-death-the-importance-of-fan-memorials/.

Likona, Thomas. *Educating for Character*. New York: Bantam, 1991.

Lixey, Kevin, ed. *Sport and Christianity: A Sign of the Times in the Light of Faith*. Washington, DC: Catholic University of America Press, 2012.

———. "Sport in the Magisterium of Pius XII." In *Sport and Christianity*, edited by Kevin Lixey, 104–20. Washington, DC: Catholic University of America Press, 2012.

———. "The Vatican's Game Plan for Maximizing Sport's Educational Potential." In *Sports and Christianity: Historical and Contemporary Perspectives*, edited by Nick J. Watson and Andrew Parker, 250–68. New York: Routledge, 2013.

Loewe, William P. *The College Student's Introduction to Christology*. Collegeville, MN: Glazier, 1996.

MacAloon, John. "Introduction: Muscular Christianity after 150 Years." *International Journal of the History of Sport* 23.5 (2006) 687–700.

MacIntyre, Alisdair. *Dependent Rational Animals*. Chicago: Open Court, 1999.

Mandelbaum, Bert. *The Win Within: Capturing Your Victorious Spirit*. Austin, TX: Greenleaf, 2014.

———. "You Were Born to Be an Athlete." *U.S. News & World Report*, July 31, 2017. https://health.usnews.com/health-care/for-better/articles/2017-07-31/you-were-born-to-be-an-athlete.

Maranise, Anthony. "Superstition and Religious Ritual: An Examination of Their Effects and Utilization in Sport." *The Sport Psychologist* 27 (2013) 83–91.

Maraniss, David. *When Pride Still Mattered: A Life of Vince Lombardi*. New York: Simon & Schuster, 2000.

Marthaler, Berard. *The Creed*. Revised ed. Mystic, CT: Twenty-Third, 2005.

Martin, James. *Learning to Pray: A Guide for Everyone*. New York: HarperOne, 2021.

Massa, Mark S. *Catholics and American Culture: Fulton Sheen, Dorothy Day, and the Notre Dame Football Team*. New York: Crossroads, 1999.

Massaro, Thomas. *Living Justice: Catholic Social Teaching in Action*. 3rd ed. Lanham, MD: Rowman & Littlefield, 2016.

Mattison, William, III. *Introducing Moral Theology: True Happiness and the Virtues*. Grand Rapids: Brazos, 2008.

Mazurkiewicz, Michal. *Sport and Religion: Muscular Christianity and the Young Men's Christian Association. Ideology, Activity and Expansion (Great Britain, the United States and Poland, 1857–1939)*. Kielce, Poland: Wydawnictwo Uniwersytetu Jana Kochanowskiego, 2018.

Mazza, Carlo. "Sport in the Magisterium of John Paul II." In *Sport and Christianity*, edited by Kevin Lixey, 121–38. Washington, DC: Catholic University of America Press, 2012.

McGuire, Martin R. P. "Numerology." In *New Catholic Encyclopedia*, edited by Berard Marthaler, 475–76. Detroit: Thomson/Gale, 2003.

McNamee, Mike. "Whose Prometheus?" In *The Ethics of Sports: A Reader*, edited by Mike McNamee, 214–23. New York: Routledge, 2010.

———. "Youth Sport and the Virtues." In *Youth Sport and Spirituality: Catholic Perspectives*, edited by Patrick Kelly, 74–87. Notre Dame: University of Notre Dame Press, 2015.

Meléndez, Juan José Sosa. "Football *Plus* Human and Spiritual Formation: The Sports Pastoral at Santo Domingo Parish, Managua." *Journal of Religion & Society* Supplement Series 20 (2019) 63–70.

Meyer, Andrew R. "Historical Relationship between Sport and Christianity." In *Sport and Christianity: Practices for the Twenty-First Century*, edited by Matt Hoven et al., 59–69. London: T. & T. Clark, 2019.

———. "Muscular Christian Themes in Contemporary American Sport: A Case Study." *Journal of the Christian Society for Kinesiology, Leisure and Sport Studies* 2.1 (2012) 1–19.

———. "Redemption of 'Fallen' Hero-Athletes: Lance Armstrong, Isaiah, and Doing Good While Being Bad." *Religions* 10.8 (2019) 1–15.

Minsberg, Talya. "When Gender Equality at the Olympics Is Not So Equal." *New York Times*, July 22, 2021. https://www.nytimes.com/2021/07/22/sports/olympics/olympics-athletes-gender.html.

Montague, James. "Hero or Villain? Ben Johnson and the Dirtiest Race in History." *CNN*, July 23, 2012. https://www.cnn.com/2012/07/23/sport/olympics-2012-ben-johnson-seoul-1988-dirtiest-race/index.html.

Mount Shoop, Marcia W. *Touchdowns for Jesus and Other Signs of the Apocalypse*. Eugene, OR: Cascade, 2014.

Munoz, Laurence, and Jan Tolleneer, eds. *L'Église, Le Sport, et L'Europe: La Fédération international catholique d'éducation physique (FICEP) À L'Épreuve du Temps (1911–2011)*. Paris: L'Harmattan, 2011.

Munoz, Laurence, et al. "Sens et enjeux d'une fédération sportive dans l'Église." In *L'Église, Le Sport, et L'Europe: La Fédération international catholique d'éducation physique (FICEP) À L'Épreuve du Temps (1911–2011)*, edited by Laurence Munoz and Jan Tolleneer, 243–60. Paris: L'Harmattan, 2011.

Nanko-Fernández, Carmen. *¡El Santo! Baseball and the Canonization of Roberto Clemente*. Macon, GA: Mercer University Press, forthcoming, 2022.

———. "Pope Francis and His 'Secular Encyclical' on Sport." *National Catholic Reporter*, March 1, 2021. https://www.ncronline.org/news/media/theology-en-la-plaza/pope-francis-and-his-secular-encyclical-sport.

National Conference of Catholic Bishops. *The Challenge of Peace: God's Promise and Our Response: A Pastoral Letter on War and Peace*. May 3, 1983. https://www.usccb.org/upload/challenge-peace-gods-promise-our-response-1983.pdf.

NCAA Research Staff. "Trends in Graduation Success Rates and Federal Graduation Rates at NCAA Division 1 Schools." November 2020. https://ncaaorg.s3.amazonaws.com/research/gradrates/2020/2020D1RES_FedGSRTrends.pdf.

Neary, Timothy. "Bishop Sheil, the CYO, and Reflections for Our Times." *Journal of Religion & Society* Supplement Series 20 (2019) 45–62. https://dspace2.creighton.edu/xmlui/bitstream/handle/10504/123125/2019-36.pdf.

———. *Crossing Parish Boundaries: Race, Sports, and Catholic Youth in Chicago, 1914–1954*. Chicago: University of Chicago Press, 2016.
Nesti, Mark. "Persons First, Athletes Second: If Aquinas Came to the English Premier League." *Journal of Religion & Society* Supplement Series 20 (2019) 94–105.
———. *Psychology in Football: Working with Elite and Professional Players*. London: Routledge, 2010.
Novak, Michael. *The Joy of Sports: End Zones, Bases, Baskets, Balls, and the Consecration of the American Spirit*. Lanham, MD: Madison, 1994.
O'Malley, William J. *God: The Oldest Question*. Chicago: Loyola, 2000.
———. *The Wow Factor: Bringing the Catholic Faith to Life*. Maryknoll, NY: Orbis, 2011.
Orobator, Agbonkhianmeghe E. *Theology Brewed in an African Pot*. Maryknoll, NY: Orbis, 2008.
Otterspeer, Willem. *In Praise of Ambiguity: Erasmus, Huizinga and the Seriousness of Play*. Leiden: Leiden University Press, 2018.
———. *Reading Huizinga*. Translated by Beverley Jackson. Amsterdam: Amsterdam University Press, 2010.
Parry, Jim, et al., eds. *Sport and Spirituality: An Introduction*. New York: Routledge, 2007.
Paul VI, Pope. *Populorum Progressio: On the Development of Peoples*. Vatican.va, March 26, 1967. https://www.vatican.va/content/paul-vi/en/encyclicals/documents/hf_p-vi_enc_26031967_populorum.html.
Pfitzner, Victor C. "Was St. Paul a Sports Enthusiast? Realism and Rhetoric in Pauline Athletic Metaphors." In *Sports and Christianity: Historical and Contemporary Perspectives*, edited by Nick J. Watson and Andrew Parker, 89–111. New York: Routledge, 2013.
Piccolomini, Aeneas Sylvius. "The Education of Boys." In *Humanist Educational Treatises*, edited by Craig W. Kallendorf, 126–259. Cambridge: Harvard University Press, 2002.
Pieper, Josef. *Leisure: The Basis of Culture*. New York: Random House, 1963.
Pike, Jon, et al. "Fair Game: Biology, Fairness and Transgender Athletes in Women's Sport." *Macdonald-Laurier Institute*, 2021. https://macdonaldlaurier.ca/files/pdf/Dec2021_Fair_game_Pike_Hilton_Howe_PAPER_FWeb.pdf.
Pinckaers, Servais. "Freedom for Excellence." *The Living Light* 32 (1996) 58–68.
———. *Morality: The Catholic View*. South Bend, IN: St. Augustine's, 2003.
Pisk, Jernej. "Mimetic Desire and Scapegoat Mechanism in Sport." *Acta Universitatis Palackianae Olomucensis, Gymnica* 42.4 (2012) 9–17.
Podium Psychology. "Coach & Athlete Resource: Pre-Performance Routines (PPR) for Olympic Weightlifters." *Podium Psychology*, 2013. https://www.teamusa.org/-/media/USA_Weightlifting/The-Wednesday-Word/pre-performance-routines-by-podium-psychology.pdf?la=en&hash=A824784D4E2E7FD473400BE222342FA2DF9697B5.
Pontifical Council for Justice and Peace. *Compendium of the Social Doctrine of the Church*. Washington, DC: Libreria Editrice Vaticana, 2005.
The Pope Video. "Sports, a Culture of Encounter—The Pope Video—August 2016." *YouTube*, August 2, 2016. https://www.youtube.com/watch?v=wb1Vfu6oS8I.
Posnanski, Joe. "The 32 Best Calls in Sports History (and a Scully vs. Buck Debate)." *NBC Sports*, October 16, 2013. https://mlb.nbcsports.com/2013/10/16/the-32-best-calls-in-sports-history-and-a-scully-vs-buck-debate/.

Power, Clark. "Playing Like a Champion Today: Youth Sport and Moral Development." In *Youth Sport and Spirituality: Catholic Perspectives*, edited by Patrick Kelly, 88–110. Notre Dame: University of Notre Dame Press, 2015.

Power, F. Clark, and Lillie Rodgers. "From Play to Virtue: The Social, Moral, and Religious Dimensions of Youth Sport." *Journal of Religion & Society* Supplement Series 20 (2019) 23–44.

Price, Joseph. *Rounding the Bases: Baseball and Religion in America*. Macon, GA: Mercer University Press, 2006.

Putney, Clifford. *Muscular Christianity: Manhood and Sports in Protestant America, 1880–1920*. Cambridge: Harvard University Press, 2001.

Rahner, Hugo. *Man at Play*. Providence, RI: Cluny Media, 2019.

Rahner, Karl. *Foundations of Christian Faith: An Introduction to the Idea of Christianity*. Translated by William V. Dych. New York: Crossroad, 1989.

Ramsay, Hayden. *Reclaiming Leisure: Art, Sport and Philosophy*. Basingstoke, UK: Palgrave Macmillan, 2005.

Rauschenbusch, Walter, and Joseph Fahey. *Walter Rauschenbusch: Essential Spiritual Writings*. Maryknoll, NY: Orbis, 2019.

Reeves, Compton. *Pleasures and Pastimes in Medieval England*. New York: Oxford University Press, 2015.

Religion of Sports. "Religion of Sports | The Space Between | Full Episode." *YouTube*, January 28, 2019. https://www.youtube.com/watch?v=zMvoETbbYdk.

Rhoden, William J. *Forty Million Dollar Slaves: The Rise, Fall and Redemption of the Black Athlete*. New York: Crown, 2006.

Rodgers, Lillie K., and F. Clark Power. "Athletics as Sacrificial Offering." In *Sport and Christianity: Practices for the Twenty-First Century*, edited by Matt Hoven et al., 97–108. New York: T. & T. Clark, 2019.

Rohr, Richard. "Transforming Pain." *Center for Action and Contemplation*, October 17, 2018. https://cac.org/transforming-pain-2018-10-17/.

Rolheiser, Ronald. *The Holy Longing: The Search for a Christian Spirituality*. New York: Doubleday, 1999.

Rothblatt, Sheldon. "James Anthony Mangan: An Appreciation." In *'Manufactured Masculinity': Making Imperial Manliness, Morality and Militarism*, edited by James Anthony Mangan, 1–8. New York: Routledge, 2012.

Saiving, Valerie. "Androgynous Life: A Feminist Appropriation of Thought." In *Feminism and Process Thought*, edited by Sheila Greeve Daveney, 11–31. New York: Mellen, 1981.

Salzman, Todd, and Michael G. Lawler. *Introduction to Catholic and Theological Ethics*. Maryknoll, NY: Orbis, 2019.

Sandel, Michael J. "Bionic Athletes." In *The Ethics of Sports: A Reader*, edited by Mike McNamee, 208–13. New York: Routledge, 2010.

Schefter, Adam. "Tebow Phenomenon Gets Eerie." *ESPN*, January 13, 2012. https://www.espn.com/nfl/story/_/page/10spot-divisional/tim-tebow-phenomenon-gets-eerie—adam-schefter-10-spot.

Scholes, Jeffrey. *Christianity, Race, and Sport*. New York: Routledge, 2021.

Scholes, Jeffrey, and Raphael Sassower. *Religion and Sports in American Culture*. New York: Routledge, 2014.

Seasoltz, Kevin. "Sacred Space." In *New Catholic Encyclopedia*, edited by Berard Marthaler, 12:500–504. 2nd ed. 15 vols. Detroit: Gale, 2003.

———. "Sacred Time." In *New Catholic Encyclopedia*, edited by Berard Marthaler, 12:504–6. 2nd ed. 15 vols. Detroit: Gale, 2003.

Sexton, John. *Baseball as a Road to God*. New York: Gotham, 2013.

Shea, Bill. "The 5 North American Major Leagues Will Have 150 Teams in 2020—But Only 1 Black Majority Owner. Why?" *The Athletic*, February 11, 2020. https://theathletic.com/1592098/2020/02/11/the-5-north-american-major-leagues-will-have-150-teams-in-2020-but-only-1-black-majority-owner-why/.

Shelton, Ron, dir. *Tin Cup*. Burbank, CA: Warner Bros. Pictures, 1996.

Sheridan, Phil. "How Roger Staubach and Drew Pearson Made the 'Hail Mary' Pass Famous." *History.com*, August 6, 2021. https://www.history.com/news/hail-mary-pass-roger-staubach-drew-pearson-1975.

Siakam, Pascal. "Taking a Chance on the Unknown." *The Players' Tribune*, December 21, 2016. https://www.theplayerstribune.com/articles/pascal-siakam-toronto-raptors-cameroon.

SI Wire. "Cubs Fans Share Stories on the Meaning of a World Series Title." *Sports Illustrated*, November 3, 2016. https://www.si.com/mlb/2016/11/03/world-series-chicago-cubs-fans-meaning.

Smart, Ninian. *The Religious Experience of Mankind*. 3rd ed. New York: Scribner, 1984.

Smith, Christian, and Melinda Lundquist Denton. *Soul Searching: The Religious and Spiritual Lives of American Teenagers*. Oxford: Oxford University Press, 2005.

Smith, James K. A. *Desiring the Kingdom*. Grand Rapids: Baker Academic, 2009.

———. *How (Not) to Be Secular: Reading Charles Taylor*. Grand Rapids: Eerdmans, 2014.

Smith, Jason M. "Praying to Win: Reflections on the Involvement of God in the Outcomes of Sport." *Theology* 123.5 (2020) 329–36.

Smith, Ronald A. *The Myth of the Amateur: A History of College Athletic Scholarships*. Austin: University of Texas Press, 2021.

Sorensen, H. J. "Numerology (In the Bible)." In *New Catholic Encyclopedia*, edited by Berard Marthaler, 476–78. Detroit: Thomson/Gale, 2003.

St. Michael's College. *Yearbook*. Toronto: St. Michael's College, 1911.

Taylor, Charles. *A Secular Age*. Cambridge: Belknap of Harvard University Press, 2007.

Tertullian of Carthage. *De Spectaculis (The Shows)*. Translated by. S. Thelwall. Ante-Nicene Fathers 3. 10 vols. http://www.tertullian.org/anf/anf03/anf03-09.htm#P910_361877.

Thompson, John, Jr. *I Came as a Shadow: An Autobiography*. New York: Holt, 2020.

Tracy, Jeff. "The Closed Door of Youth Sports." *Axios*, March 20, 2021. https://www.axios.com/hard-truths-deep-dive-sports-youth-aa7f7e44-ccc3-4114-ba68-20532e28a9d8.html?utm_source=newsletter&utm_medium=email&utm_campaign=newsletter_axiosam_sports_merge&stream=top.

Trothen, Tracy. *Spirituality, Sport, and Doping: More Than Just a Game*. New York: Springer, 2018.

———. *Winning the Race?: Religion, Hope, and Reshaping the Sport Enhancement Debate*. Macon, GA: Mercer University Press, 2015.

Twietmeyer, Gregg, et al. "Sport, Christianity and Social Justice? Considering a Theological Foundation." *Quest* 71.2 (2019) 121–37.

Utrup, Alex. "A Coach's Fight to Pray: A Public High School Coach's Case Involving the First Amendment." *Marquette Sport Law Review* 31.2 (2021) 325–41.

Van Reybrouck, David. *Congo: The Epic History of a People*. Translated by Sam Garrett. New York: HarperCollins, 2014.

Vanysacker, Dries. "The Attitude of the Holy See toward Sport during the Interwar Period (1919–1939)." *The Catholic Historical Review* 101.4 (2015) 794–808.
The Vatican—Archive. "Pope Francis' Prayer Intentions for August 2016." *YouTube*, August 2, 2016. https://www.youtube.com/watch?v=OMfsnLsekQU&t=56s.
Vatican Council. *Schema constitutionis pastoralis de ecclesia in mundo huius temporis: Textus recognitus et relationes*. 2 vols. Vatican City: Vatican, 1965.
Vatican II. *Gaudium et Spes*. *Vatican.va*, December 7, 1965. http://www.vatican.va/archive/hist_councils/ii_vatican_council/documents/vat-ii_const_19651207_gaudium-et-spes_en.html.
———. *Lumen Gentium*. *Vatican.va*, November 21, 1964. https://www.vatican.va/archive/hist_councils/ii_vatican_council/documents/vat-ii_const_19641121_lumen-gentium_en.html.
Verducci, Tom. "Why MLB Issued Historic Punishment to Astros for Sign Stealing." *Sports Illustrated*, January 13, 2020. https://www.si.com/mlb/2020/01/13/houston-astros-cheating-punishment.
Wagamese, Richard. *Indian Horse*. Vancouver: Doublas & McIntryre, 2012.
Ward, Graham. "A Question of Sport and Incarnational Theology." *Studies in Christian Ethics* 25.1 (2012) 49–64.
Washington Nationals. "Green Ballpark." https://www.mlb.com/nationals/ballpark/information/green-ballpark.
Watson, Nick J., and Andrew Parker. *Sport and the Christian Religion: A Systematic Review of Literature*. Newcastle-Upon-Tyne, UK: Cambridge Scholars, 2014.
Whitaker-Moore, Aja. "Strong Barriers to the Business Side of Sport Remain." *Axios*, March 20, 2021. https://www.axios.com/hard-truths-deep-dive-sports-business-9d9eacc9-f1ae-4bed-a0a6-dac892d6f9de.html.?utm_source=newsletter&utm_medium=email&utm_campaign=newsletter_axiosam_sports_merge&stream=top.
Williams, Corey L. "Religion and Sport in Multireligious Nigeria: The Case of Kaduna City Interfaith Football Club." In *Global Perspectives on Sports and Christianity*, edited by Afe Adogame et al., 114–28. New York: Routledge, 2018.
Williams, M. E., and D. A. Lane. "Eschatology (In Theology)." In *New Catholic Encyclopedia*, edited by Berard Marthaler, 5:342-52. 2nd ed. 15 vols. Detroit: Gale, 2003.
Windle, Lauren. "'God Is the One Who Directs My Life'—The Christian Faith of Simone Biles." *Premier Christianity*, July 29, 2021. https://www.premierchristianity.com/stories/god-is-the-one-who-directs-my-life-the-christian-faith-of-simone-biles/5303.article.
Winston, Kimberly. "Serena Williams' Secret Weapon: The Surprising Faith of the Wimbledon Champ." *The Washington Post*, July 11, 2015. https://www.washingtonpost.com/news/acts-of-faith/wp/2015/07/11/the-surprising-faith-of-tennis-champ-serena-williams/.
Wojtyla, Karol. *Love and Responsibility*. San Francisco: Ignatius, 1993.
Yerkovich, Jim. "WE." In *Youth Sport and Spirituality: Catholic Perspectives*, edited by Patrick Kelly, 208–28. Notre Dame: University of Notre Dame Press, 2015.
Zhang, Luke. "Who Has the Most Game Winners in NBA History." *Dunk or Three*, August 20, 2021. https://dunkorthree.com/most-buzzer-beaters-nba/.
Zogry, Michael. *Anetso, the Cherokee Ball Game: At the Center of Ceremony and Identity*. Chapel Hill: University of North Carolina Press, 2010.
Zuesse, Evan. "Ritual." In *Encyclopedia of Religion*, edited by Lindsay Jones, 11:7833–48. 2nd ed. 15 vols. Detroit: Macmillan Reference USA, 2005.

www.ingramcontent.com/pod-product-compliance
Lightning Source LLC
Chambersburg PA
CBHW031428150426
43191CB00006B/439